IMAGES
of Aviation

MARINE AIR GROUP 25
AND SCAT

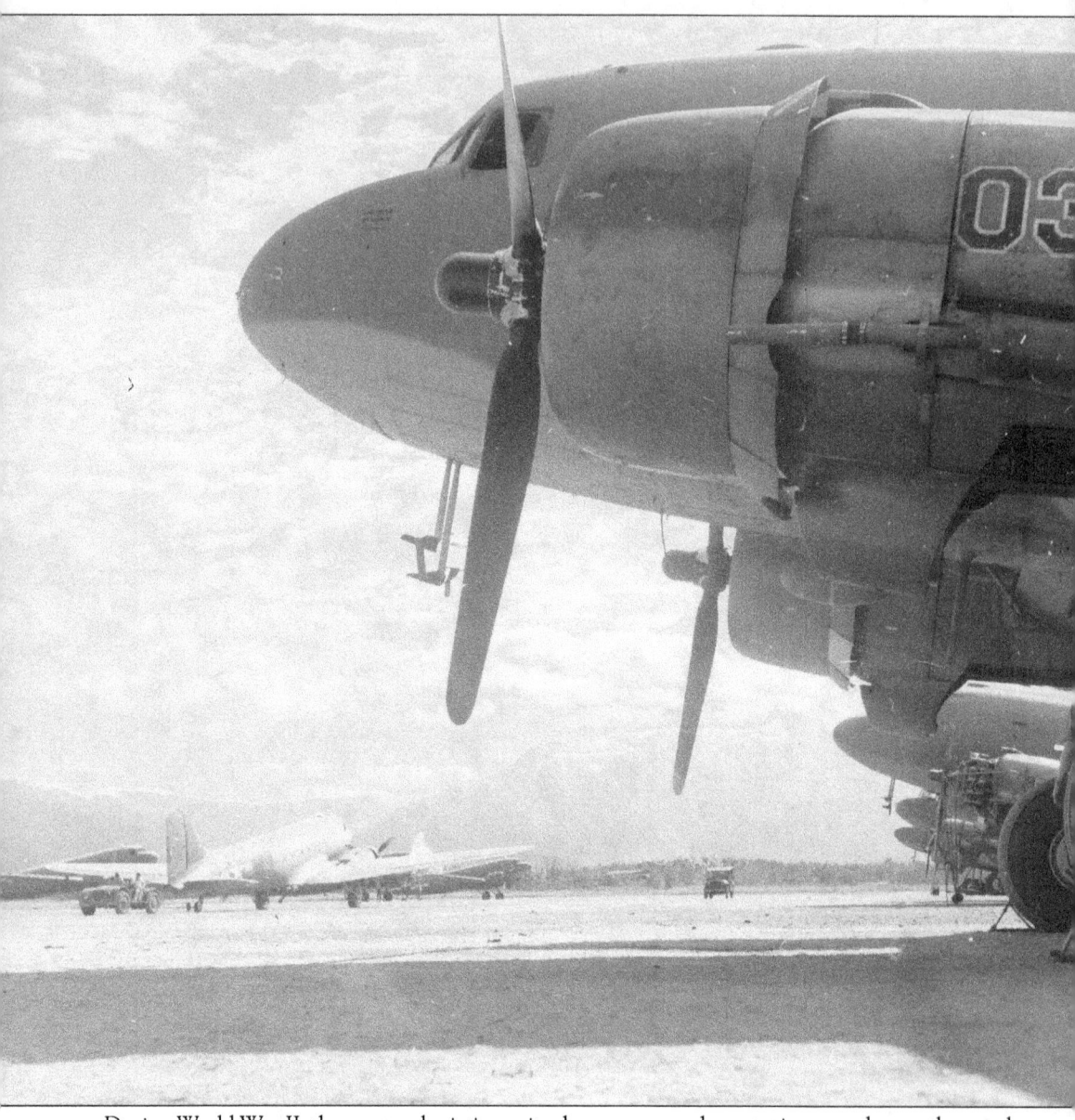

During World War II, there was a logistics unit whose name and reputation were known by nearly everyone throughout the South Pacific: SCAT. SOPAC (South Pacific) Combat Air Transport Command, with Marine Air Group 25 as its core, was an outstanding joint-service transport unit operating across the vast theater in support of frontline units. These SCAT R4D aircraft were photographed by famed photojournalist David Douglas Duncan in New Caledonia. (National Archives and Records Administration.)

ON THE COVER: Crowding around a SCAT R4D from Marine Air Group 25, medical personnel receive casualties from Guadalcanal at a hospital in the New Hebrides (now Vanuatu) in the South Pacific. The aircraft's crew, charged with overseeing the unloading process, stand by ready to assist. Out of all of its important missions SCAT was best known for aeromedical evacuation. (National Archives and Records Administration.)

IMAGES
of Aviation

MARINE AIR GROUP 25
AND SCAT

William M. Armstrong

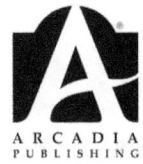

ARCADIA
PUBLISHING

Published by Arcadia Publishing
Charleston, South Carolina

Library of Congress Control Number: 2017939676

For all general information, please contact Arcadia Publishing:
Telephone 843-853-2070
Fax 843-853-0044
E-mail sales@arcadiapublishing.com
For customer service and orders:
Toll-Free 1-888-313-2665

Visit us on the Internet at www.arcadiapublishing.com

*For Joshua, Riley, and Elizabeth, and in loving memory
of Capt. William E. and Virginia DuRoss.
Dedicated to the veterans of MAG-25 and SCAT.*

CONTENTS

Acknowledgments   6

Introduction   7

1.   Origins   9

2.   Preparing for War   15

3.   Guadalcanal and SCAT   21

4.   Siege of Rabaul   51

5.   From Peleliu to Tsingtao   109

6.   Korea   121

Selected Bibliography   127

ACKNOWLEDGMENTS

I would like to begin by thanking the members of Marine Air Group 25 and SCAT Veterans of World War II, especially Dr. H. Jesse Walker, Bob Stitt, John Diehl, Stan Bieber, Paul "Hookie" Wynn, Roland La Forest, Dick Haven, John Duboise, Leland Blackwell, and Cliff Arthur. My wife and I would like to give special thanks to our friends Harold Klesath and Anita Young, whose company was the highlight of every reunion that we attended. My first reunion experience would not have been possible without the kind guidance of Bud Wegener, Bill Sears, Oliver Jones, Art Noe, and Grant Parks. My friend Ted Schwartz has spent decades preserving and promoting MAG-25's legacy, including the collection and digitization of the unit's newspaper, the *Ton-Tooter*. Although I never met him, I am heavily indebted to Robert Biggane, who steered the organization for decades and preserved valuable photographs and other records.

No individual did more to inspire this book than my late grandfather, Bill DuRoss, who indulged my childhood fascination with the air war in the South Pacific, although he seldom spoke of his own experiences. As always, my wife, Elizabeth, has helped at every stage of the book's development, offering valuable insights and guidance. Our children, Riley and Joshua, have been extraordinarily patient as I spent countless hours on yet another project involving old pictures. I hope that this book will have a special meaning for them as the great-grandchildren of a MAG-25 veteran.

I would also like to thank Holly Reed and the staff of the Still Pictures Branch of the National Archives and Records Administration (NARA), College Park, Maryland, who have been facilitating my periodic searches for MAG-25 and SCAT photographs for over 15 years, and Sylvester Jackson and Maranda Gilmore at the Air Force Historical Research Agency (AFHRA), Maxwell Air Force Base, Alabama. Additional photographs come from the Naval History and Heritage Command (NHHC) and the archives of the former Marine Air Group 25 and SCAT Veterans of World War II Inc. (MAG-25/SCAT). Photographs from the author's collection, except where noted, come from the family albums of William and Virginia DuRoss.

INTRODUCTION

When Japan attacked Pearl Harbor on December 7, 1941, inadequate combat airlift capability can be counted among the many ways in which the United States was unprepared for war. Although the war in Europe had led to a renewed interest in air transport, and promising designs were in development, transport units and adequate transport aircraft were few and far between. The immediate solution was to mass-produce an adaptation of a popular and successful commercial airliner, the Douglas DC-3, for military service, and quickly train thousands of skilled men to fly and maintain them.

That process was well underway when the United States launched its first offensive against the Japanese Empire on the remote island of Guadalcanal (code name "Cactus") in the Solomon Islands. There, the Japanese had begun construction of an air base that could threaten the approaches to Australia and New Zealand. The enemy proved tenacious, and supplies were short due to early Japanese dominance of the waters surrounding the island.

Back in the United States, a transport squadron had just been formed around a talented pool of experienced airline pilots, members of the Marine Corps Reserve. Their aircraft was the new Douglas R4D, although crews often still referred to it as the DC-3, or simply "DC." Marine Utility Squadron 253 (VMJ-253) and its parent unit, newly established Marine Air Group 25 (MAG-25), received the urgent word to deploy to New Caledonia, a Free French enclave in the South Pacific, to support the Guadalcanal operation. Meanwhile, a veteran Marine squadron, VMJ-152, also prepared to deploy. It had recently exchanged its motley collection of utility aircraft for R4Ds. Although many of its wartime personnel were new to the Marine Corps, during the preceding decade the squadron had played a critical role in the development of Marine Corps air transport, and several key MAG-25 officers were veterans of the unit.

MAG-25, initially consisting of Headquarters Squadron 25 and the flight echelon of VMJ-253, arrived at Tontouta Air Base, New Caledonia, in September 1942, and almost immediately began flights to Guadalcanal. VMJ-152 was assigned to MAG-25 and arrived in New Caledonia in October 1942. That same month, a US Army Air Forces (USAAF) unit, the 13th Troop Carrier Squadron (TCS), was attached to MAG-25, kicking off an impressive feat of interservice cooperation. The USAAF, like the Marine Corps, had begun rapidly expanding its air transport capability with aid from experienced airline pilots. The 13th TCS had been activated in December 1940. In November 1942, Marine Service Squadron 25 (SMS-25) was activated to provide maintenance for the group.

On November 24, Commander, Aircraft, South Pacific Force (COMAIRSOPAC), Vice Adm. Aubrey Fitch, directed that this cooperative effort be organized under a new command, SOPAC Combat Air Transport Command (SCAT), operating under the 1st Marine Aircraft Wing. Throughout SCAT's existence, it would be led by the senior officer of MAG-25 and would operate with a mix of US Marine Corps, Army, and Navy personnel.

The units of SCAT flew daily in support of Guadalcanal operations, at times proving vital to the success of air operations on the island. By the time of VMJ-253's first missions to the island, the Marines ashore had taken to calling the invasion "Operation Shoestring," rather than the official "Operation Watchtower," due to their lack of resources and the tenuous supply chain to the island. Guadalcanal's defense against frequent Japanese air attacks fell largely to the ragtag "Cactus Air Force," a heroic mix of overtaxed US Navy, Marine Corps, and USAAF units who struggled against the odds to keep their battered aircraft airworthy. Engineers fought a near-constant battle to keep the island's airstrips operational despite Japanese bombardment.

There was little that SCAT did not fly to the island. Cargoes included small arms, ammunition, grenades, food, mail, bombs, torpedoes for the US Navy's PT boats, aircraft engines and other replacement parts, aviation gasoline, fuel tanks, medical supplies, and replacement personnel. On nearly every return trip, the transports evacuated casualties. Little deterred the crews of these famously "unarmed and unarmored" transports, who flew day and night and were grounded by only the severest of weather. On Guadalcanal they often landed, unloaded, reloaded, and departed under fire. Rarely did they receive fighter escorts. Yet SCAT's greatest dangers were combinations of mechanical trouble and geography—especially severe, unpredictable weather. SCAT shared in a Distinguished Unit Citation for the Guadalcanal campaign.

In the waning days of the fight for Guadalcanal, SCAT was joined by the USAAF's pioneering 801st Medical Squadron, Air Evacuation Transport, fresh from the United States after a truncated training period. In March 1943, another new squadron, VMJ-153, also began arriving from the United States. SCAT forged an efficient and reliable transportation network spanning the vast South Pacific theater, moving ever northward as the Allies advanced across the Solomon Islands. In August 1943, the USAAF 403rd Troop Carrier Group also joined SCAT.

Operation Cartwheel, a two-pronged Allied advance through the Solomons in the east and New Guinea in the west, targeted the major Japanese air and naval base at Rabaul, New Britain, in the Bismarck Archipelago east of New Guinea. SCAT supported the eastern thrust, which by mid-1944 had isolated and largely neutralized the once formidable stronghold, earning a Navy Unit Commendation. In recognition of their now established role as dedicated transport units, MAG-25's squadrons were redesignated Marine transport squadrons (VMR). That July, SCAT's US Army components began departing to support Gen. Douglas MacArthur's operations in the Southwest Pacific. Meanwhile, VMR-253 was detached to the Central Pacific, where the squadron's expertise was employed to augment the SCAT-patterned Transport Air Group (TAG).

SCAT, now officially Solomons Combat Air Transport Command, later supported the Allied advance into the Philippines, although its role there largely shifted to exclusive support of the Marine air units fighting in what was overwhelmingly an Army campaign, under the command and dominance of General MacArthur. In February 1945, SCAT was disbanded altogether as an administrative entity, although MAG-25 operations continued as before. When the war ended, MAG-25 was still supporting combat operations in the Philippines and on Bougainville, and had begun escorting and transporting Marine air units to Okinawa and other distant islands. The first phase of the Allied invasion of Japan, Operation Olympic, was scheduled for November 1945.

After Japan's surrender, MAG-25 was repositioned to northern China in what, in retrospect, was a prelude to the Cold War in East Asia. It remained there into the summer of 1946, at which point it returned to the United States and was deactivated. In 1950, MAG-25 was reactivated, seeing further service during and after the Korean War, and again providing outstanding logistical support to frontline combat units.

In wartime, an exceptional logistics unit can gain fame, earning the lasting respect of the fighting units who rely upon it. SCAT was one such unit. One measure of SCAT's reputation during the war may be the sheer volume of its photographic record. Many photographers documented its activities throughout the war, including David Douglas Duncan, then a Marine Corps officer. Indeed, there are few units of any type whose activities have been so thoroughly documented in official photographs. Many of those photographs, including many never before published, are presented in this book.

One

ORIGINS

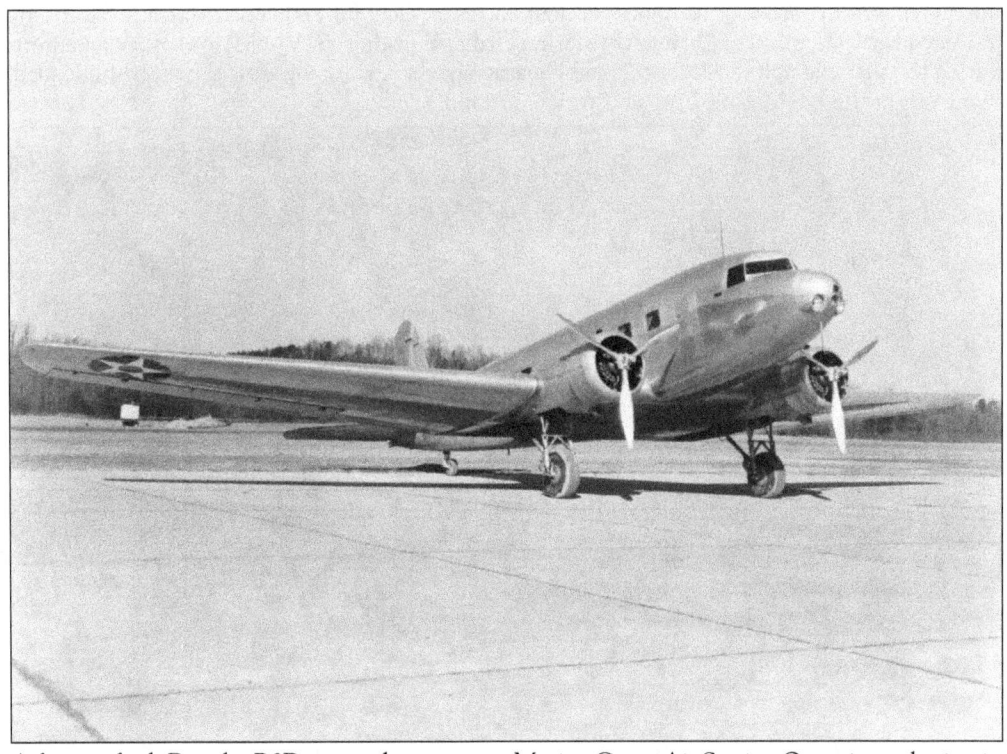

A factory-fresh Douglas R2D sits on the tarmac at Marine Corps Air Station Quantico, ushering in a new era of Marine air transport. Quantico's utility squadron—whose pilots might fly a transport mission one day and a pesticide spraying mission the next—was typically the first to receive the Marine Corps' latest models. Eventually known as VMJ-152, the squadron played a pioneering role in developing combat airlift capability. (NARA.)

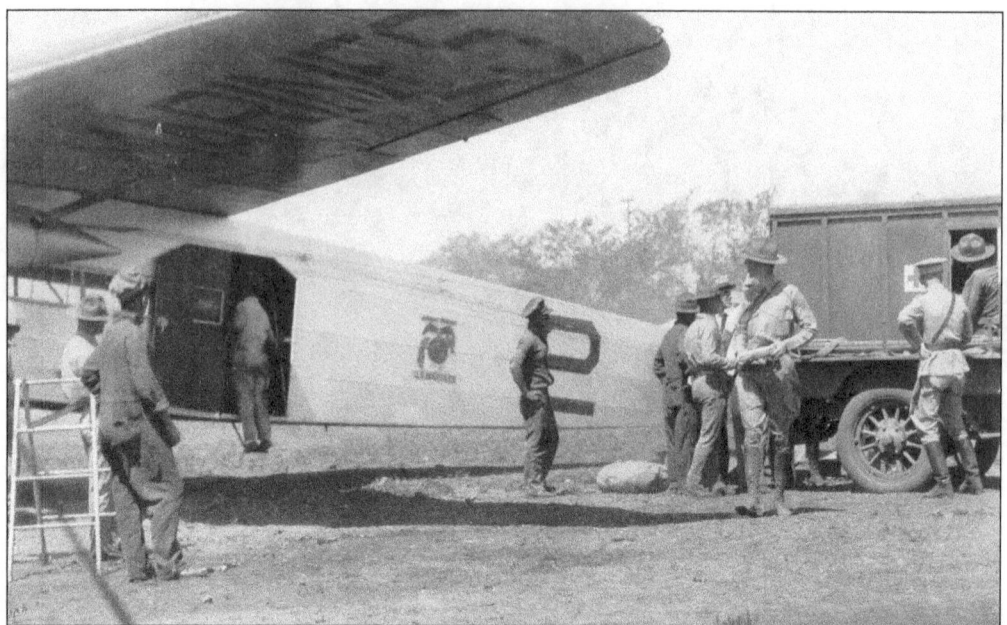

The Fokker TA-1 trimotor was the first practical Marine Corps transport aircraft. It could fly at the then impressive speed of 102 miles per hour and carry eight fully equipped Marines. Beginning in December 1927, pilots of Quantico's Marine Utility Squadron 6 (VJ-6M) and other squadrons ferried the first examples to US-occupied Nicaragua, where this aircraft is shown being loaded. (Courtesy of the US Marine Corps History Division.)

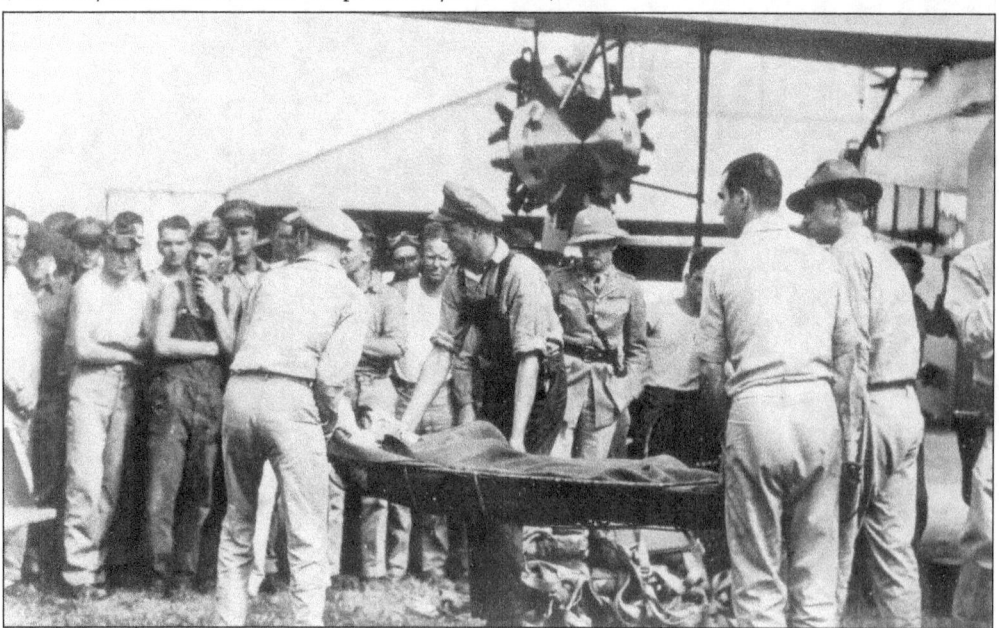

Despite their limited numbers, the Marines' five TA-1 aircraft revolutionized US military air transport, making the first ever airlift of American combat troops within days of arriving in Nicaragua. They cut timetables for deployment and resupply over rugged terrain from days to hours. Soon, the aircraft were being used for other missions, such as casualty evacuation (shown) and supply airdrops. These experiences would have a lasting impact. (MAG-25/SCAT.)

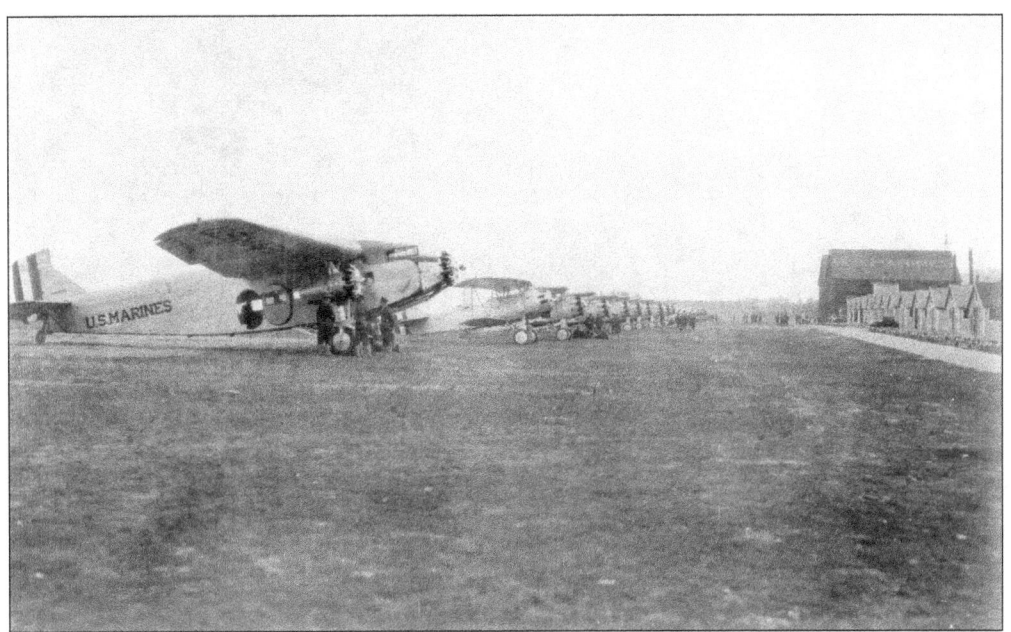

In September 1928, the designation "VJ-6M" was given to the deployed transport unit in Nicaragua, which, on paper, left the East Coast Expeditionary Force at Quantico without a utility squadron, although personnel there remained unchanged. Quantico took delivery of the Marine Corps' first Ford JR-2 trimotor transport in 1929, assigning it to Marine Fighting Squadron 5 (VF-5M). Here, the JR-2 sits prominently at Quantico's Brown Field in 1930. (NARA.)

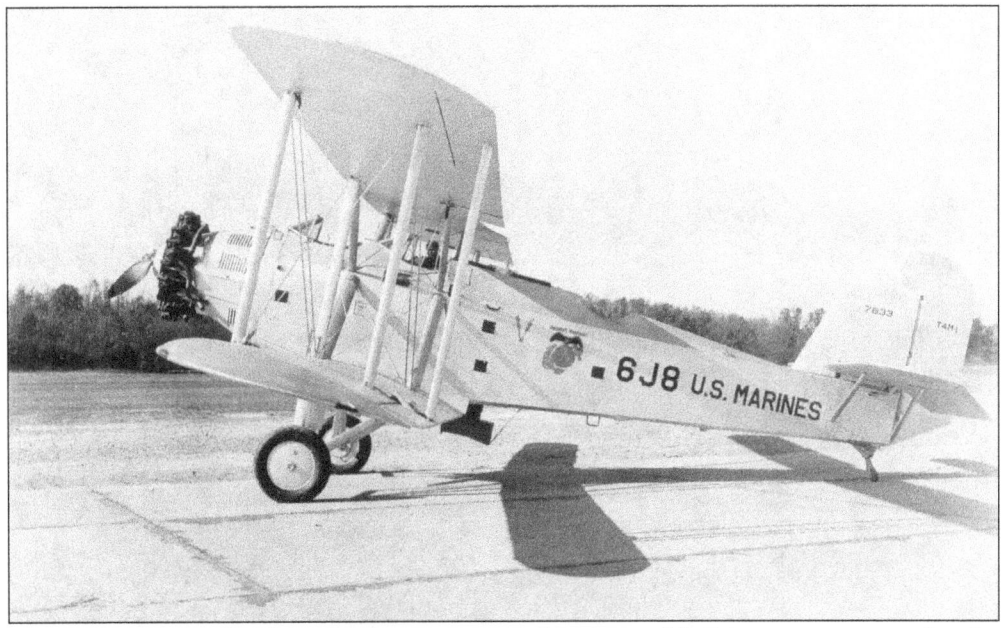

In 1933, with the end of the US military mission in Nicaragua, VJ-6M was again assigned to the East Coast Expeditionary Force at Quantico. The squadron now had three Ford trimotors (their designation changed from JR to RR in 1931), but still operated a mix of aircraft. It flew 11 types, totaling 16 airplanes, including this aged Martin T4M-1 torpedo bomber equipped with a belly-mounted sprayer for pesticides. (NARA.)

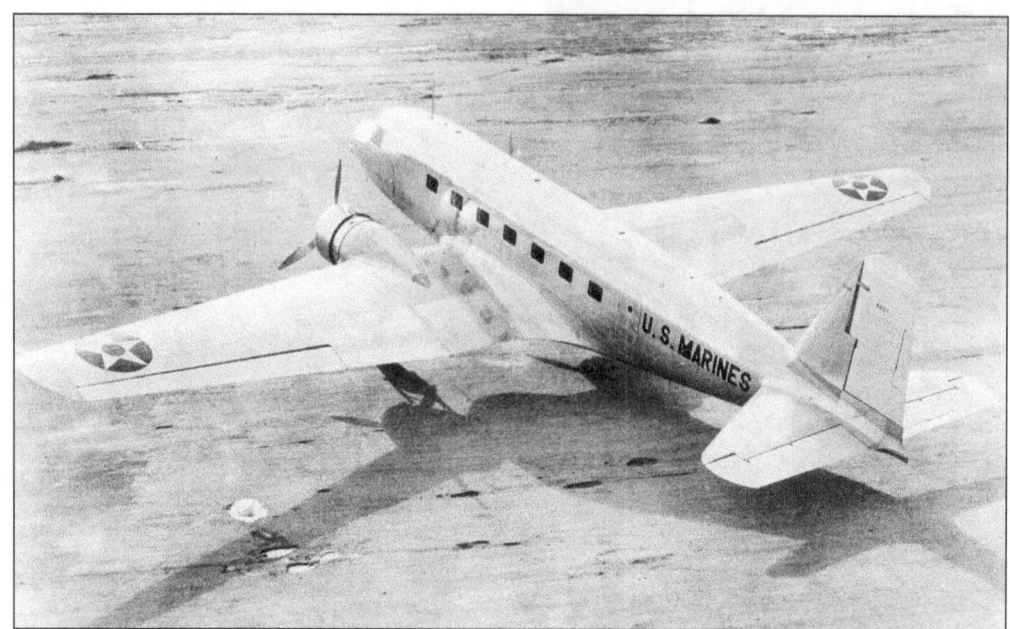

In December 1934, VJ-6M reached another milestone: accepting the Marines' first Douglas R2D-1. The R2D, based on the DC-2 commercial airliner, offered unprecedented speed, safety, and cargo capacity. In those lean times, funds for a large-scale procurement did not exist, and only two found their way into Marine Corps service, both at Quantico. Aircraft Squadrons, East Coast Expeditionary Force, had by now been renamed Aircraft One, Fleet Marine Force. (NARA.)

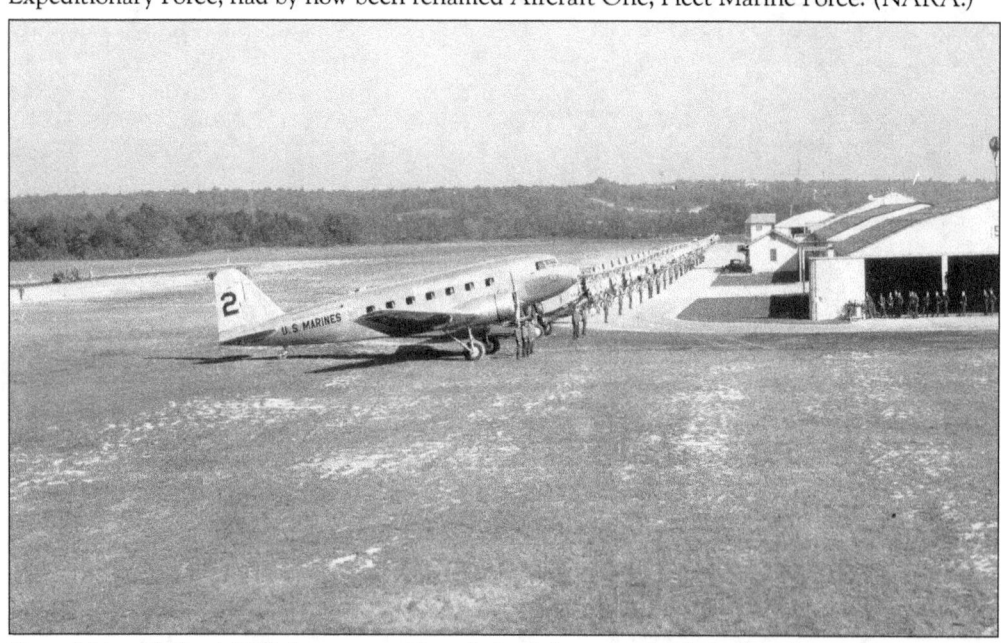

One of Aircraft One's R2D-1 transports dwarfs the fighters on the flight line during an inspection at Turner Field in July 1937. This photograph was taken just weeks after VJ-6M was redesignated Marine Utility Squadron 1 (VMJ-1), using a revised US Navy alphanumeric coding system still in use today. Among the squadron pilots who flew the transport was Capt. Allen Koonce, who would later command SCAT. (NARA.)

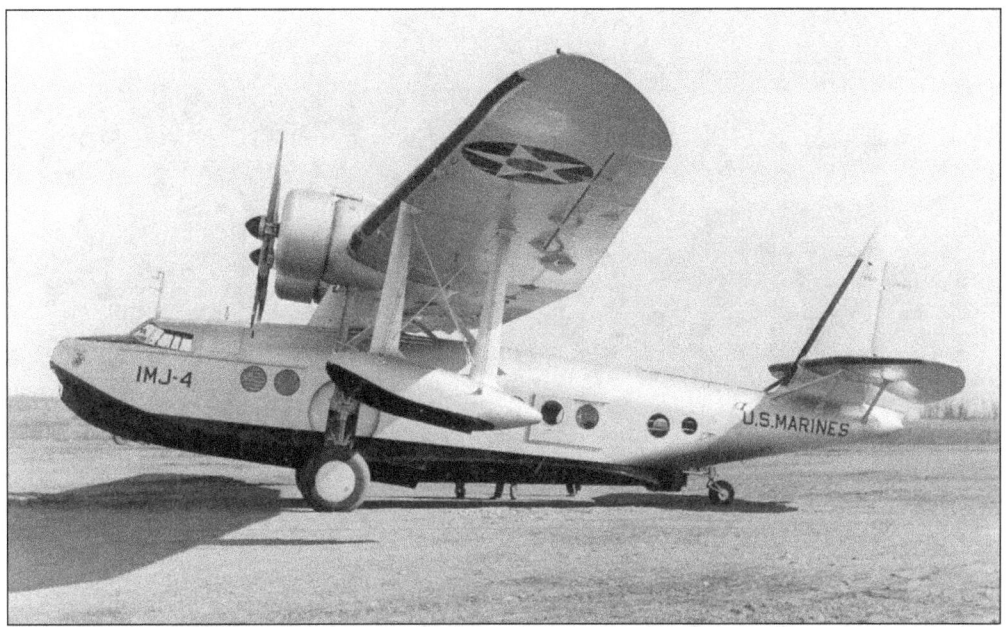

Captain Koonce of VMJ-1 flew this Sikorsky JRS-1 from the factory to Quantico in February 1938. That year, Aircraft One became the 1st Marine Aircraft Group; its commanding officer remained Col. Roy S. Geiger, later to gain fame at Guadalcanal. In 1939, this aircraft would participate in the successful rescue of submariners from the sunken USS *Squalus*, flying in divers and supplies. (Courtesy of the National Naval Aviation Museum.)

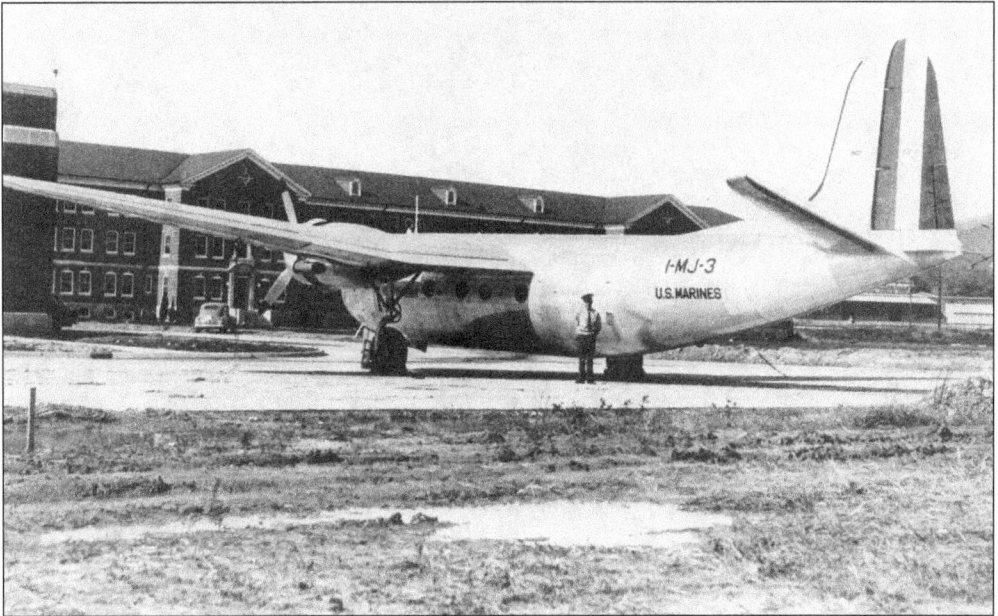

In 1940, VMJ-1 enjoyed another leap forward in airlift capability when it received the Marine Corps' first Douglas R3D-2 aircraft, the third of which is shown at Quantico in 1941. The R3D was the naval version of the short-lived DC-5 airliner, aborted due to wartime demands. It outperformed the R2D, with a top speed of 230 miles per hour, range of 1,600 miles, and maximum load of 24 passengers. (NARA.)

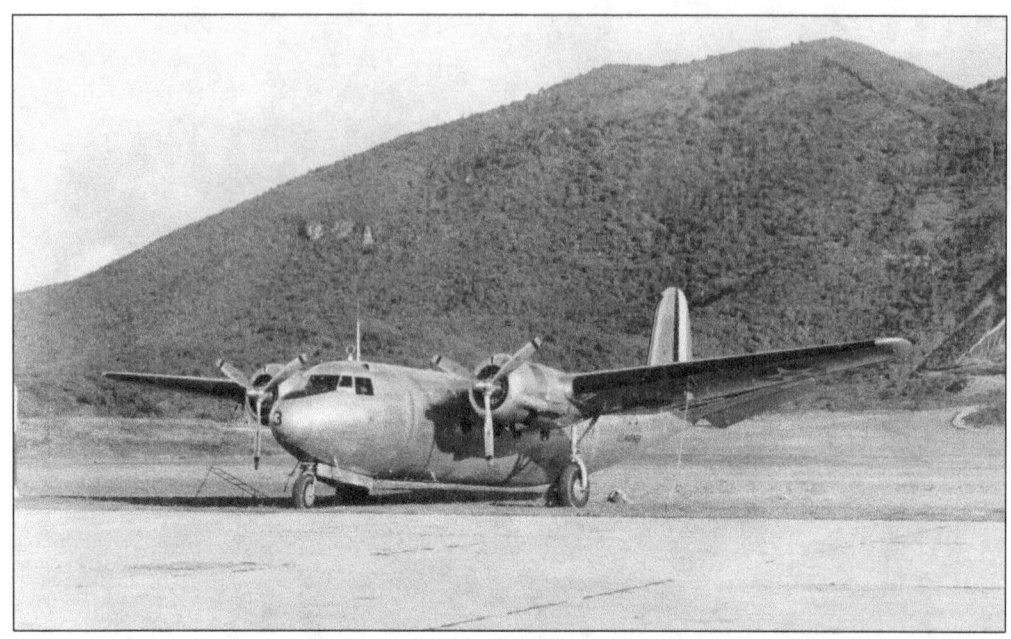

One of VMJ-1's R3D-2 aircraft is shown during Fleet Landing Exercise (FLEX) 7, likely at Bourne Field, St. Thomas, Virgin Islands, in February or March 1941. By this time, VMJ-1's pilots were highly proficient in long-distance instrument flight. In addition, a number of experienced airline pilots were attached to Quantico as reserve officers. On June 28, after returning from the Virgin Islands, VMJ-1 would be redesignated VMJ-152. (NARA.)

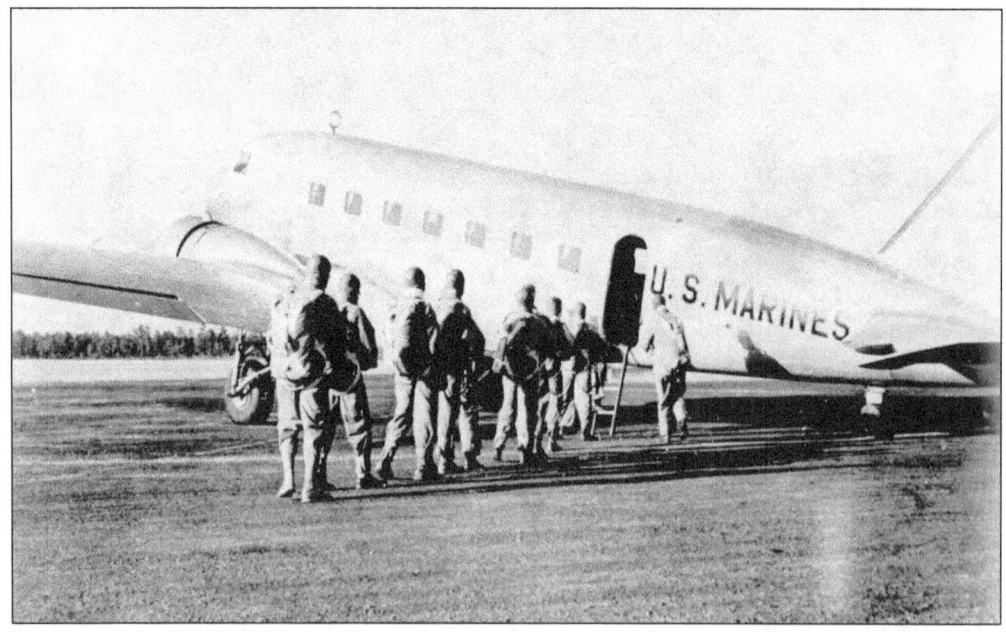

Paramarines of the 1st Parachute Battalion board an R2D while training with VMJ-152 in 1941. Marine parachute units would only jump while training during the war (including at New Caledonia) but would serve with distinction in the Pacific. On July 7, the 1st Marine Aircraft Group became the 1st Marine Aircraft Wing. VMJ-152 would be attached to the 1st Marine Aircraft Wing throughout its World War II combat service. (NARA.)

Two

PREPARING FOR WAR

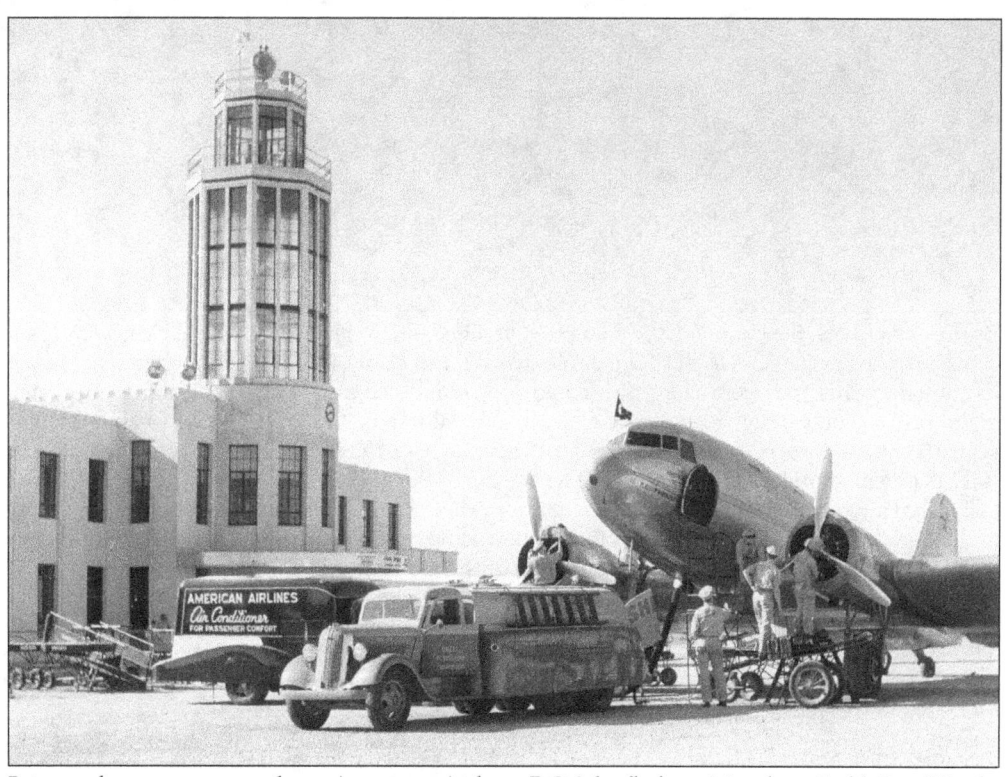

Prior to the war, crews ready an American Airlines DC-3 for flight at Meacham Field, Fort Worth, Texas. In 1942, Marine Corps Reserve pilots from American and other leading airlines formed the nucleus of VMJ-253. During the war, the American Airlines Naval Training School at Meacham Field trained new naval aviators destined for R4D units. (Courtesy of the Smithsonian National Air and Space Museum [NASM 00130926].)

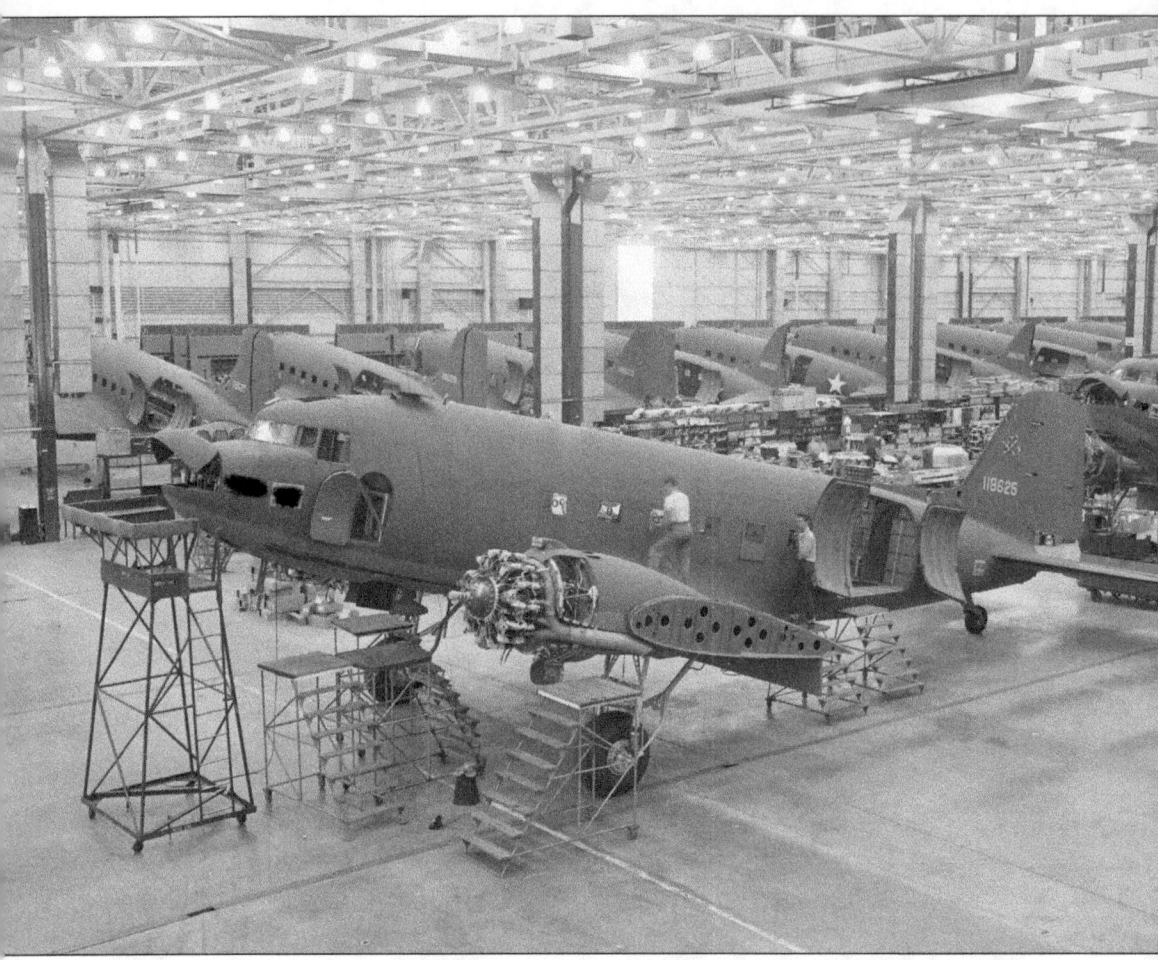

By the end of 1941, the popular DC-3 had been modified into a capacious and reliable new military transport, the Douglas C-47/R4D. Larger than the R2D and R3D, its most obvious differences from its civilian counterpart were a large side cargo door, reinforced cargo floor, navigator's astrodome, and a tail assembly designed to tow gliders. Its official name, "Skytrain," never entirely caught on with crews—MAG-25 preferred "Flying Boxcar." MAG-25's initial aircraft complement were R4D-1s procured under Navy contract. The US Navy Bureau of Aeronautics (BuAer) procured additional aircraft through larger Army contracts, their designations simply switched from C-47 and C-47A to R4D-1 and R4D-5, respectively, upon delivery. Navy aircraft also received new BuAer serial numbers. Photographer Alfred T. Palmer of the US Office of War Information visited the Douglas Aircraft Company plant in Long Beach, California, in October 1942 documenting the production surge of this invaluable aircraft. His work is shown on this and the following page. This aircraft, C-47 41-18625, later served with SCAT in the South Pacific (see page 87). (Courtesy of the Library of Congress.)

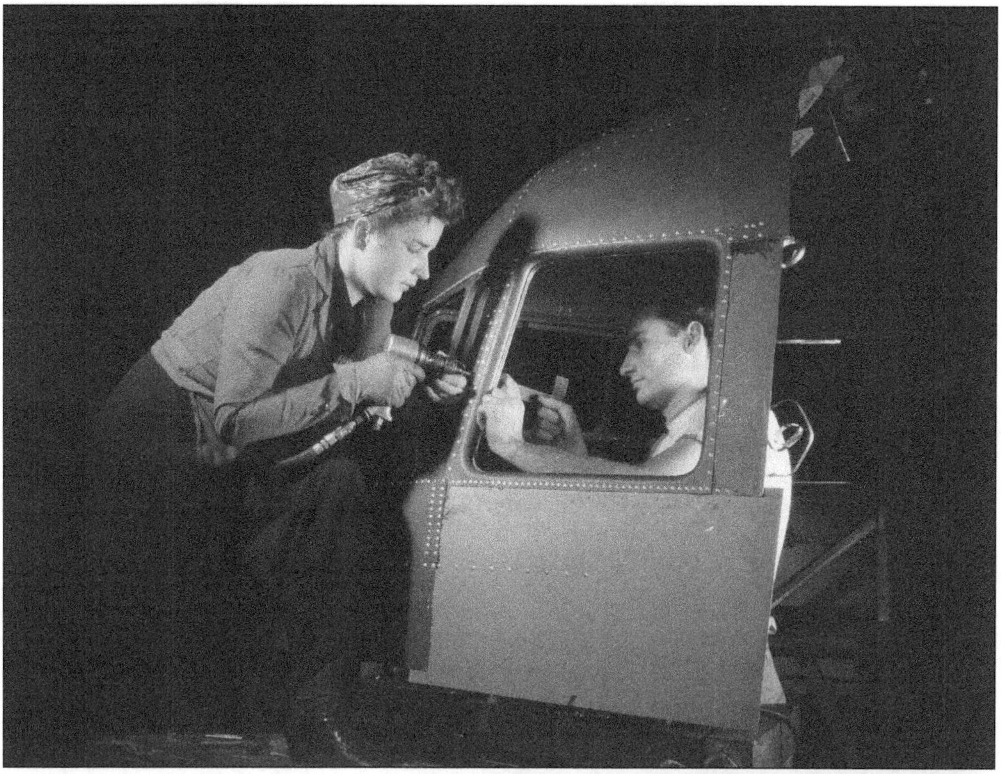

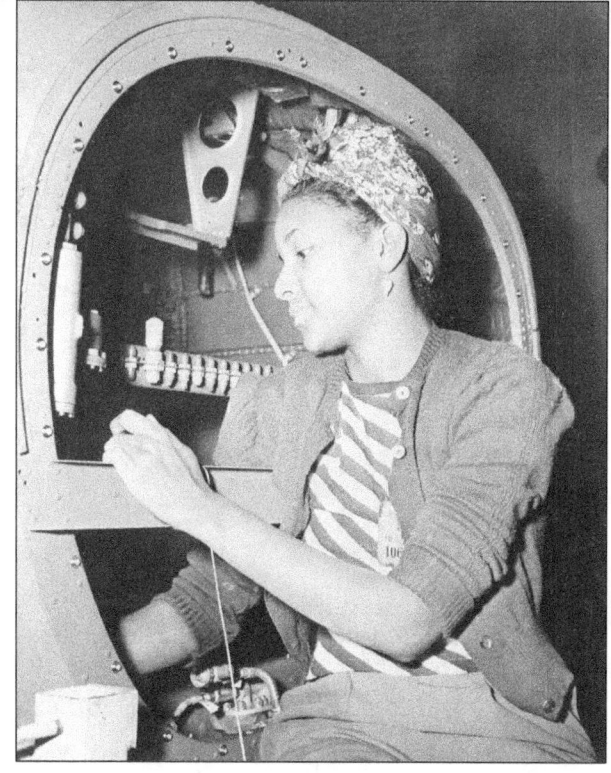

"Rosie the Riveter" was a crucial part of SCAT's story, as women filled vital manufacturing positions at Douglas and other manufacturers. Here, a riveting team at Long Beach works on a C-47's cockpit assembly, featuring the iconic Douglas window design introduced with the DC-1 in 1933. (Courtesy of the Library of Congress.)

Deloris Aldridge works on the nose compartment of a C-47 at Long Beach. Production of the important transport later expanded to Douglas plants in Santa Monica and Oklahoma City. Douglas built over 10,000 C-47s during the war, the military variant vastly outnumbering its civilian DC-3 counterpart. Many continued in service for decades with a mix of military and civilian operators. (Courtesy of the Library of Congress.)

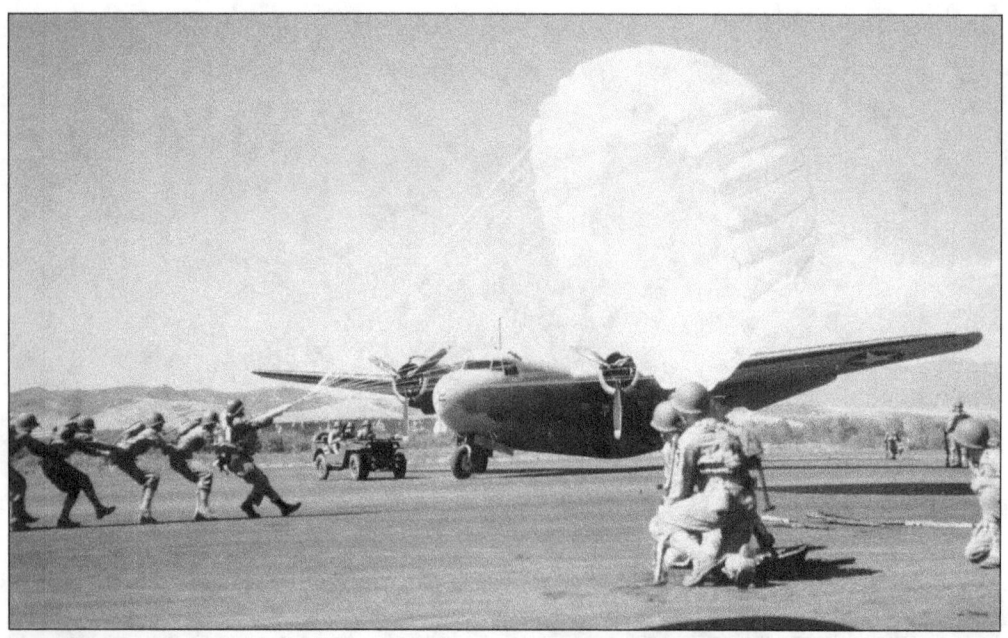

Paramarines train with VMJ-152 at Camp Kearny, California, a former World War I training camp, in the summer of 1942. The entire 1st Marine Aircraft Wing had relocated to Camp Kearny from Quantico by December 21, 1941. At least two of VMJ-152's four R3D-2 aircraft were modified to accommodate paratroopers. This example is painted in the blue-gray over light gray camouflage common to US naval aircraft in 1941–1942. (NARA.)

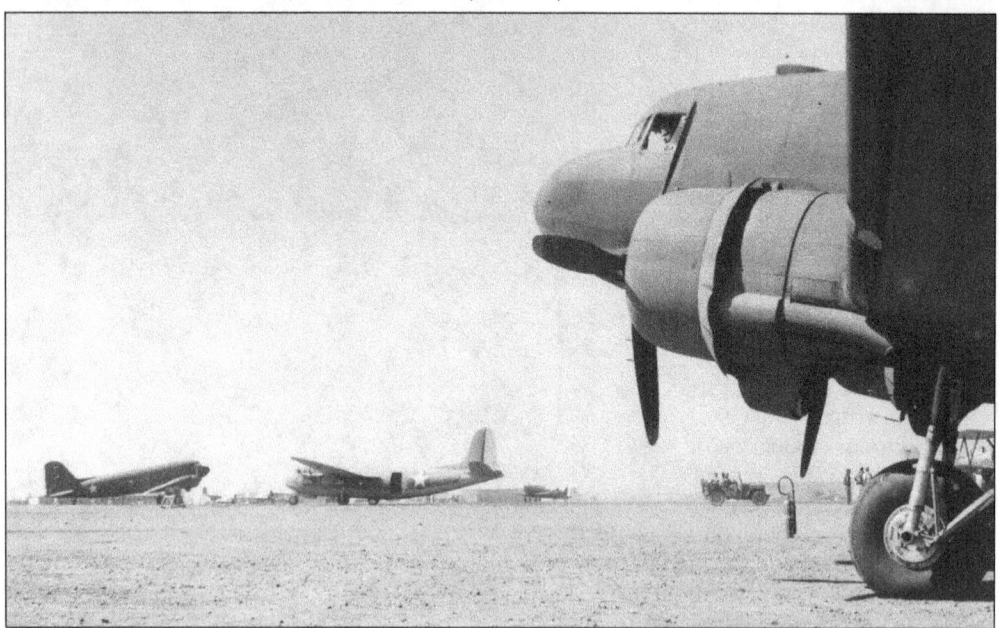

US naval aviation expanded rapidly, and many of the 1st Marine Aircraft Wing's experienced veterans were promoted to leadership positions in newly formed squadrons. Wartime volunteers were trained to take their places. VMJ-152 was soon assigned to MAG-15, which initially functioned as the Marines' R4D training unit. These MAG-15 R4Ds and a lone R3D are shown at Camp Kearny early in the war. (Courtesy of the National Naval Aviation Museum.)

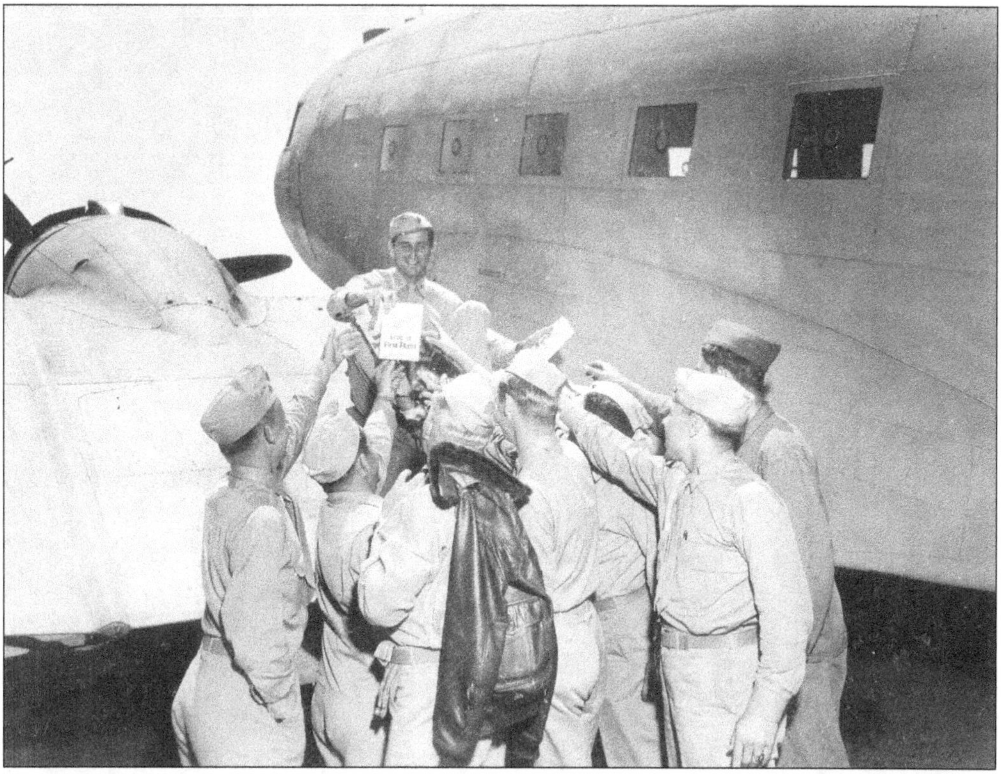

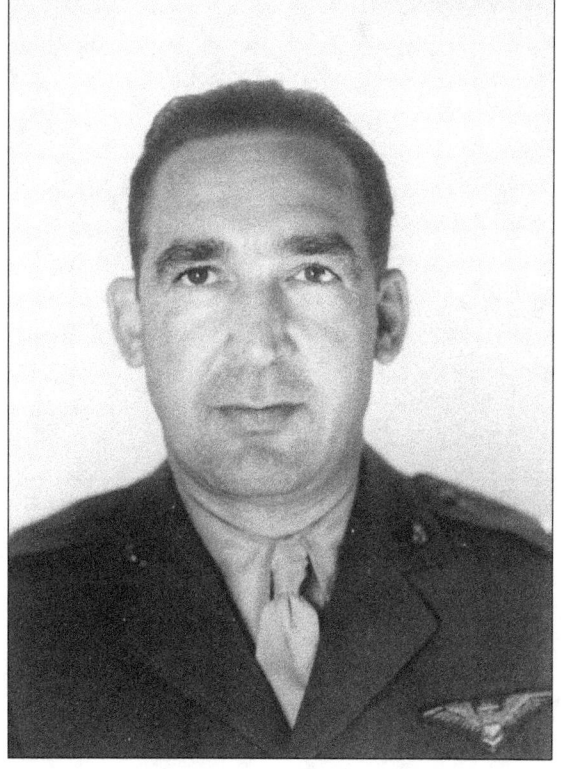

Navigator John Otis Carney of Headquarters Squadron, MAG-15, hawks his novel *Love at First Flight*, coauthored with Charles Spalding, in this posed photograph at Camp Kearny in 1943. Carney would later serve with VMJ-153. MAG-15 specialized in familiarization training, its instructors introducing green crewmen to the R4D. MAG-15 would continue training aircrews for overseas service with MAG-25 and other units until it deployed overseas itself in early 1944. (NARA.)

Lt. Col. Perry "P.K." Smith was MAG-25's first commanding officer and later the first commander of SCAT. A career Marine Corps officer, Smith's prewar assignments included VJ-6M at Quantico and VJ-7M (later VMJ-2 and VMJ-252) in San Diego and Hawaii. He was given command of VMJ-253 in March 1942, then MAG-25 in June 1942, remaining with the group until July 1943. Smith retired as a brigadier general in 1954. (NARA.)

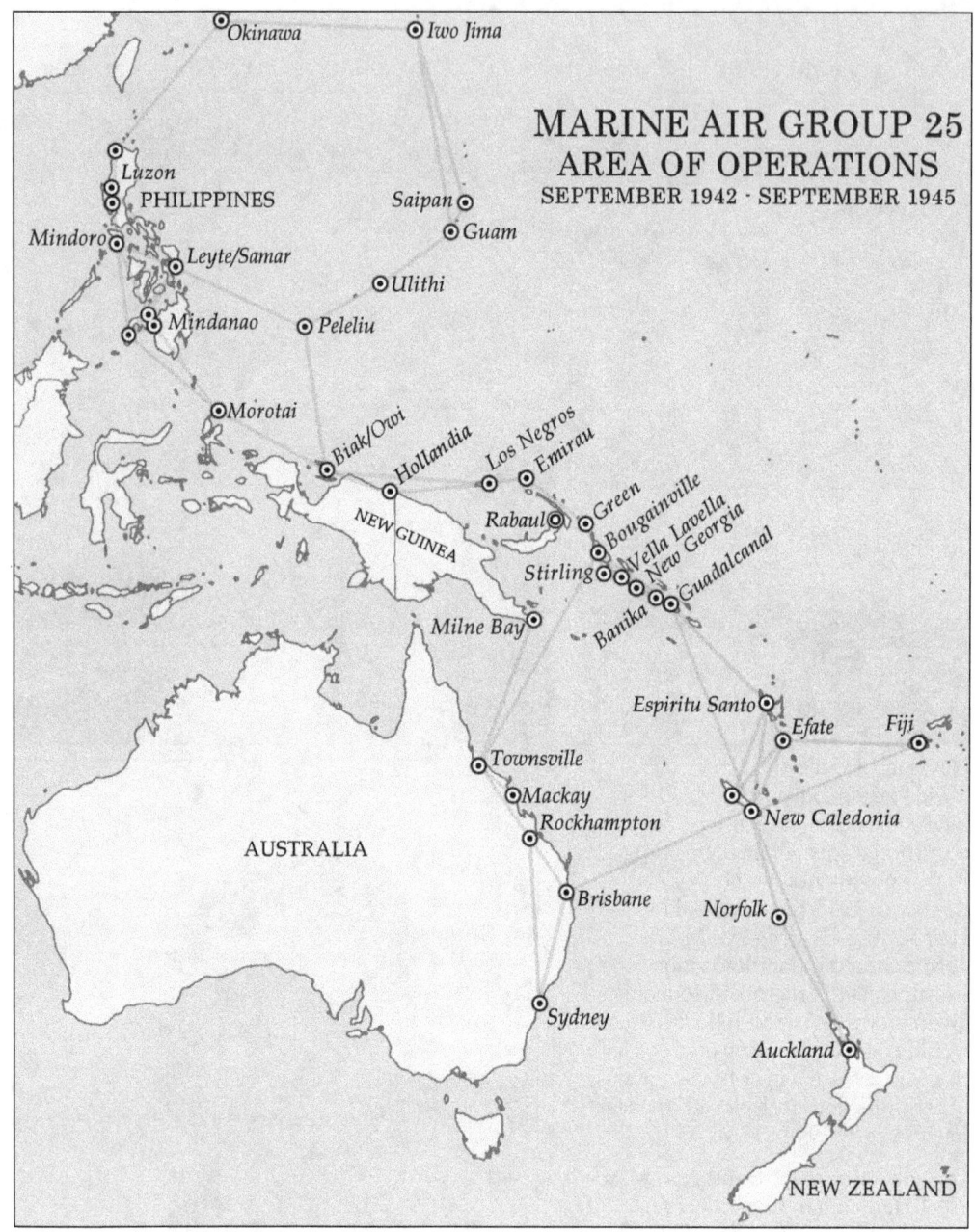

MAG-25's route from San Diego to New Caledonia included stops at Marine Corps Air Station Ewa, Hawaii (a 2,618-mile nonstop flight), Palmyra, Canton, and Fiji, a total distance of about 6,733 miles. Prior to Japan's surrender, MAG-25 would encompass an operational area that grew to roughly 5,340,000 square miles (4,032,000 square nautical miles), most of which was ocean. (Author illustration.)

Three

GUADALCANAL AND SCAT

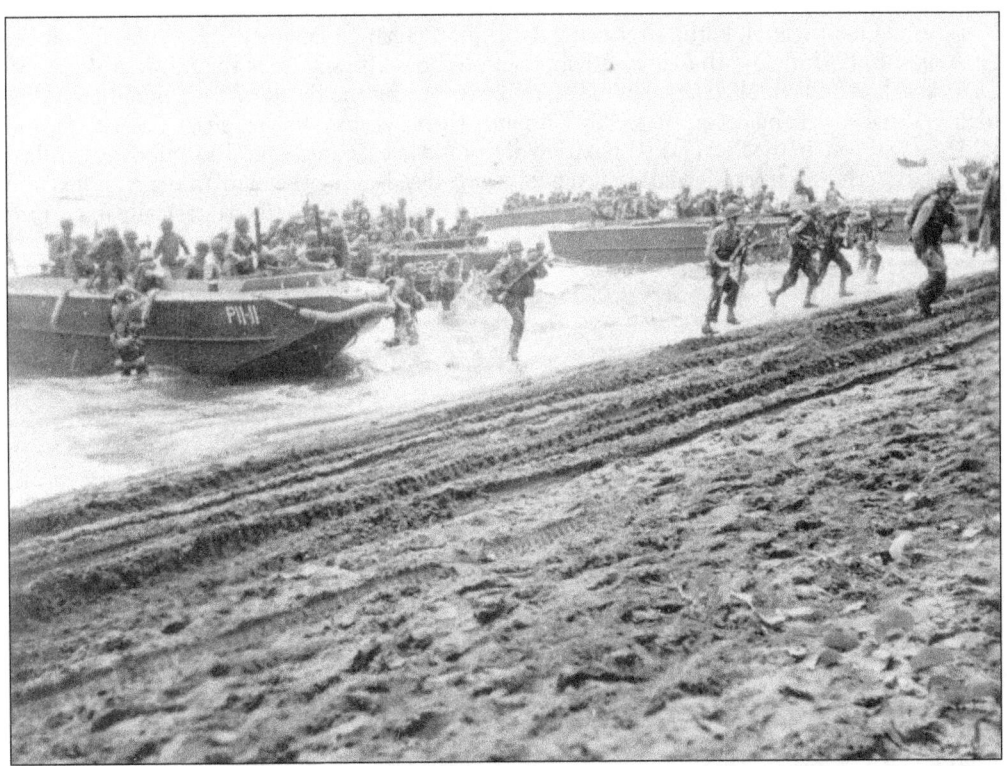

The 1st Marine Division storms ashore on Guadalcanal on August 7, 1942. The initial landing was unopposed, and the Marines soon held a perimeter around the partially constructed airfield, soon named Henderson Field after a fallen Marine aviator. The Japanese, caught by surprise, retreated into the jungle. Yet Japan quickly rushed naval, air, and ground forces to the island, and the ensuing battle for Guadalcanal would ultimately last six months. (NARA.)

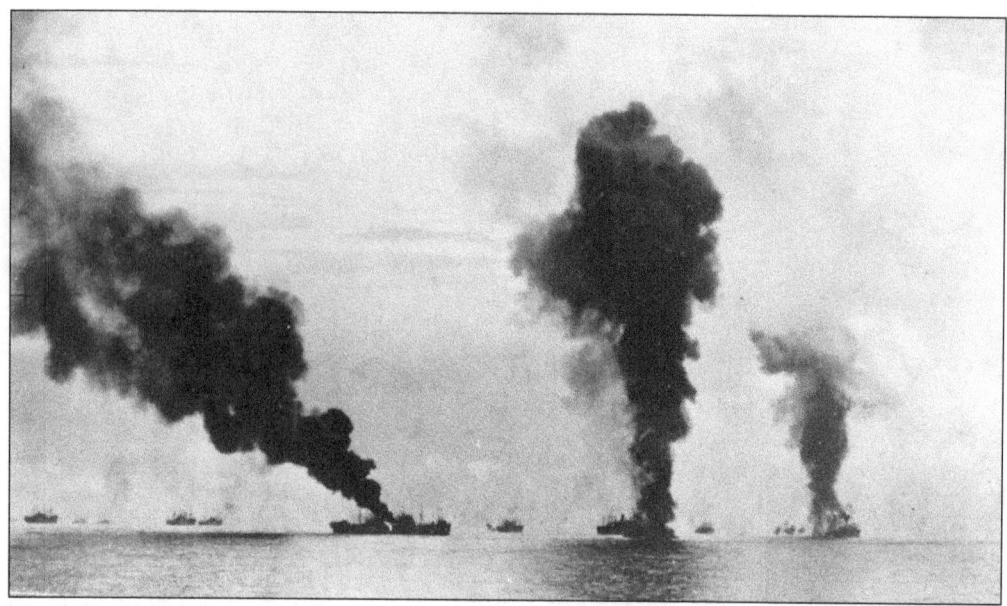

The enemy ashore proved elusive, but naval and air attacks soon jeopardized the landings. Above, the mortally damaged transport USS *George F. Elliott* (at center left), which had brought Marines to Guadalcanal, burns after being struck by a crashing Japanese G4M "Betty" bomber on August 8, 1942. Below, this captured photograph shows the demise of the heavy cruiser USS *Quincy*, ablaze and engulfed by Japanese searchlights during the Battle of Savo Island later that night. Also lost were heavy cruisers USS *Vincennes* (likely visible afire, at left), USS *Astoria*, and HMAS *Canberra*. In the face of this unexpectedly formidable Japanese naval and air threat, Allied transports withdrew from Guadalcanal the following day, leaving the men ashore stranded and without vital supplies. It now became imperative to devise lifelines to the strategically important island, by sea and by air. (Both, NHHC.)

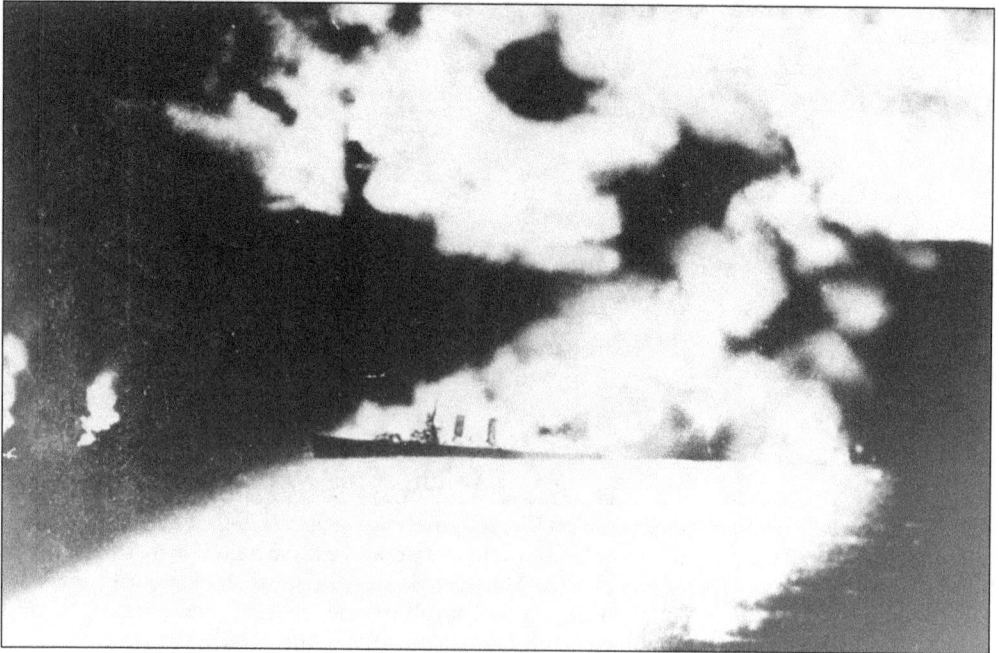

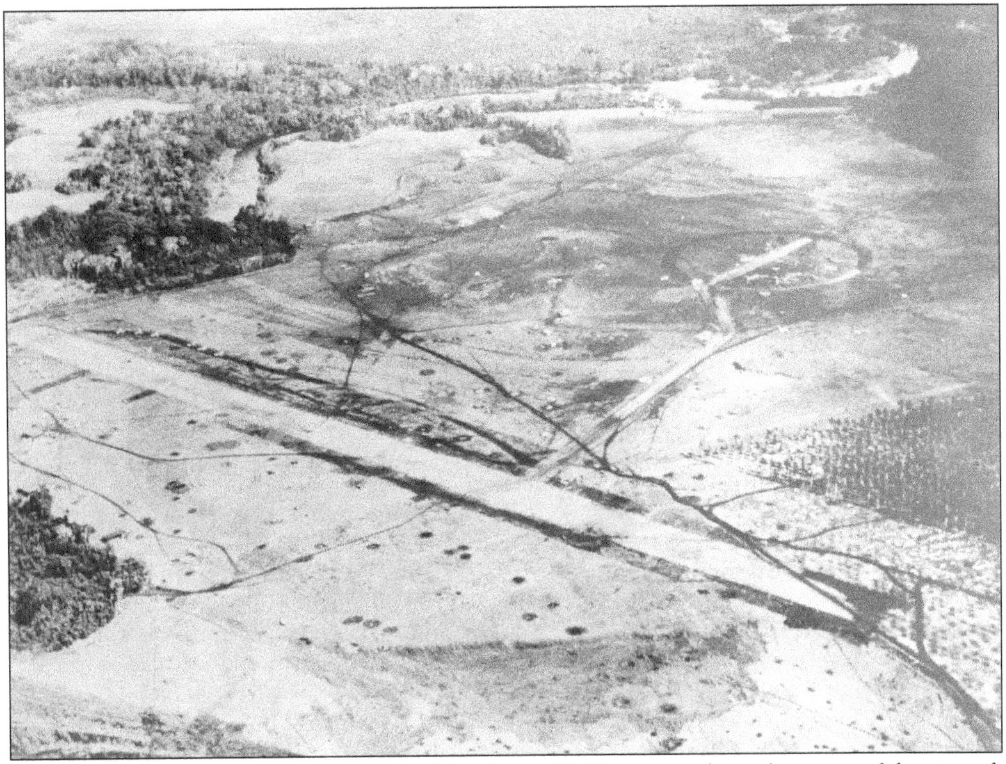

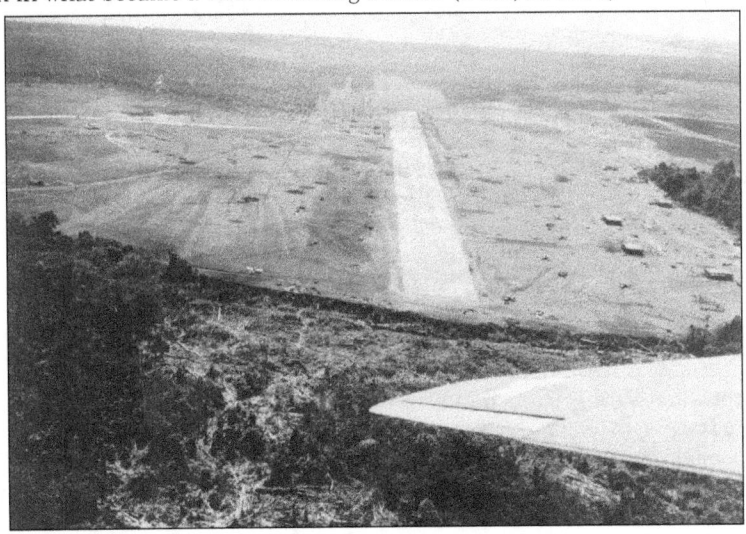

These August 1942 views show primitive Henderson Field, as seen above from one of the aircraft of USS *Saratoga* (CV-3) and below from a USAAF B-17 Flying Fortress. Completion of the crude runway begun by the Japanese became a high priority, and the first aircraft—F4F Wildcat fighters and SBD Dauntless dive-bombers—touched down on August 20. On August 23, the first aircraft of MAG-25 departed San Diego. Lt. Col. P.K. Smith landed the first transport on Guadalcanal on September 3, 1942, carrying Maj. Gen. Roy S. Geiger. Geiger would command the 1st Marine Aircraft Wing from the embattled island. Just two days later, after landing under fire, Lt. Col. W. Fiske Marshall became the first to airlift casualties from the battlefield, inaugurating MAG-25's participation in what became a vital lifesaving service. (Both, NARA.)

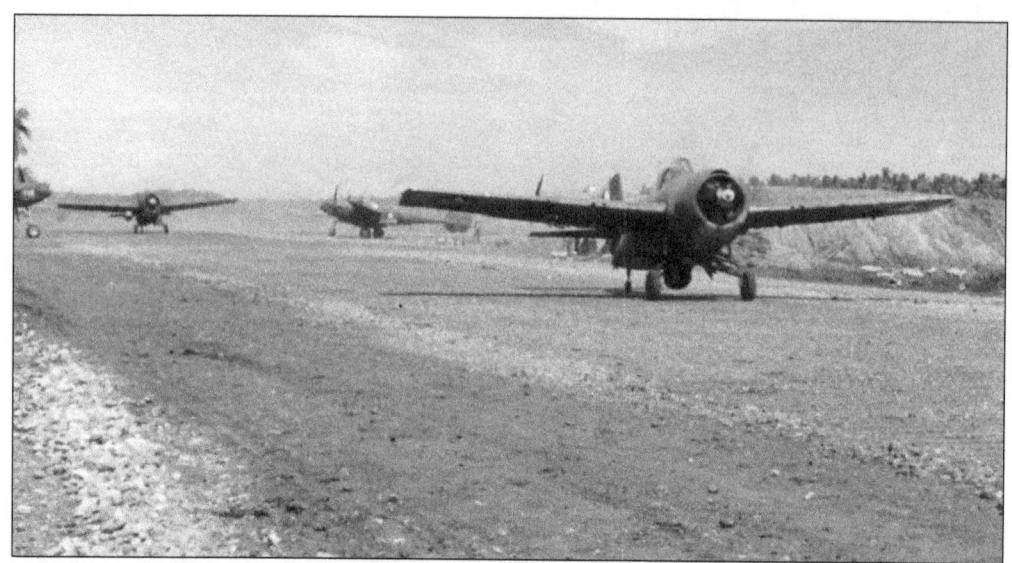

F4F Wildcats of Marine Fighting Squadron 121 (VMF-121) and P-38 Lightnings of the USAAF 347th Fighter Group taxi out in late 1942. The "Cactus Air Force" struggled to keep its aircraft flying, facing fuel and spare parts shortages, combat losses, and numerous accidents on Guadalcanal's crude, battered runways. SCAT proved a vital lifeline, particularly in mid-October as the sole source of aviation gasoline. (Courtesy of the National Museum of Naval Aviation.)

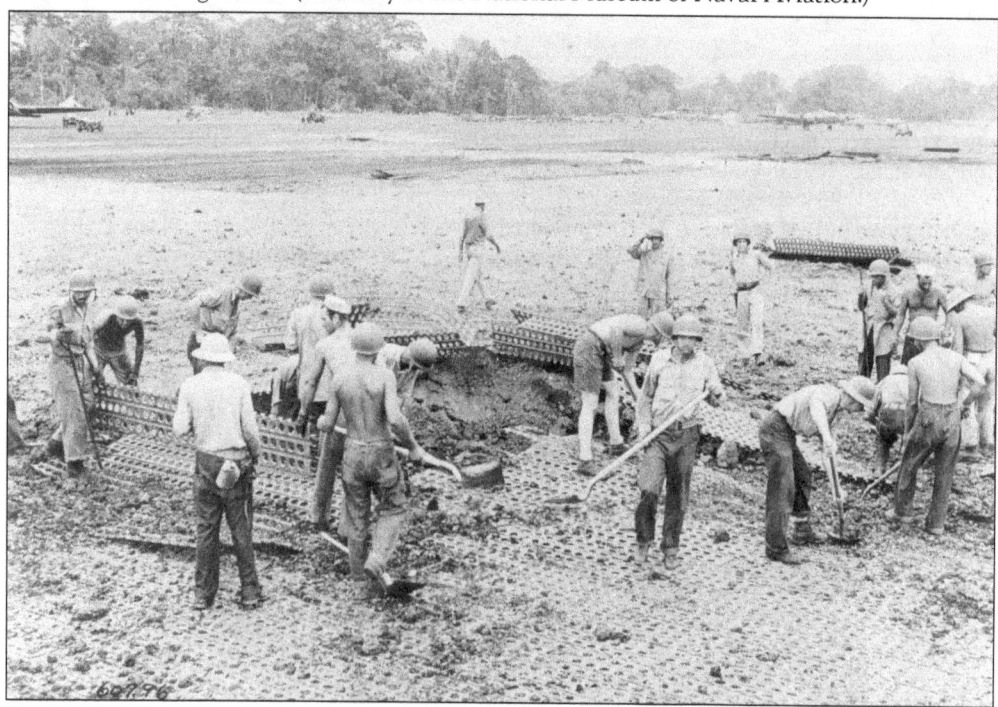

Japanese bombers and warships made Henderson Field a hazardous place throughout the campaign. These men are starting to repair a bomb crater on the airstrip on October 13, 1942. Early transport flights into Guadalcanal were frequently targeted and occasionally hit by enemy fire, both on the ground and in the air. The "Cactus Air Force" sometimes escorted transport aircraft into and out of the airspace immediately around Guadalcanal. (NARA.)

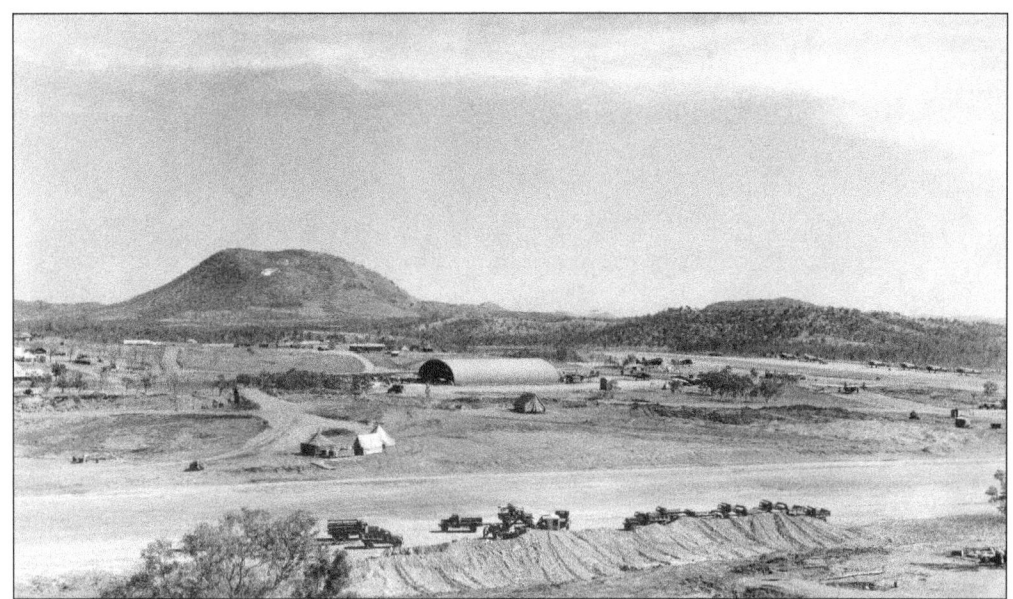

The view above shows Tontouta Air Base's intersecting runways, looking west-southwest. SCAT aircraft can be seen in the distance, by the maintenance hangar and runway 3/21. The former air base is now La Tontouta International Airport, and only runway 11/29 in the foreground remains. Below, Seabees of the 53rd Naval Construction Battalion resurface runway 3/21 in 1943. On October 9, 1942, MAG-25 suffered its first casualties when VMJ-253's executive officer, Maj. Walter "Skip" Kimball, a highly experienced airline pilot, took off at night with a heavy load in poor visibility from this runway and struck the distant hill, known afterward as "Kimball Hill." Also killed aboard R4D-1 01981 were copilot 2nd Lt. Donald Griffin, flight mechanic Cpl. Charles Mottram Jr., navigator Cpl. John Troup, and radio operator Pfc. Charles Vestal, as well as three passengers. (Both, NARA.)

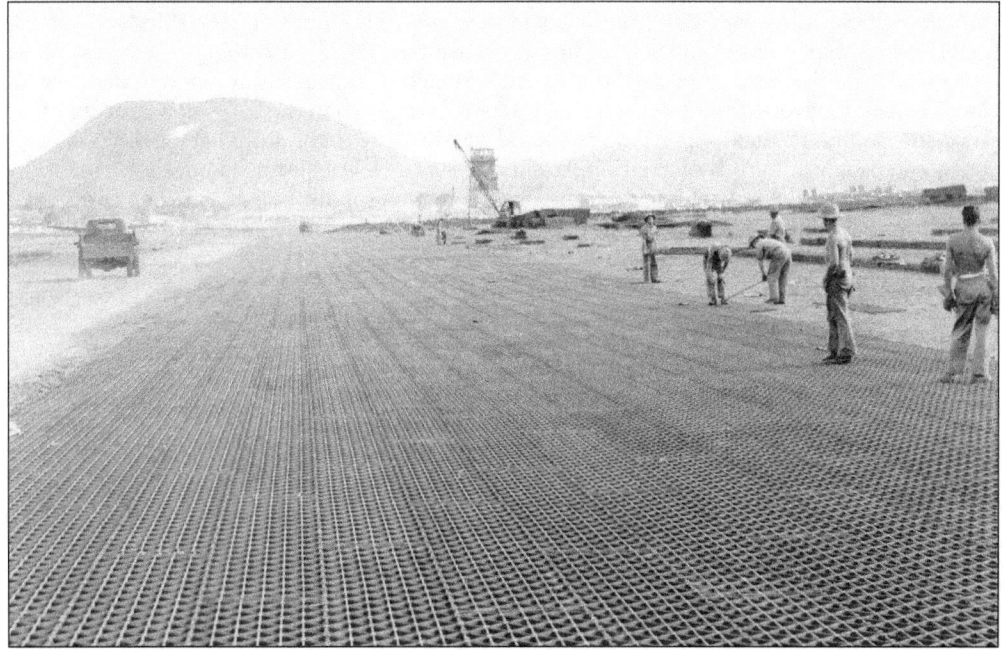

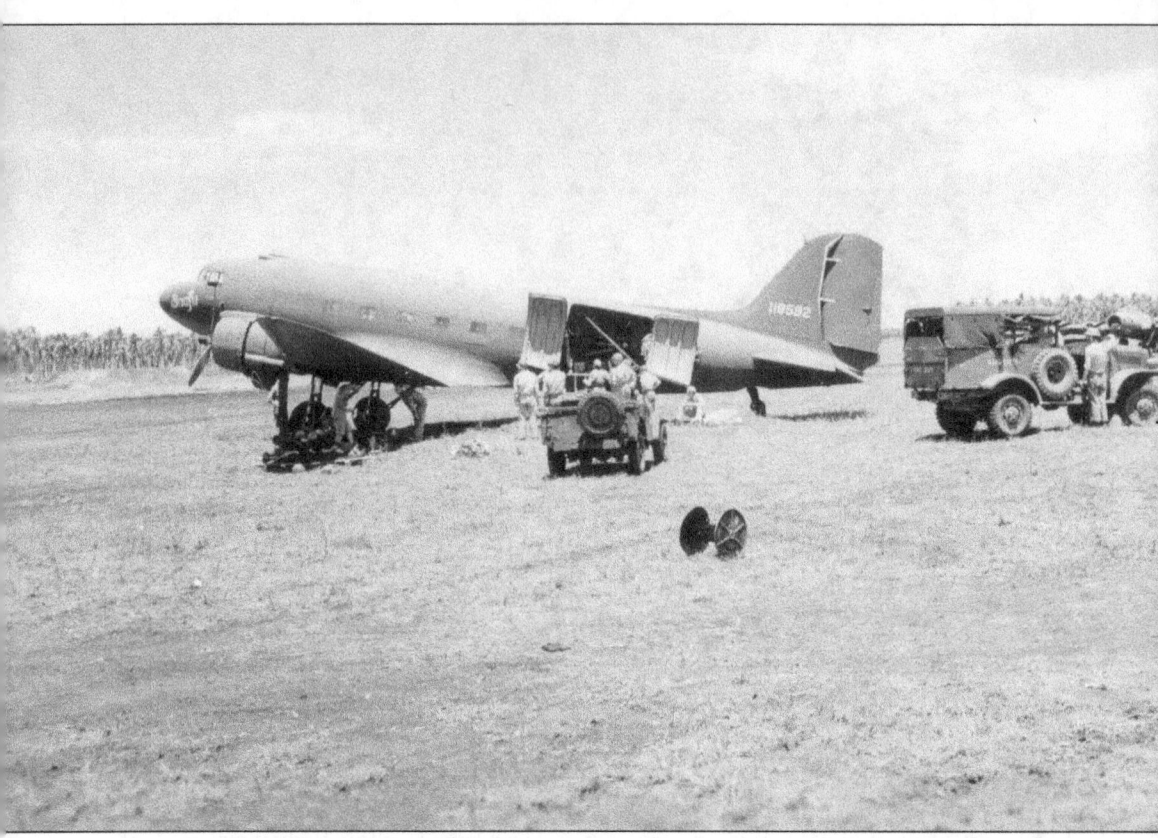

This image of *Snafu* of the 13th TCS (C-47 41-18582), taken on November 15, 1942, is a rare view of transport operations at Henderson Field during the Battle of Guadalcanal. Allied victory in the three-day Naval Battle of Guadalcanal had just blocked Japan's final attempts to bombard Henderson Field using warships. SCAT would never carry the most cargo—ships such as the LST (landing ship, tank) would deliver far more when they could get through—but was valued for its speed and flexibility, especially during emergencies. Flying mostly at night, under cover of clouds or near wavetop height, they were a far stealthier target than the large, slow-moving LSTs. Ammunition and medical supplies were aboard nearly every flight, although at times cargoes consisted entirely of barrels of aviation gasoline. Yet SCAT was just as famous for its morale-boosting cargo: cigarettes, whiskey, candies, and sometimes mail from home. The transports' arrivals were often eagerly awaited, and in the early weeks, Japanese gunners made deliberate efforts to disable them using small arms and artillery. (NARA.)

In January 1943, five MAG-25 officers received the Silver Star for actions during the Battle of Guadalcanal. Standing at Tontouta's parade ground, from left to right, are 2nd Lt. James M. Walker (VMJ-253), Lt. Col. Fiske Marshall (Headquarters), Maj. Owen Ross (Headquarters), Lt. Comdr. Tom Flaherty (MAG-25 senior medical officer), and Capt. John Whitaker (VMJ-253). All had safely evacuated casualties under heavy fire; Marshall and Walker both evaded Japanese fighter attacks. (MAG-25/SCAT.)

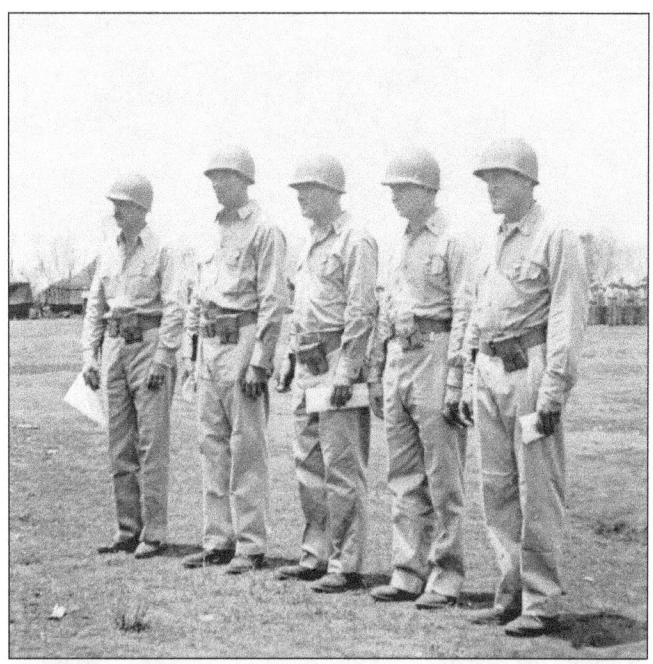

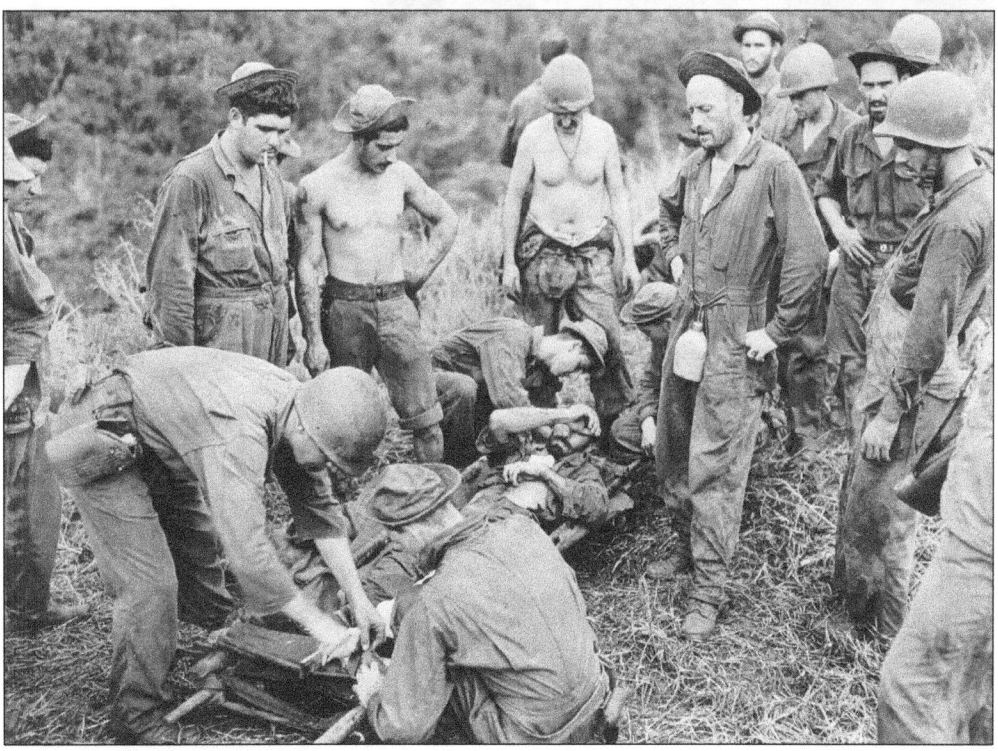

Soldiers of the 35th Infantry Regiment, 25th Infantry Division, evacuate a wounded man behind the front lines southwest of Henderson Field on January 15, 1943. By the end of 1942, SCAT's units had evacuated 3,202 casualties from forward areas, approximately 1,600 of whom were wounded in action during the fight for Guadalcanal. Many other patients suffered from infectious disease or combat stress. (Courtesy of the Library of Congress.)

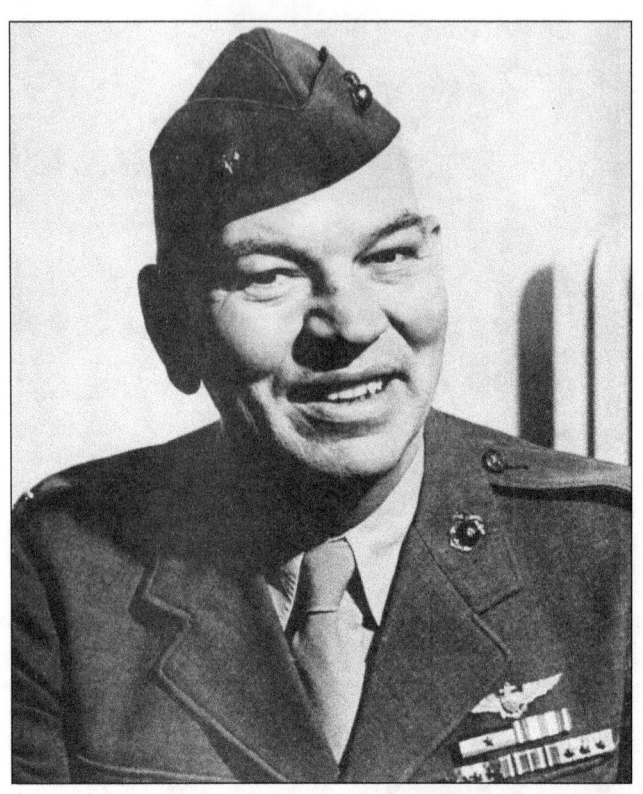

Col. Wyman Fiske Marshall, a reserve officer, commanded MAG-25 and SCAT from July 10 to December 23, 1943. A World War I veteran, Marshall had a distinguished career at Northwest Airlines and saw prewar duty with VMJ-1 in Puerto Rico. He joined MAG-25 as executive officer in July 1942. In December 1942, he took on the dual role of SCAT executive officer. Marshall later served in the Korean War. (MAG-25/SCAT)

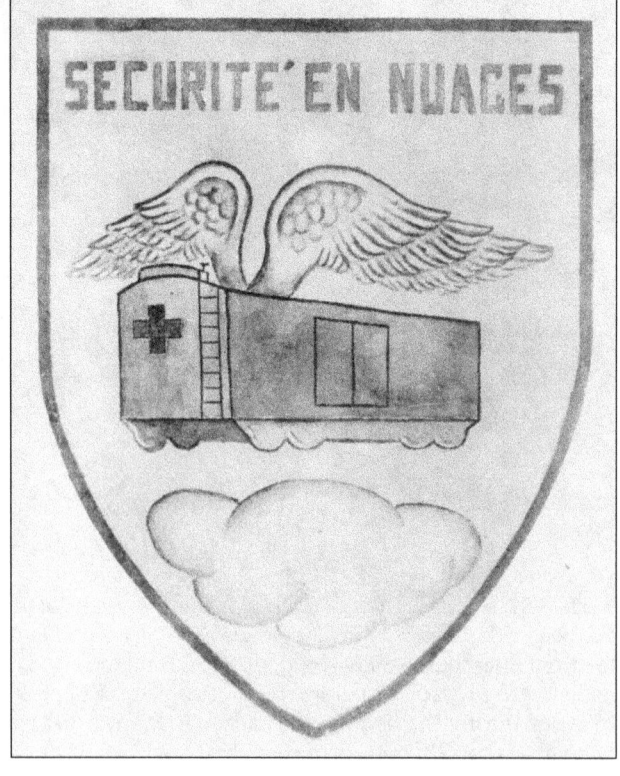

Walt Disney Studios drew MAG-25's "flying boxcar" insignia at the request of T.Sgt. Ray Alexander, MTSgt. William Dickman, and T.Sgt. Thomas Efstathiou in early 1943. The motto "Securité en Nuages," intended as "Security in Clouds," references the unit's preferred method of avoiding prowling enemy fighters. The red cross and angel wings symbolize MAG-25's role in aeromedical evacuation. Efstathiou was killed in action while serving with VMF-122 in June 1943. (MAG-25/SCAT).

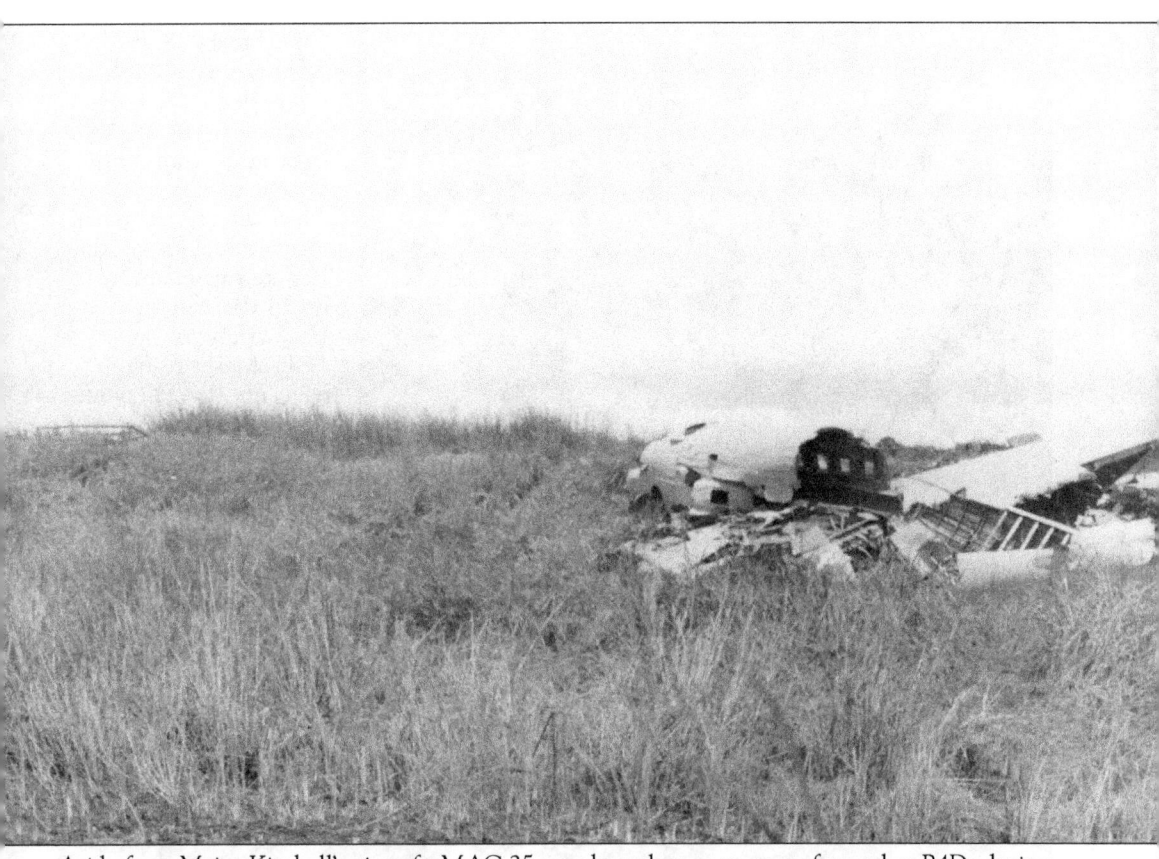

Aside from Major Kimball's aircraft, MAG-25 may have lost as many as four other R4Ds during the Guadalcanal campaign, but records are spotty. Least fortunate was VMJ-253's R4D-1 04696, piloted by S.Sgt. Arthur Dowers Jr., which reportedly exploded and crashed on approach off the coast of Guadalcanal's Kukum Bay the evening of November 13, 1942, with no survivors. Other members of the crew were 2nd Lt. Joseph Abel, Cpl. Roman Freise, Pfc. John Matuszak, and PhM3c. Paul Westerman. The wreck pictured here, almost certainly a MAG-25 aircraft, sat in the kunai grass south of Henderson Field on January 24, 1943. It is probably the aircraft recorded as destroyed when an SBD of VS-3 crashed into it on takeoff on September 20, but there is at least one vague account of other abandoned SCAT R4Ds, one reportedly due to artillery damage, another due to landing gear collapse. Its identity appears to be a mystery, but it may be either 01648 or 01978, both of which were nonfatal operational losses while assigned to VMJ-253 in late 1942. (NARA.)

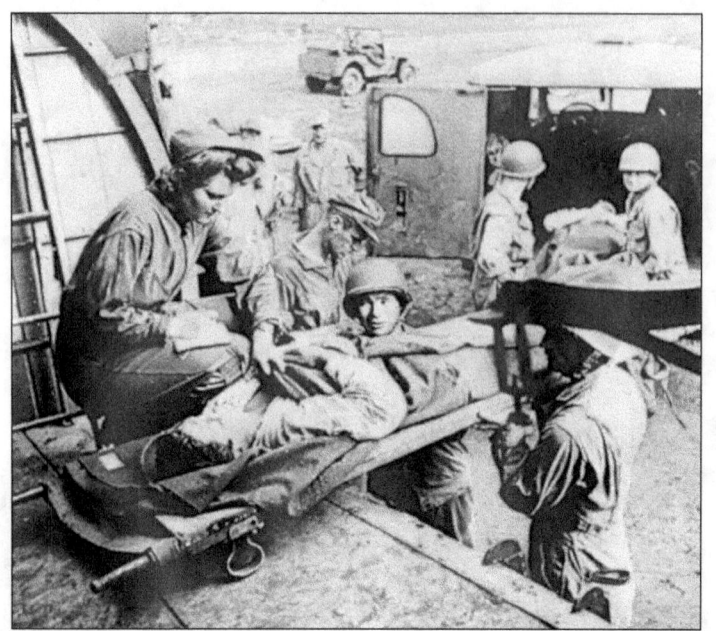

On February 28, 1943, flight nurse 2nd Lt. Mae Olson (left) of the 801st Medical Squadron, Air Evacuation Transport, became the first American servicewoman to arrive on Guadalcanal. Her crewmates aboard R4D-1 03135, from VMJ-253, were copilot 1st Lt. Mosby Cardozo, navigator Pvt. Junior Clark, flight mechanic Sgt. John Peak Jr., radio operator Sgt. Walker Stewart, and pilot Maj. John Walsh Jr. (Courtesy of the US Air Force.)

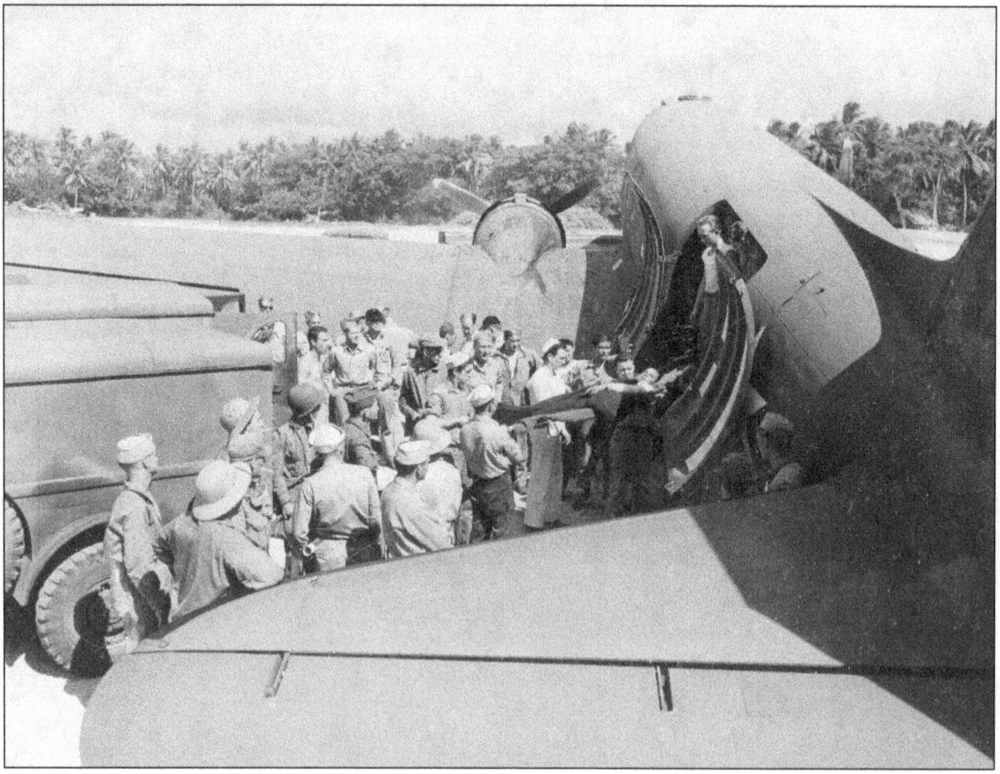

Medical personnel and aircrew, a mix of US Army, Navy, and Marine Corps personnel, stand by while litter patients from Guadalcanal are removed from a MAG-25 R4D, at Espiritu Santo or Efate. Some members of the flight crew, standing just behind the wing, wear blue baseball caps then popular among Marine fliers. From September 1942 through July 1944, SCAT's squadrons evacuated a total of 42,462 casualties from forward areas. (NARA.)

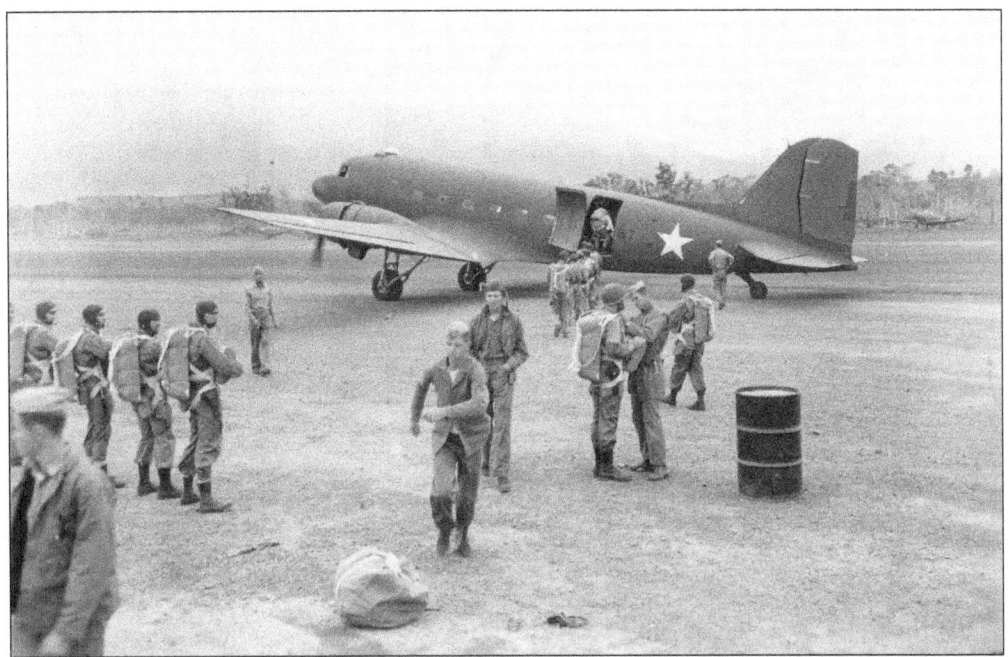

Marines of the 1st Parachute Battalion prepare to make their daily training jump aboard R4Ds of VMJ-253 at Tontouta on February 1, 1943. The 1st Parachute Battalion was encamped at nearby Camp Kiser, where it had recuperated after seeing intense combat on Guadalcanal and several neighboring islands. The unit would only ever jump in training, in part because even SCAT possessed too few aircraft to make a mass parachute drop. Above, Marines file aboard R4D "57" (likely 05057). Below, another group boards R4D "52" (likely 05052). Last in line is United Press war correspondent Edgar Rice Burroughs, the famed novelist and creator of the characters Tarzan and John Carter of Mars. (Both, NARA.)

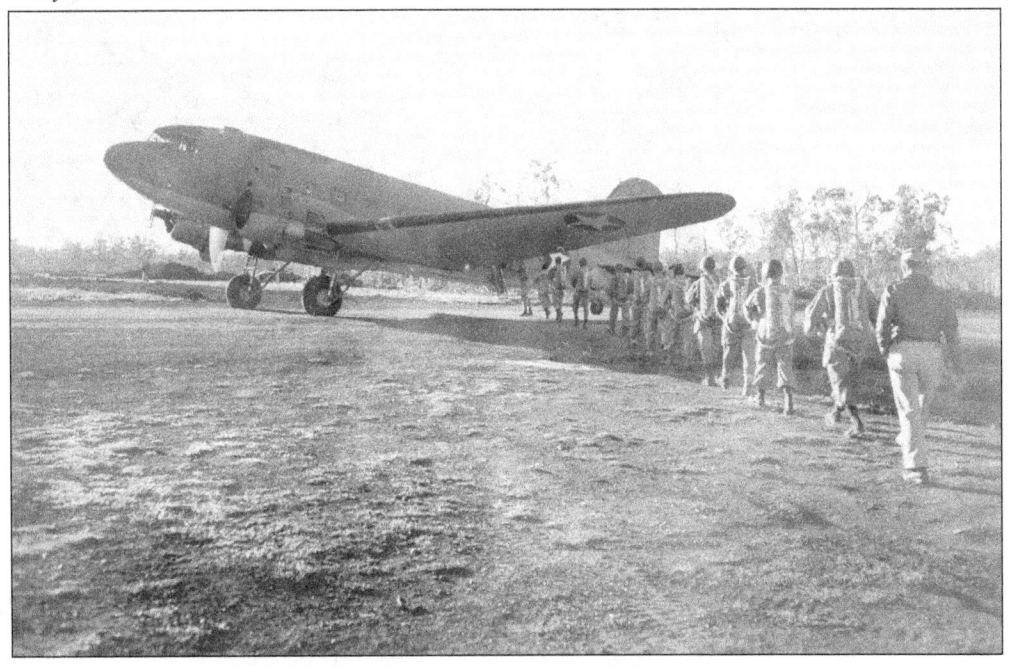

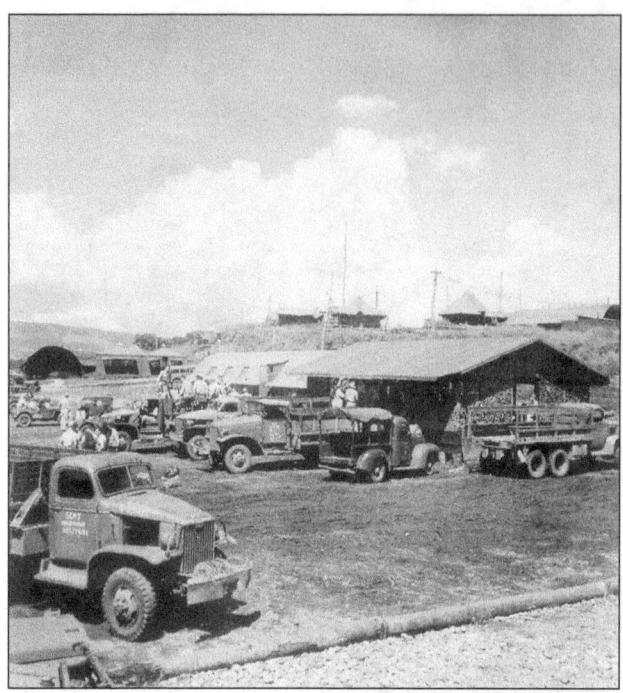

Development of Guadalcanal as a major Allied base began even before the island was secured, and accelerated after the last Japanese forces evacuated on February 8, 1943. In March 1943, SCAT's passenger office was in full operation near Henderson Field. Although Japanese ground forces no longer posed a threat, Guadalcanal's airfields were still subject to periodic minor Japanese air raids. (NARA.)

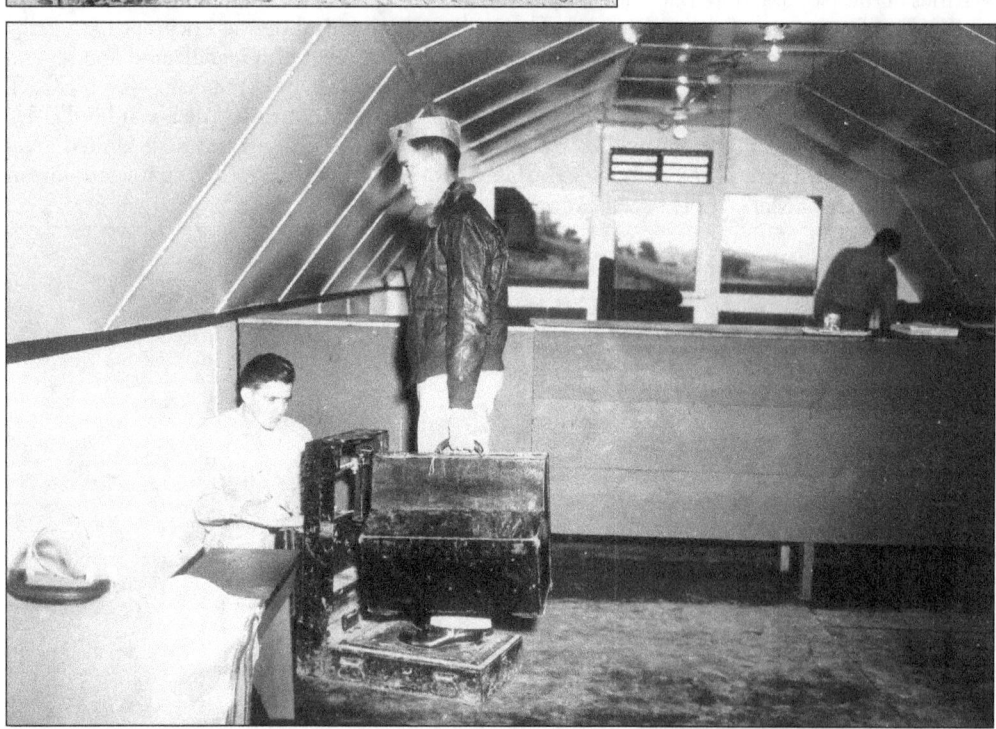

Every scheduled passenger was required to weigh in at the SCAT operations office. Here, a Marine and his luggage are weighed by Sgt. Marion Schoeny of Headquarters Squadron 25 at Henderson Field. SCAT ran a tight operation, and passengers were expected to check in at least an hour before their scheduled departure time and report to their aircraft no later than a half hour prior to takeoff. (NARA.)

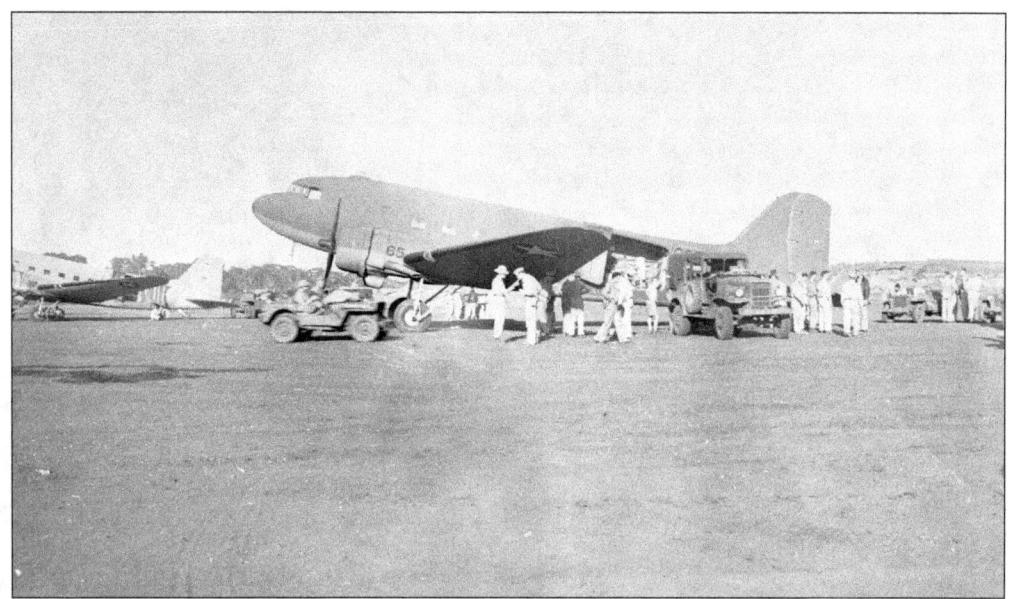

As SCAT flights to and from Guadalcanal became more routine, so did photographic coverage of the group's operations. In March 1943, these aircraft brought needed supplies and continued to evacuate casualties, most suffering from debilitating tropical disease. Above, R4Ds "82" (left) and "65" prepare to exchange cargo for patients. Below, parked on Guadalcanal, *Hitler's Hearse* (C-47 41-18574) of the 13th TCS appears to have found itself in the wrong hemisphere. Like many aircraft of the "Thirsty Thirteenth," it sported a second name, *Black Cat 13*, painted on the starboard side. A noticeable cultural difference within SCAT was that the USAAF typically assigned regular crews to individual aircraft, whereas the Marines operated a pool system with crew composition and aircraft assignments typically changing with each mission. Names and nose art were conspicuously absent on Marine R4Ds. (Both, NARA.)

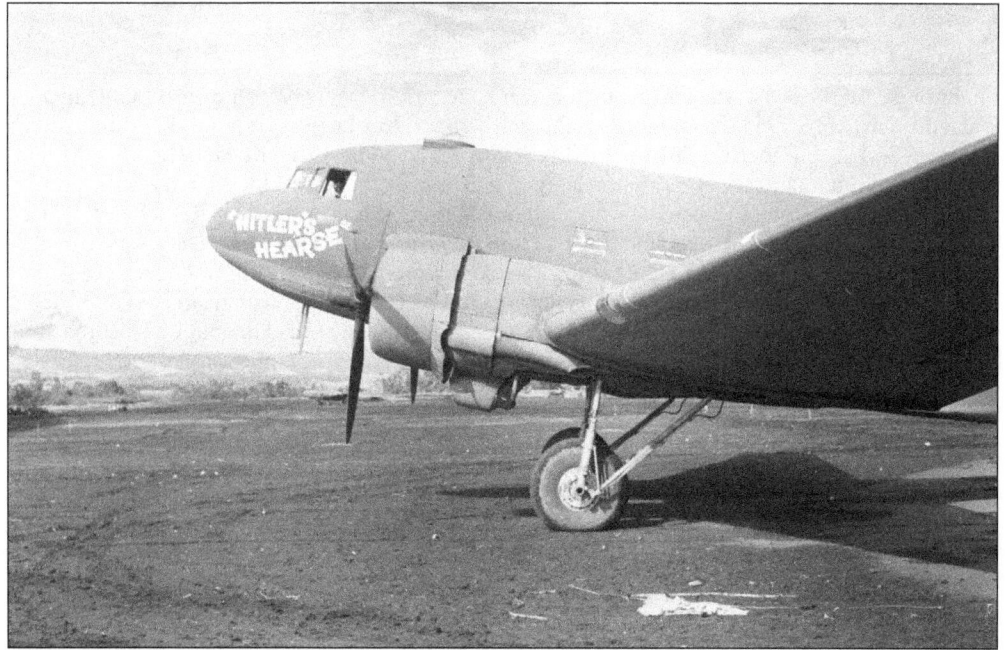

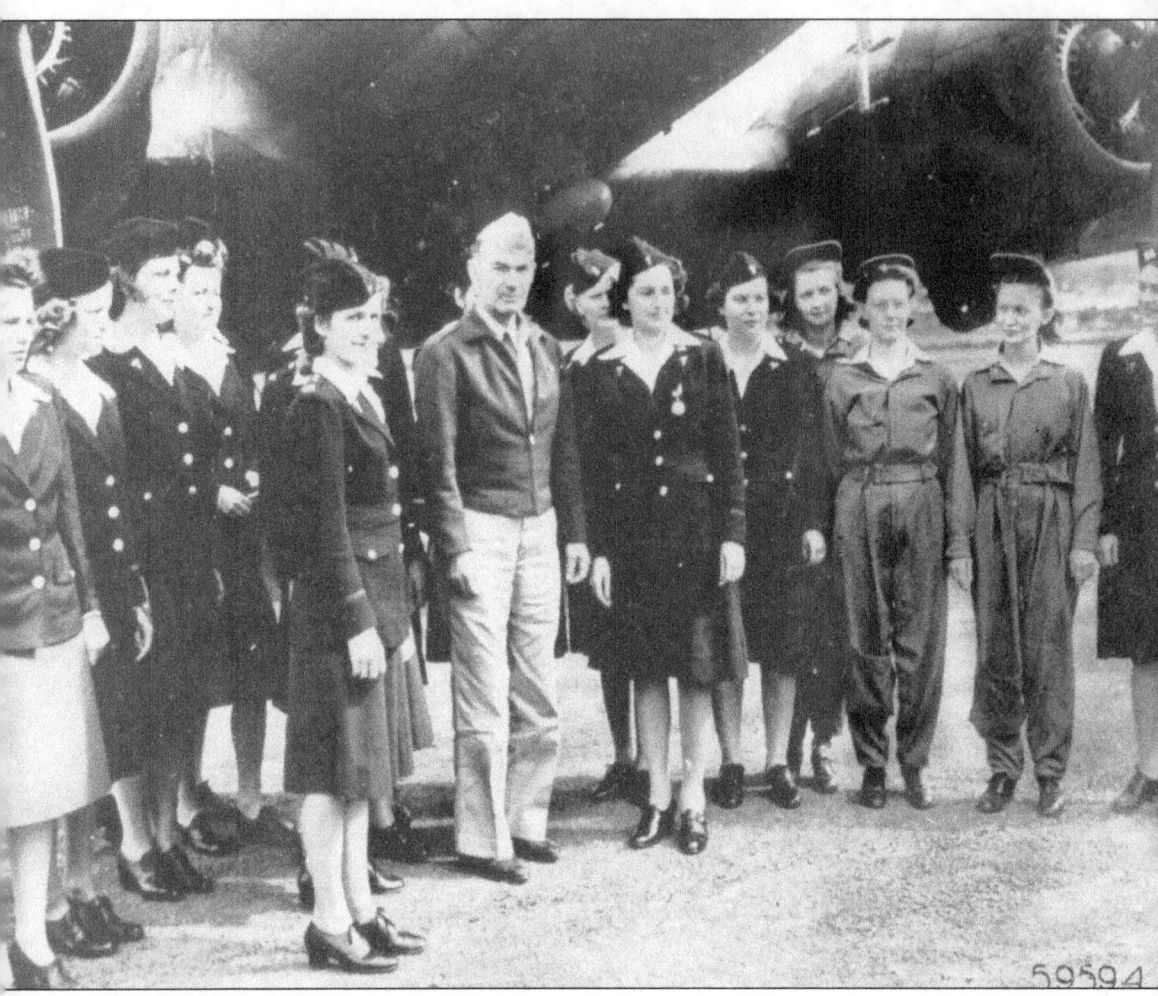

Flight nurses of the 801st Medical Squadron, Air Evacuation Transport, pose with a C-47 in New Caledonia in April 1943. From left to right (visible) are 2nd Lt. Jeraldine Jones, 2nd Lt. Edith Ahlgren, 2nd Lt. Elizabeth Sullivan, 2nd Lt. Mae Olson, 2nd Lt. Ethel Kovach, Lt. Gen. Millard Harmon (commander of US Army forces in the South Pacific), 2nd Lt. Martha Boss, 2nd Lt. Dorothy Shikoski, 2nd Lt. Joyce Boisvert, 2nd Lt. Wanda Gustafson, 2nd Lt. Beryl Laird, 2nd Lt. Cora Conerly, and Capt. Boyer. The 801st, organized at Bowman Field, Kentucky, was rushed to the South Pacific and was the first air evacuation squadron to deploy. Its flight surgeons took part in air evacuation missions during the final phase of the Guadalcanal campaign, and its complement of nurses and medical corpsmen arrived at Tontouta shortly after Guadalcanal was secured. The 801st Medical Squadron quickly became an integral part of SCAT operations. Most SCAT flights to forward areas included a USAAF nurse, flight surgeon, or medical corpsman from the 801st, or a US Navy hospital corpsman from Headquarters Squadron 25. (NARA.)

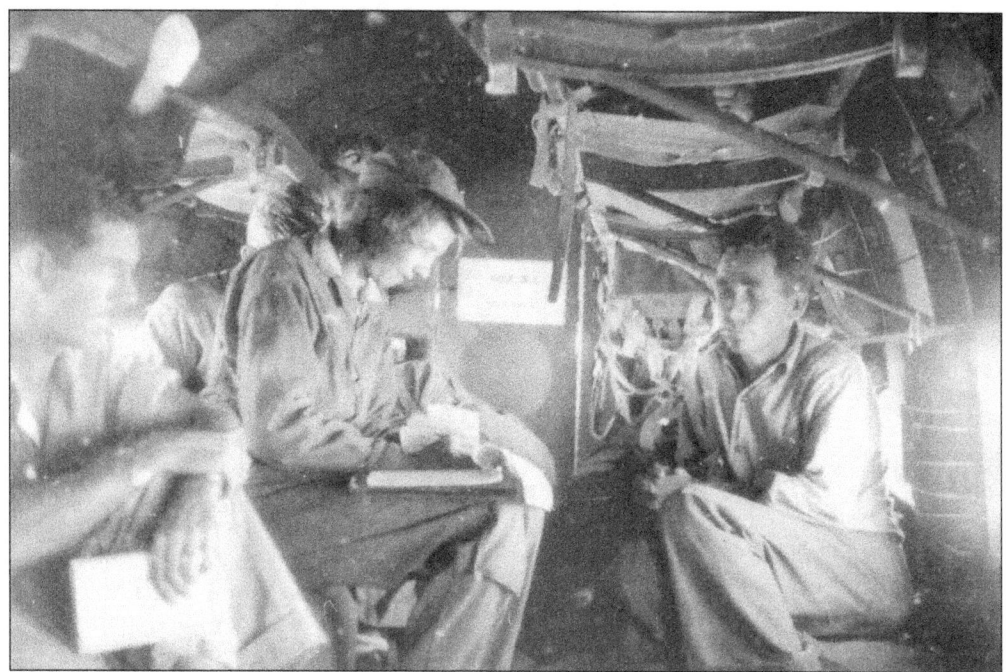

Flight nurse 2nd Lt. Wanda Gustafson of the 801st Medical Squadron interviews ambulatory patients during an April 1943 flight from Guadalcanal. Most aboard were likely suffering from malaria and other tropical diseases, which had afflicted the vast majority of American combatants and caused roughly two thirds of all American casualties during the fight for the island. In May, the 801st was redesignated a Medical Air Evacuation Transport Squadron (MAETS). (NARA.)

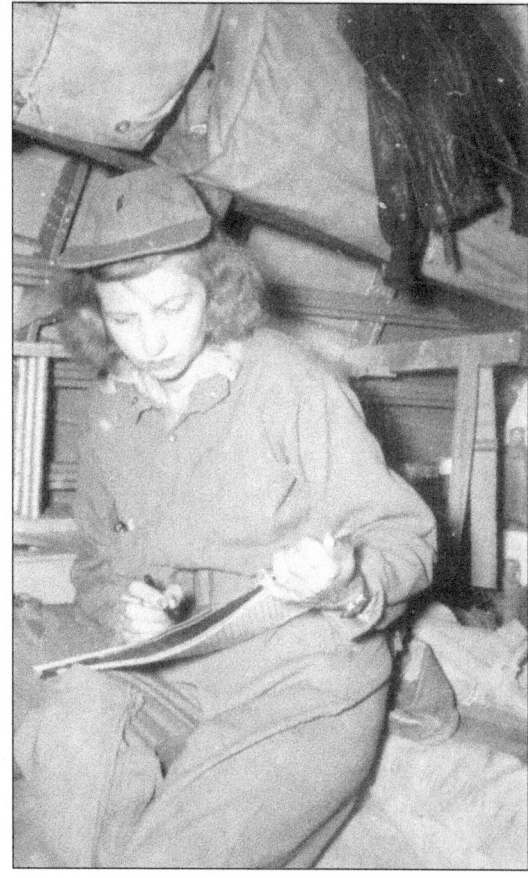

Lieutenant Gustafson reviews patient records during the flight to a rear area hospital. The nurses and corpsmen of the 801st were the only SCAT personnel with extensive training in aeromedical evacuation. Gustafson entered the service shortly after the Pearl Harbor attack. She later served during the Korean War and retired from the US Army as a lieutenant colonel in 1964, having earned a total of seven Air Medals. (NARA.)

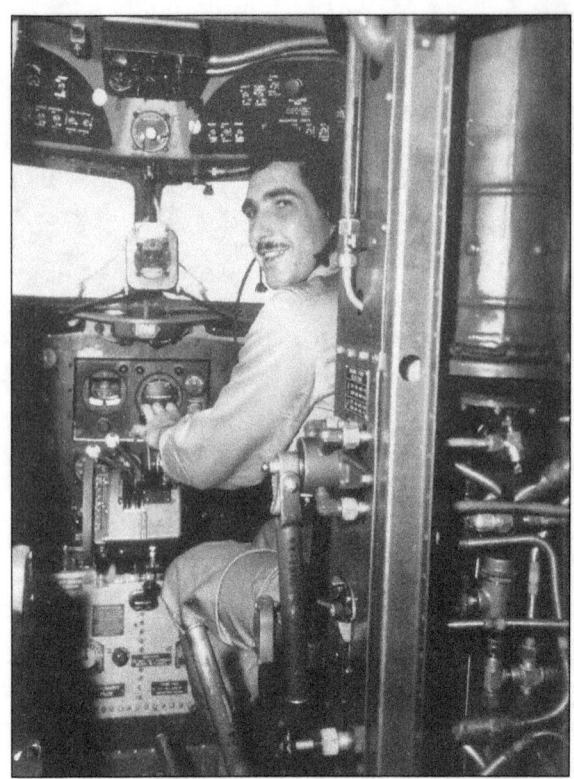

First pilot 1st Lt. Richard Nickerson of VMJ-253, who flew during the Guadalcanal campaign and received the Distinguished Flying Cross, poses in the copilot's seat of R4D-1 01982 at Henderson Field in May 1943. This aircraft, now derelict, flew for many years as N220GB. Even MAG-25's copilots were rated first pilots in the R4D before arriving overseas and were typically promoted to MAG-25 first pilot before their second combat tour. (NARA.)

Nearly all SCAT flights included a crew chief or flight mechanic as part of the crew. Here, two VMJ-253 Guadalcanal veterans, crew chiefs T.Sgt. Eldon Dennis and T.Sgt. Frank Geist, check the engine on R4D "82" (likely R4D-1 01982) at Henderson Field in May 1943. Both men were promoted to master technical sergeant shortly after this photograph was taken. (NARA.)

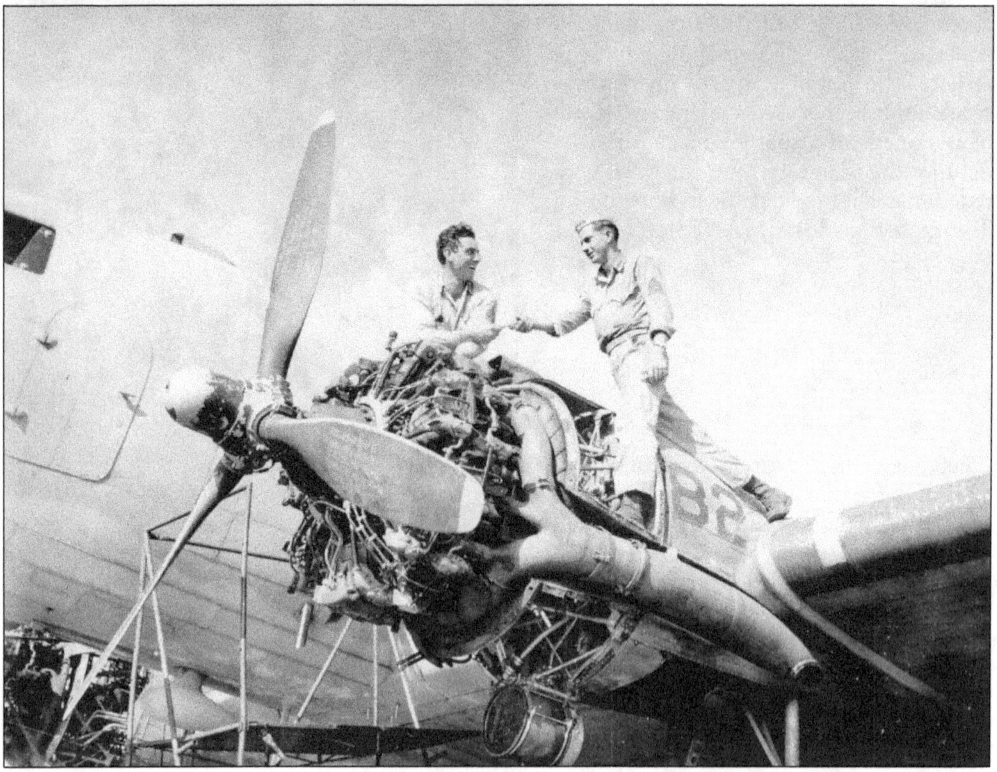

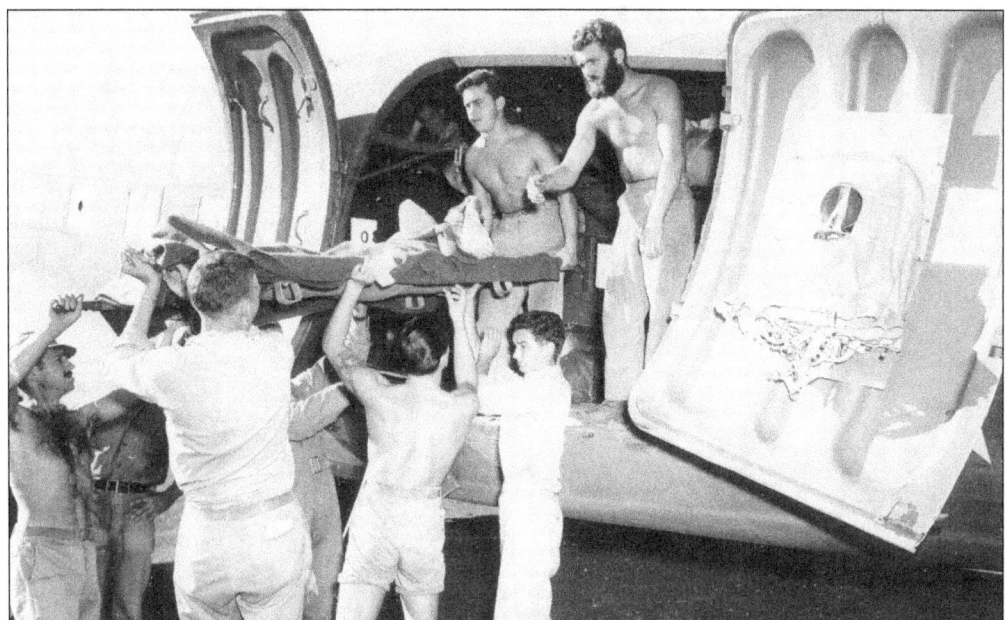

SCAT continued to evacuate a relatively small number of critically wounded men from Guadalcanal for months after the battle ended, some of them victims of Japanese air or naval attacks, others injured in accidents. Casualties would spike again during the New Georgia campaign in July. This man was likely destined for Espiritu Santo or Efate. "Mae West" life jackets, carried aboard every aircraft, are stacked on the cargo door. (NARA.)

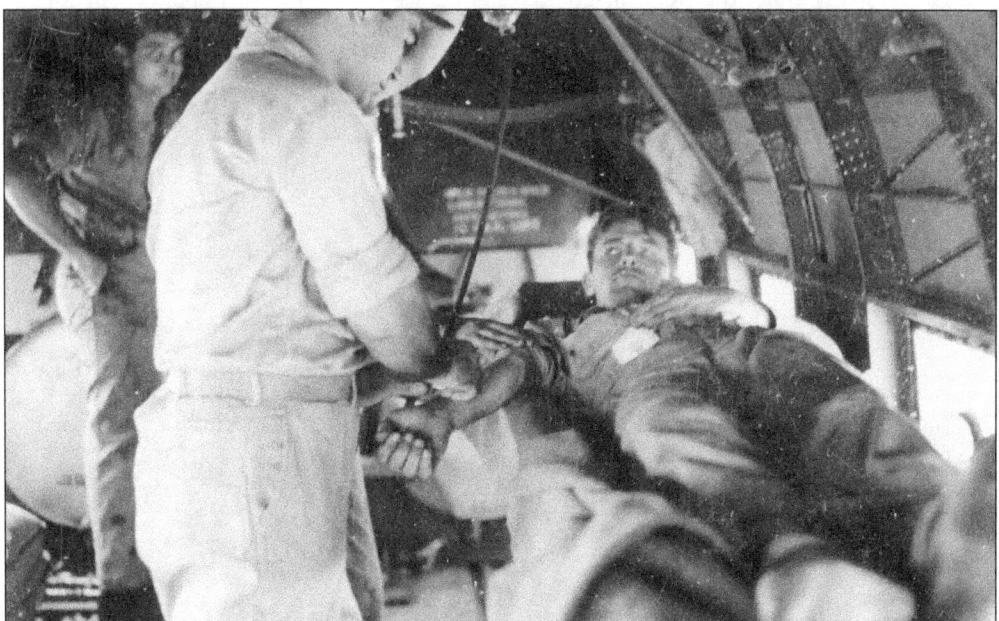

Lt. Harold Lyons of the US Navy Medical Corps (foreground) attends to disease-stricken Pfc. Herman Hudson Jr., a VMJ-152 radio operator, aboard one of the squadron's R4Ds in May 1943. Behind Lieutenant Lyons, corpsman PhM2c. Julius Thomas of Headquarters Squadron 25 suspends an intravenous drip. At left is crew chief T.Sgt. Walter Fellman. This aircraft is likely 05064. Hudson recovered, earning an Air Medal during the New Georgia campaign. (NARA.)

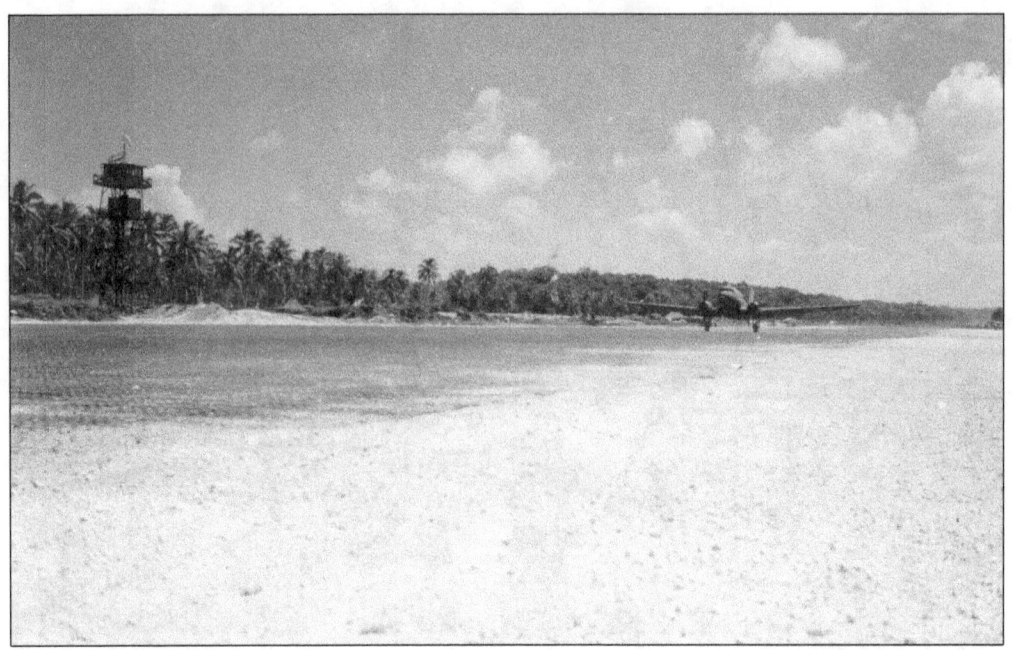

SCAT R4D "64," likely 05064, touches down on Espiritu Santo in the New Hebrides (above) and is guided to the parking area (below). Although some veterans recalled one or two blue-gray aircraft being present, at least the vast majority of MAG-25's aircraft were accepted from Douglas in USAAF colors: olive drab on top and neutral gray on the bottom. Olive drab varied in color, and faded rapidly under the tropical sun. Later aircraft received a factory-applied camouflage pattern of forest green on the edges of the wings and stabilizers. Aircraft numbers, always two-digit, initially appeared in black on the nose, engine nacelles, and aft fuselage (on the port side it typically appeared on the rear cargo doors). Numbers on early MAG-25 aircraft appear to have matched their BuAer serial numbers. (Both, NARA.)

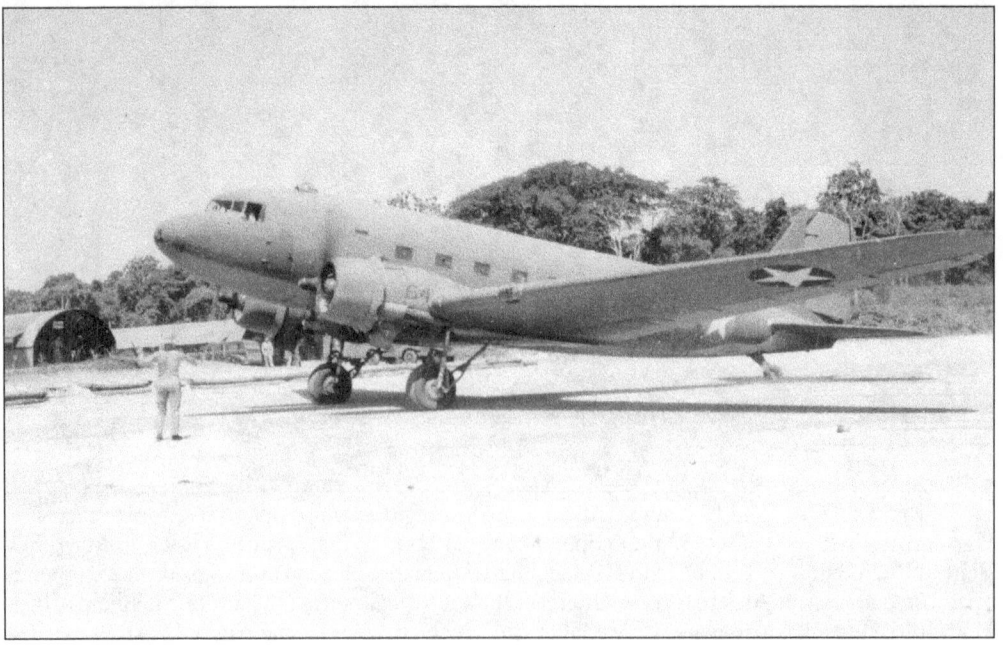

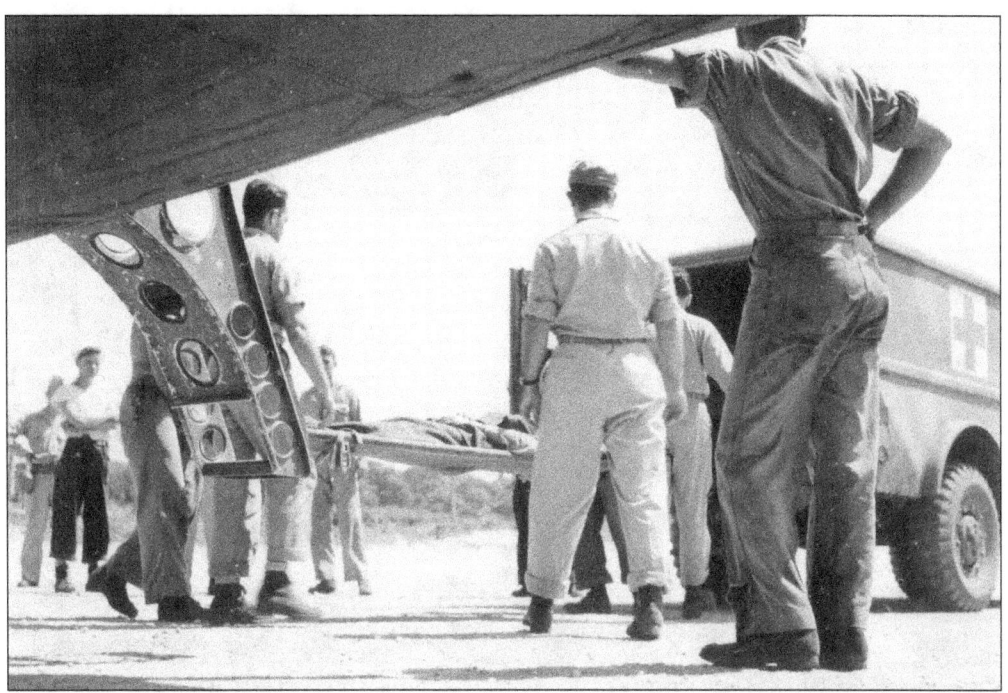

R4D "64" offloads stretcher patients destined for one of Espiritu Santo's two base hospitals. Above, the first of the patients is carried to a waiting ambulance. Below, additional ambulances soon arrive, while a fuel truck helps ready "64" for its next mission. Flying the wounded presented challenges, especially since altitude restrictions aimed at maintaining patients' blood pressure inhibited pilots' ability to fly above severe weather. "Santos," as it was frequently misidentified by crews, with its air base complex and harbor, first played a prominent role in support of the Guadalcanal campaign. Due to its importance, it still endured the occasional Japanese air raid for two months after these photographs were taken. (Both, NARA.)

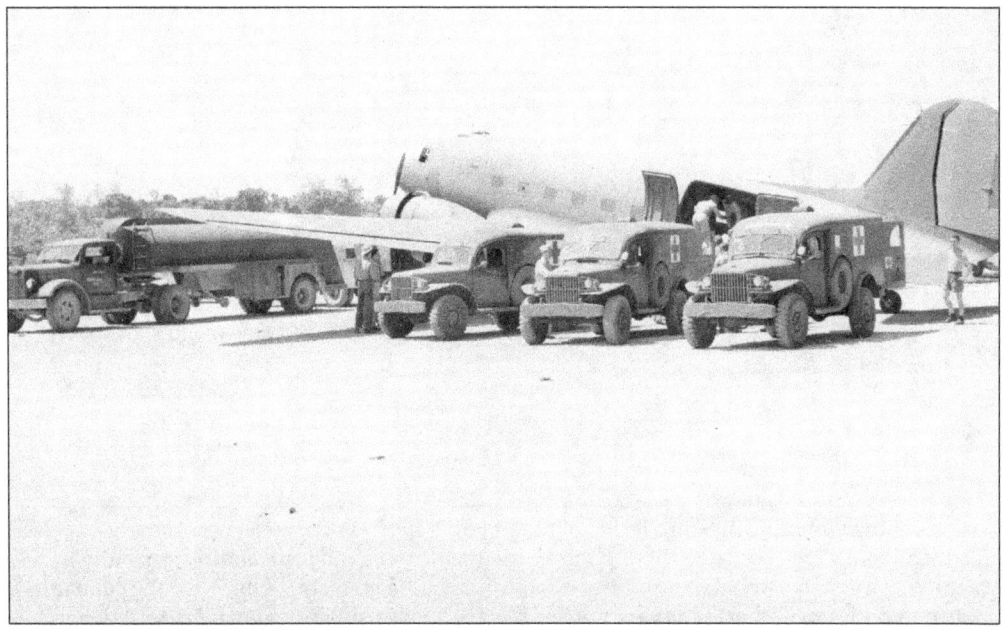

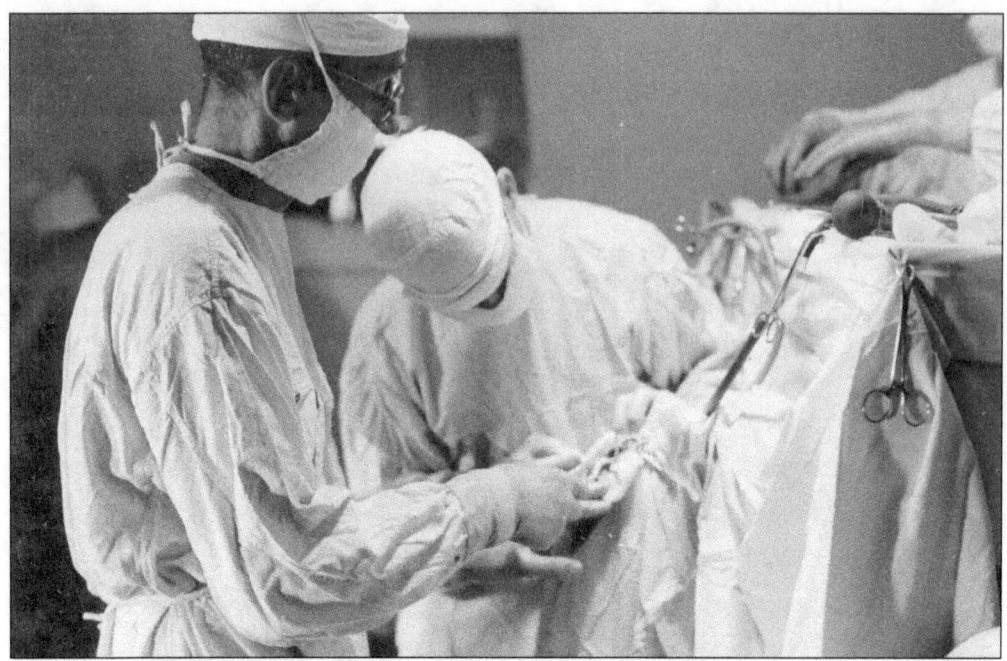

Cdr. Theodore Reynolds (left) assists Lt. Hannibal Hamlin (center) in preparing a patient's head wound for surgery at Base Hospital 3 on Espiritu Santo in April or May 1943. The patient, with shrapnel lodged in his brain and leg, had just been flown in on a SCAT R4D. Reynolds and Hamlin were both members of the US Navy Medical Corps. (NARA.)

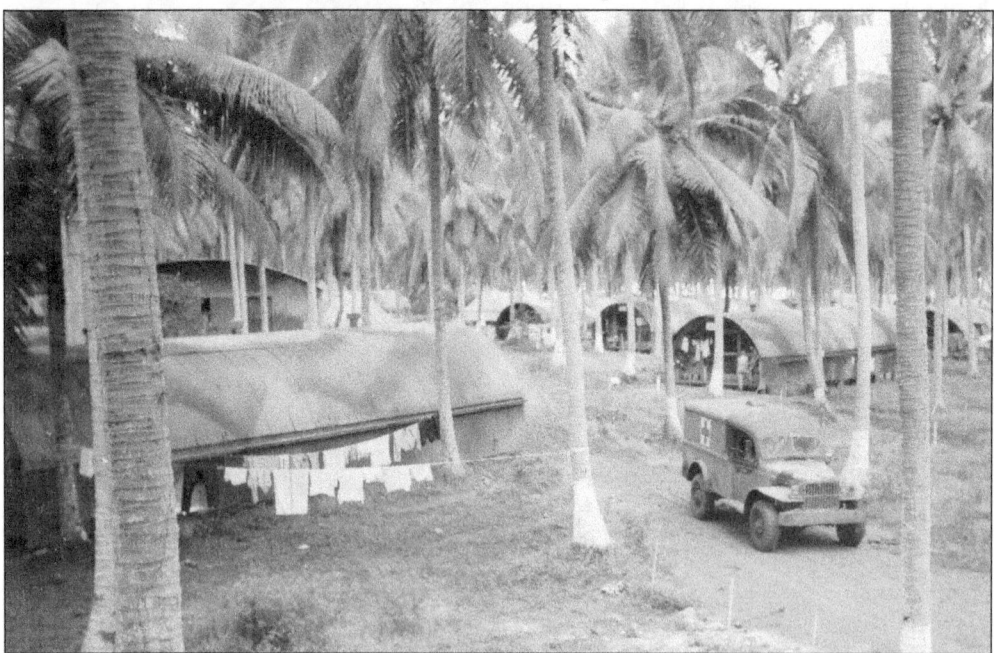

Base Hospital 3 on Espiritu Santo is shown around May 1943. Once stable, patients who received treatment here were evacuated to hospitals in the rear for rest and recuperation, typically by sea. Later in the war, some would be evacuated directly to the United States by air. Note the camouflage applied to both the Quonset huts and, unusually, the Dodge WC54 ambulance. (NARA.)

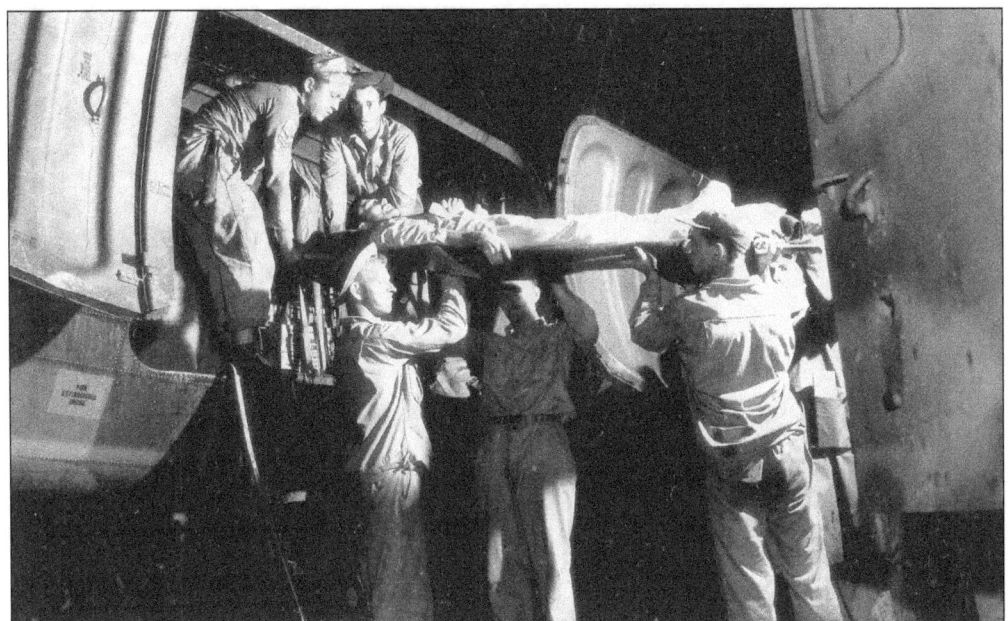

Guadalcanal would eventually house advanced medical facilities, but in June 1943, the most serious and urgent cases still required a flight to hospitals on Espiritu Santo or Efate in the New Hebrides. Here, well before dawn on June 4 at Henderson Field, medical personnel load stretcher cases into a SCAT R4D headed to a base hospital in the rear. Nighttime departures and arrivals were common for SCAT aircraft. (NARA.)

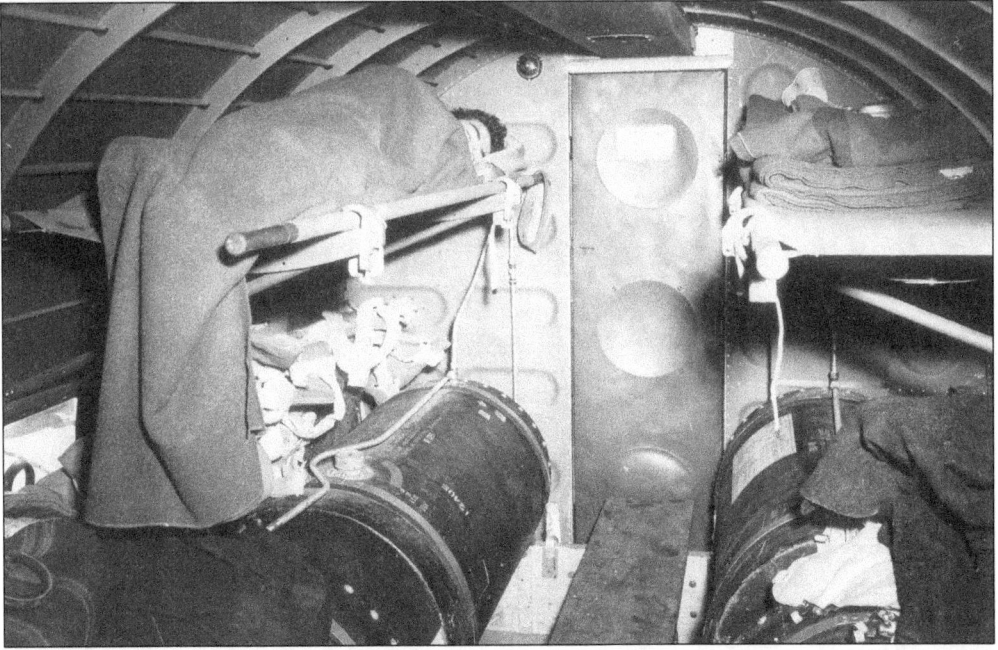

The C-47/R4D had an 804-gallon fuel capacity, which could be increased with multiple auxiliary fuel tanks mounted in the cargo compartment. Here, a patient aboard a SCAT transport shares space with the long-range tanks. SCAT aircraft frequently utilized two 100-gallon (roughly 600-pound) auxiliary tanks as shown due to their long flights over water. (NARA.)

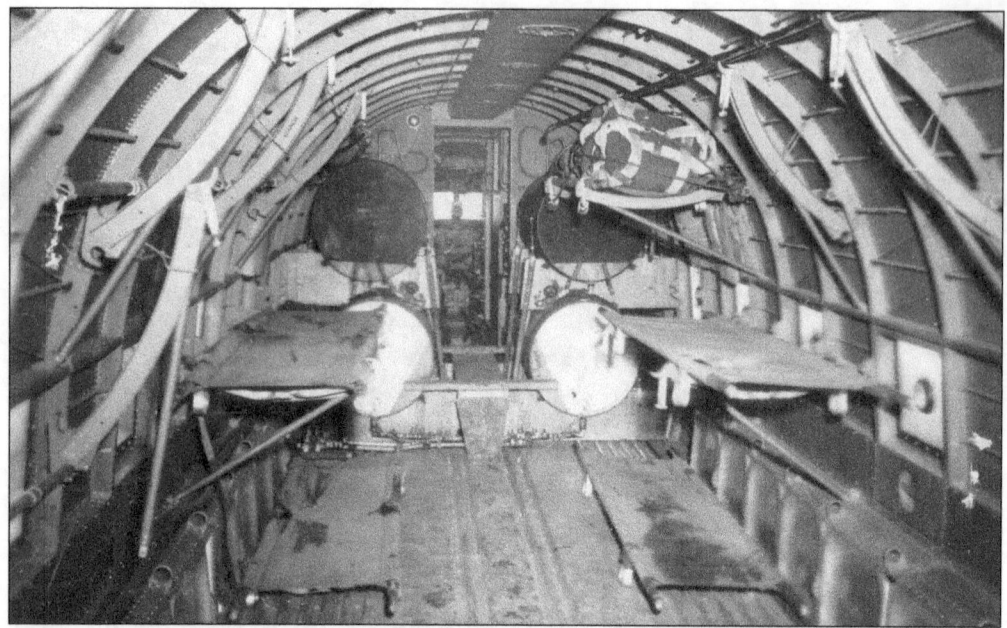

This SCAT R4D shows a four-tank configuration for cargo and five stretchers. The folding bench seats for passengers are stowed on each side. At least two standard auxiliary tank designs were used: an ovular cylinder, and the circular cylinders shown here, manufactured by United States Rubber Company. Extra fuel provided a comforting margin of safety when pilots were forced to fly around severe weather. (NARA.)

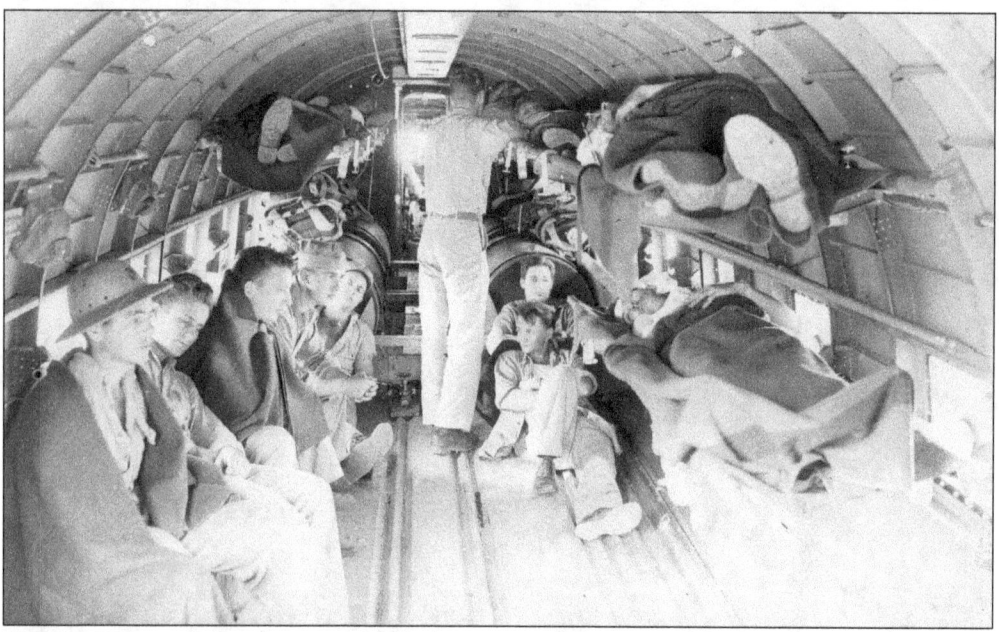

This SCAT aircraft flying a mix of ambulatory and stretcher patients displays yet another four-tank configuration. The transport was designed to carry up to 27 seated passengers or 18 stretcher patients, or some combination thereof. Total cargo, including added fuel tanks, was officially not to exceed 5,000 pounds. Another 3,000 pounds could be added in an emergency, with the caveat that 3,000 pounds of fuel be consumed before landing. (NARA.)

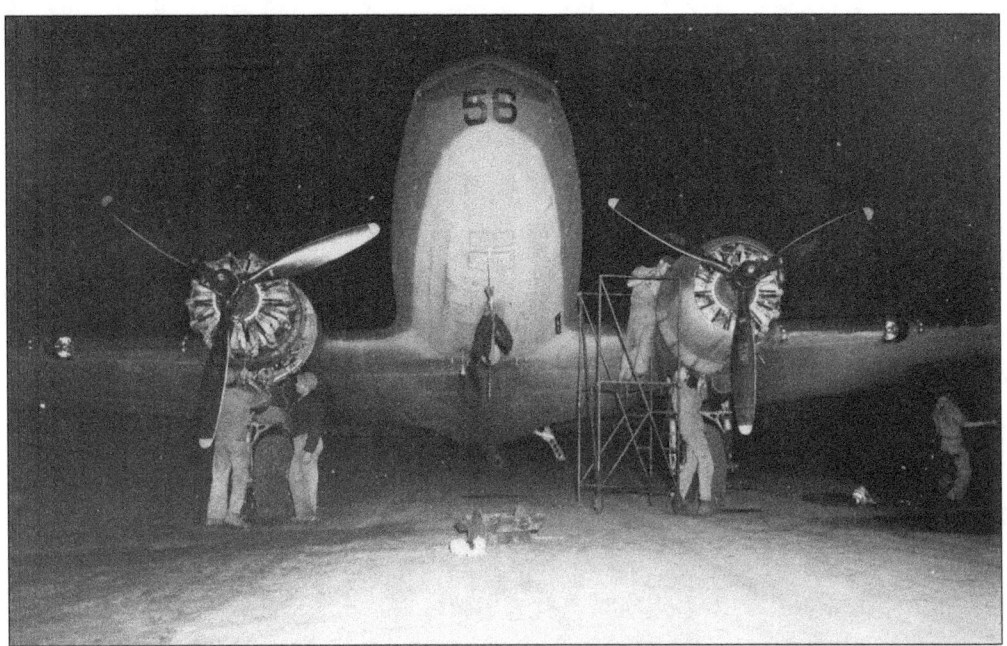

SCAT's mission requirements made round-the-clock and all-weather maintenance a necessity. Service Squadron 25 (SMS-25), organized in November 1942, was responsible for heavy maintenance on SCAT aircraft. They augmented the services of each squadron's own flight mechanics and other maintenance personnel, who had initially been forced to perform maintenance with only the rudimentary tool kits stowed aboard each aircraft. Here, aided by floodlights, ground crewmen service the Pratt and Whitney R-1830-92 Twin Wasp engines of R4Ds "56" (above) and "76" (below) on Guadalcanal. In the early months, similar scenes took place nightly at Tontouta, where overhauls were carried out. SCAT ground crews performed exemplary work and were aided by the Douglas transports' ruggedness and reliability. (Both, NARA.)

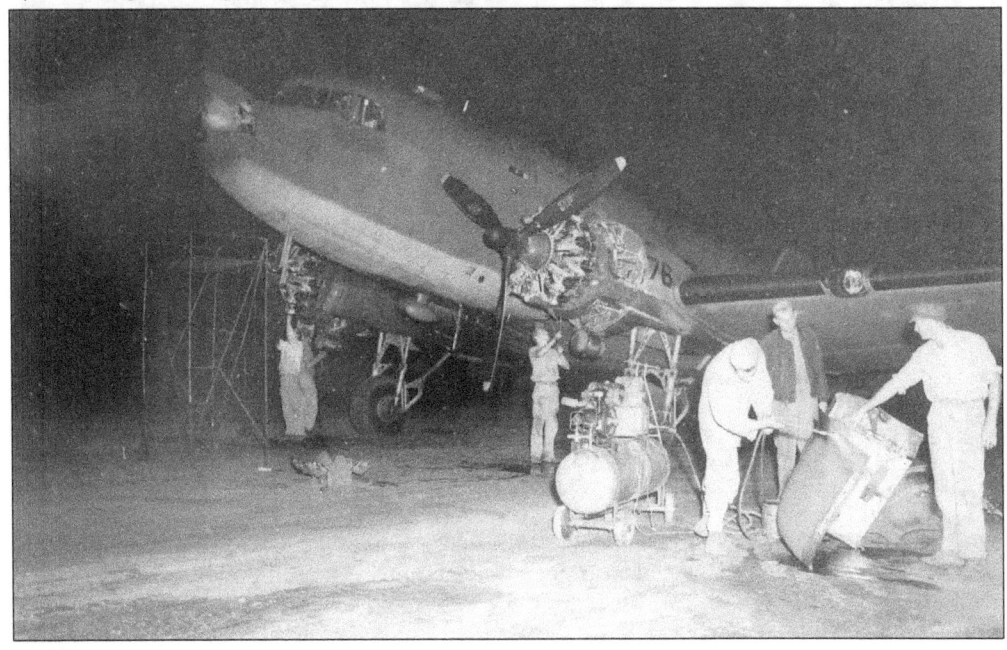

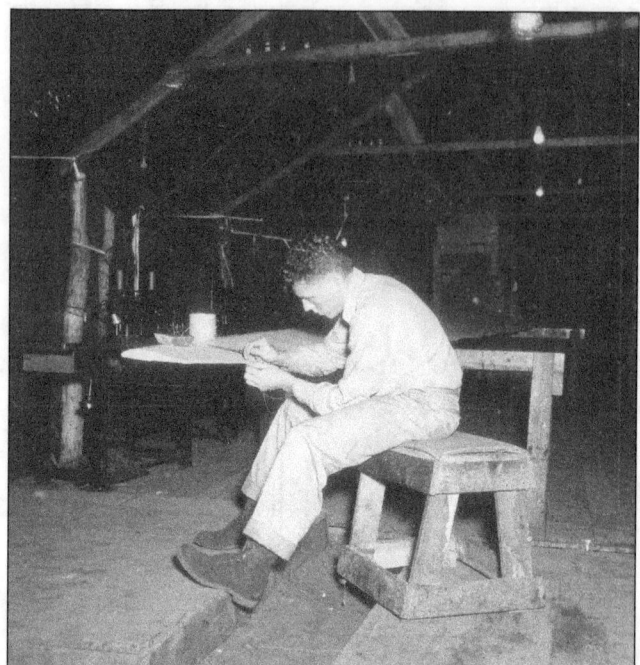

Harking back to an earlier era, Cpl. Richard Meckley of SMS-25 uses a sewing kit to make overnight repairs to an R4D's fabric-covered aileron. Like many aircraft at the time, the C-47/R4D was all metal-framed and covered mostly with riveted sheet aluminum, but retained dope-sealed fabric, used since the early days of aviation, to cover its control surfaces (ailerons, flaps, and rudder). (NARA.)

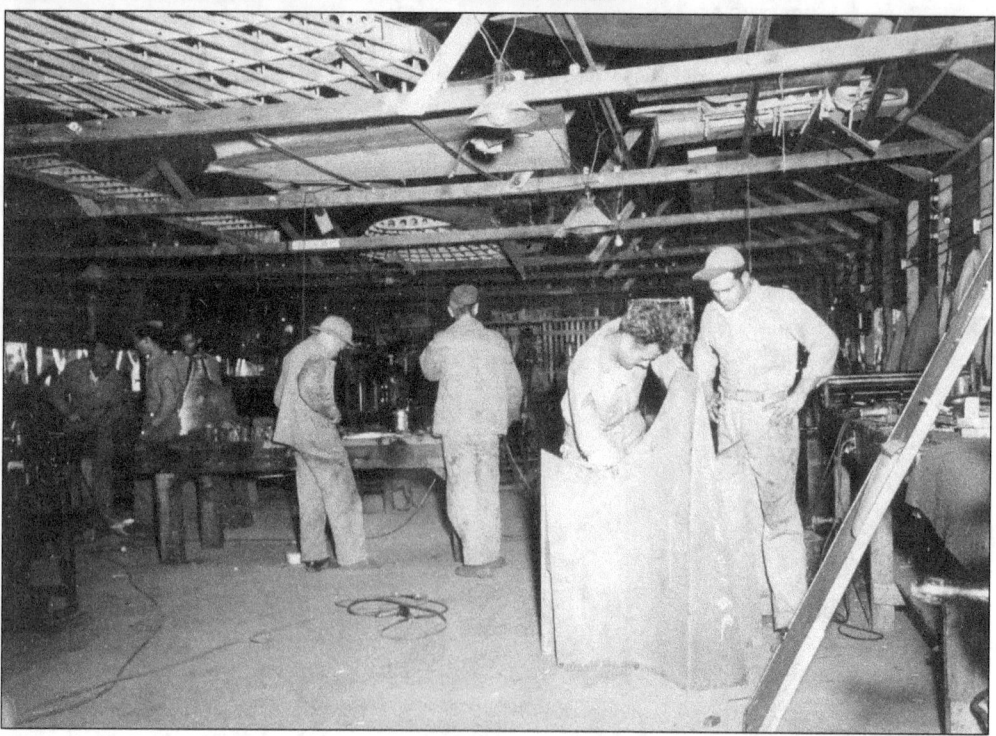

S.Sgt. Leslie Lewis (foreground, left) and Pfc. Otis Perry (foreground, right) make repairs to the tail cone of R4D "62" in SMS-25's metal shop on Guadalcanal, one of the squadron's 15 specialty repair shops. Various replacement airframe components are stowed on the joists above. In addition to shops in the rear area, crews from SMS-25 would serve at many of SCAT's forward outposts. (NARA.)

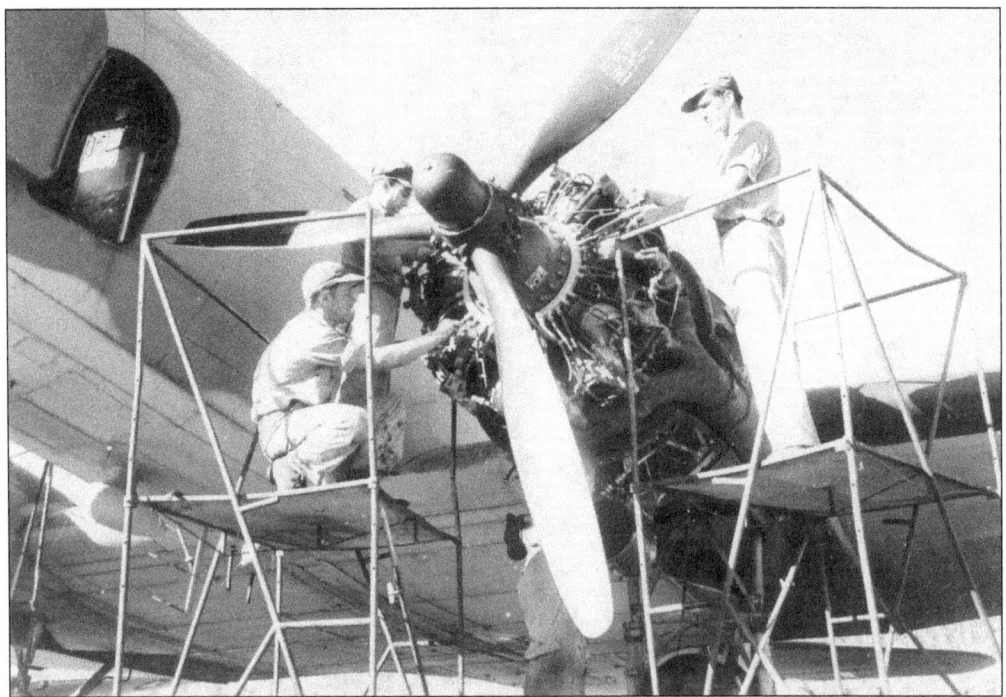

SCAT aircraft underwent engine checks and maintenance at regular intervals, although the schedule was difficult to keep during the Guadalcanal campaign. When these photographs of R4D "01" were taken on Guadalcanal in June 1943, engine replacements had become commonplace and the hard-worked aircraft were scheduled to return to the United States after 900 flying hours. That schedule did not entirely hold, however; by 1945, some aircraft had over 2,000 hours of flying time, a tribute to the efforts of maintenance crews. Above (left to right), Sgt. George Sodl, S.Sgt. Nathan Miller, and Sgt. Reid Garris of VMJ-253 work on the port engine. (Both, NARA.)

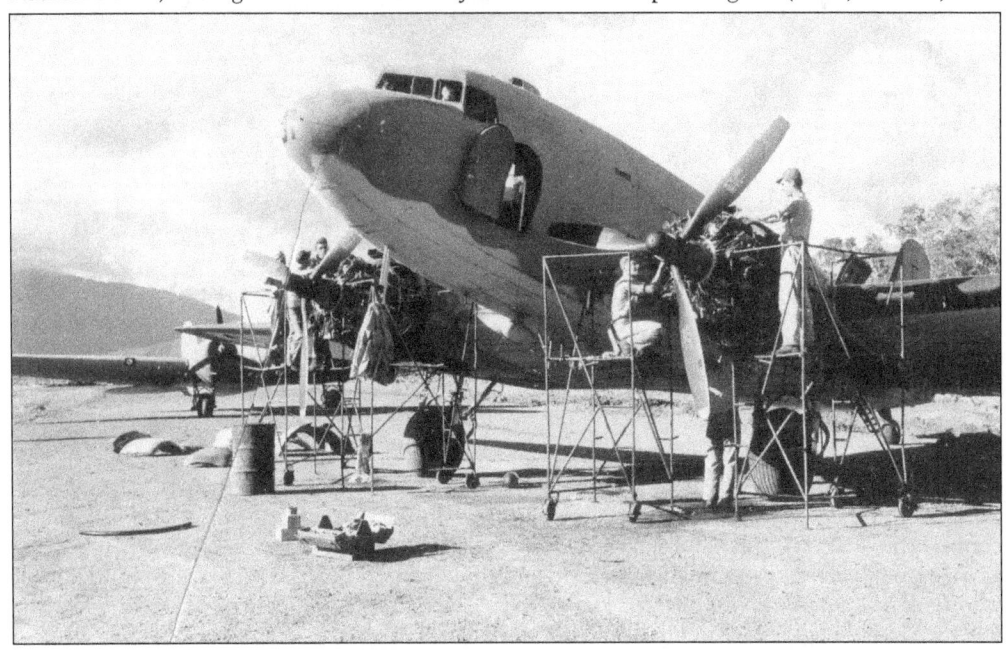

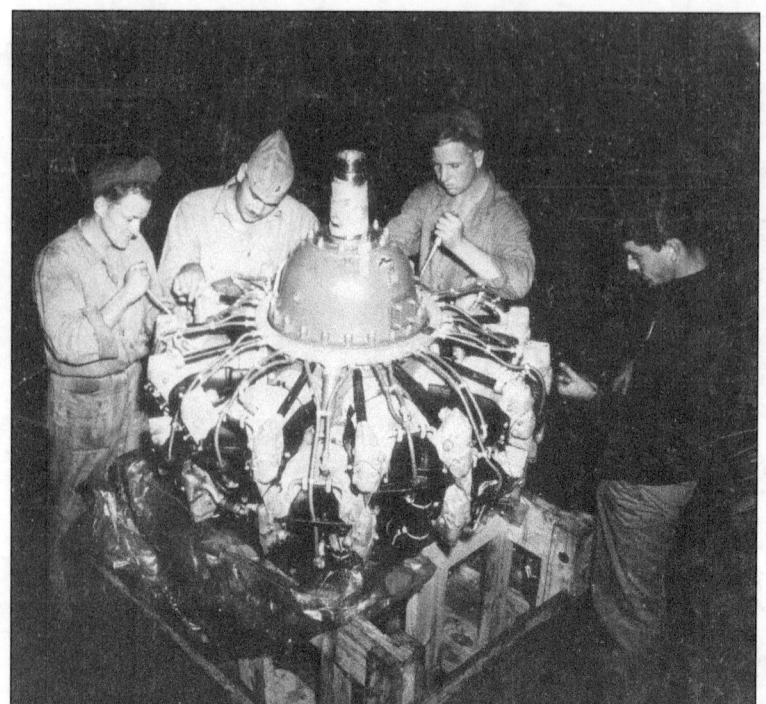

A SCAT support crew works after dark to prepare a Pratt and Whitney R-1800 aircraft engine for shipment to a forward base. From left to right are S.Sgt. Marcus Berkley Jr. and 1st Lt. Anthony Flasco of SMS-25, Pfc. Frank Gother of Marine Air Depot Squadron 1, and Cpl. James Mora of VMJ-152. Flasco is giving instruction to the enlisted men. (NARA.)

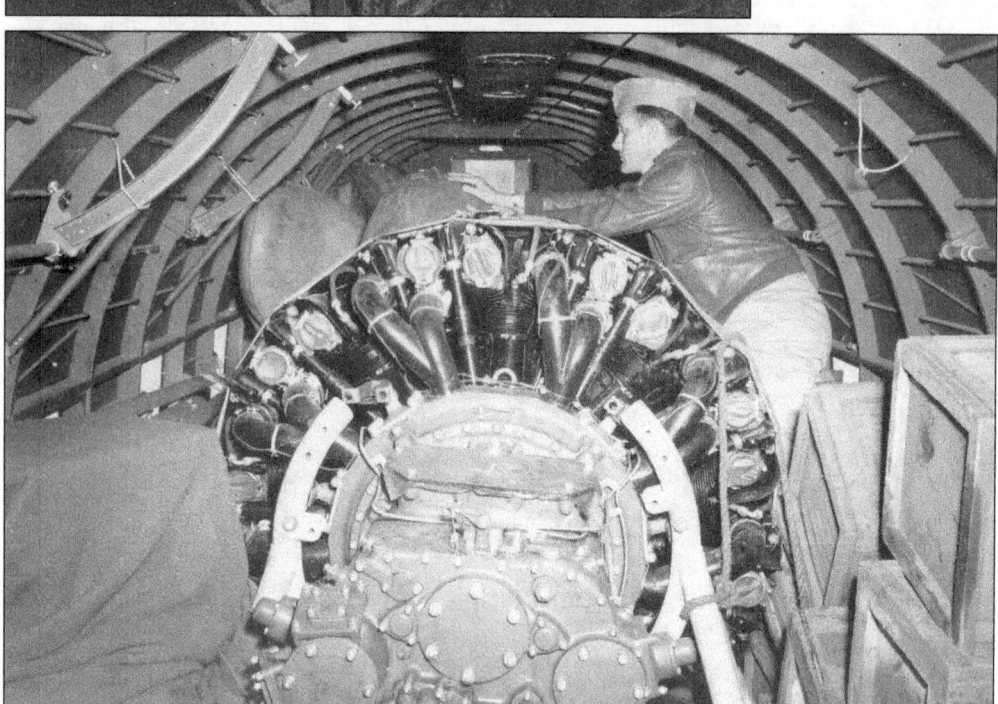

A MAG-25 officer supervises the loading of an R4D on Guadalcanal in June 1943. This image conveys the often eclectic nature of SCAT's cargo, a Pratt and Whitney R-2800 aircraft engine and external fuel tanks seemingly wedged in among spare parts boxes. The Marine photographer who took this image reported that a typical SCAT load was 1,500 pounds above the factory-specified limit, a figure that veterans did not dispute. (NARA.)

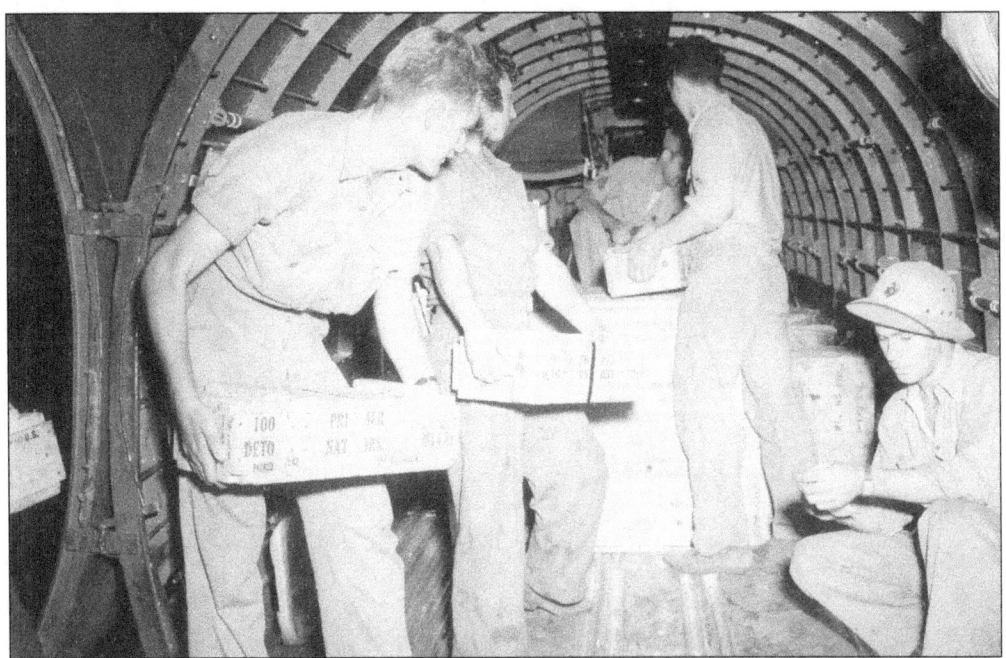

Personnel of Headquarters Squadron 25 load M14A1 primer detonators into an R4D on Guadalcanal on a June night in 1943. The detonators were used in general purpose (GP) aerial bombs and were destined for one or more American bomber squadrons at a forward base. Passing the crates are Pvt. Harley Winge (far left) and Pvt. Ernest Hoff (second from left). Pvt. Herman Rose (far right) keeps inventory. (NARA.)

Capt. Cecil Ray, SCAT cargo officer (standing on the tarmac), makes a final check of the cargo manifest with Capt. Thomas Heard, squadron executive officer (crouching at the edge of the cargo door), prior to an R4D's predawn departure from Henderson Field in June 1943. Both men were with Headquarters Squadron 25. Effective cargo loading required attention to many details, including weight distribution, secure stowage, and item priority. (NARA.)

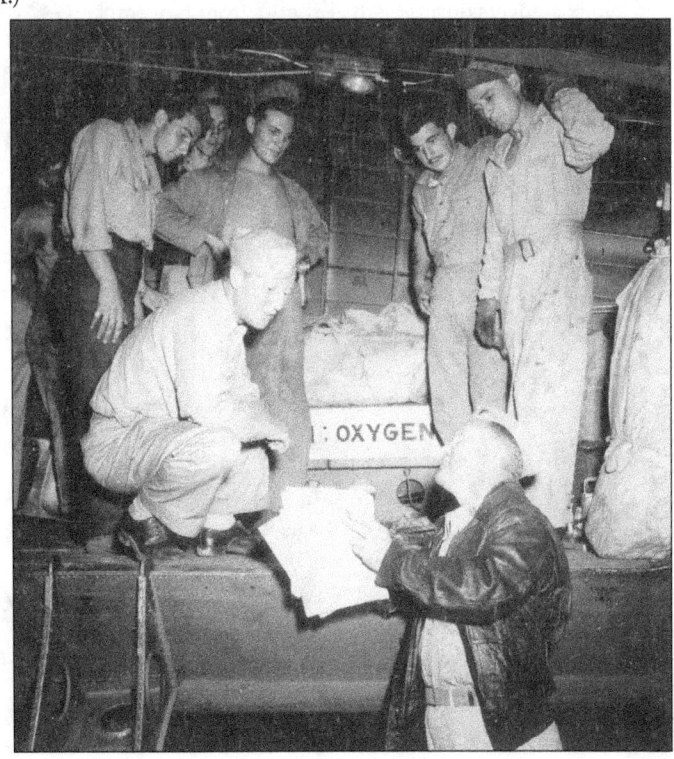

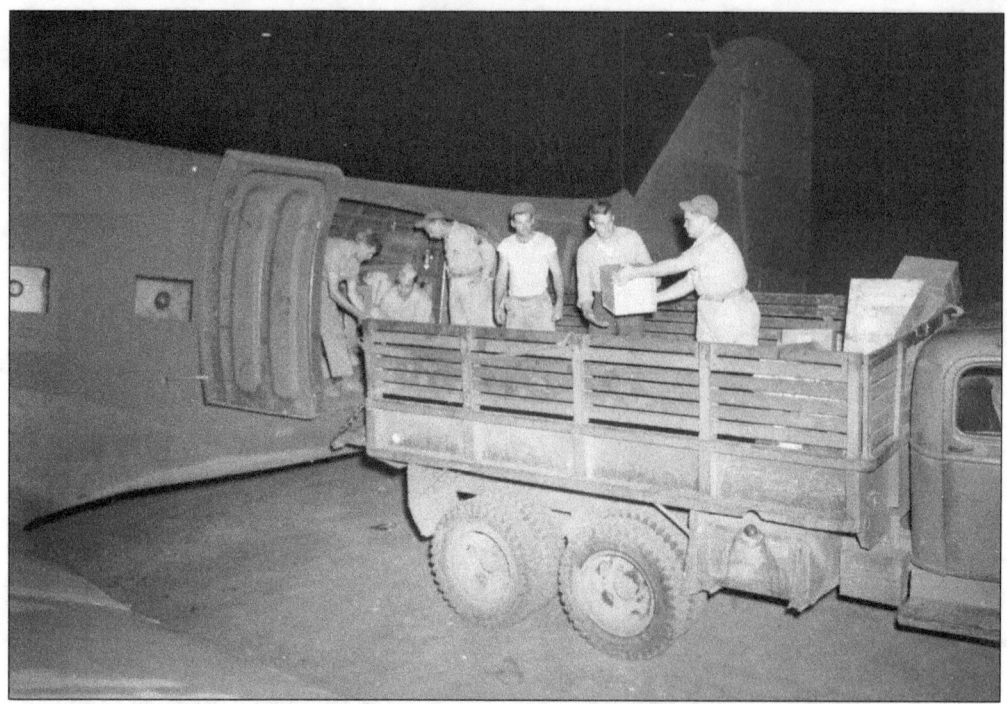

Army and Marine personnel load a truckload of medical supplies aboard an R4D, likely destined for forward hospital facilities on Banika in the Russell Islands. Loading of SCAT aircraft on Guadalcanal often went on throughout the night. SCAT flew 43,626,495 pounds of cargo and 235,596 passengers during 34,834 flights from November 1942 through June 1944. (NARA.)

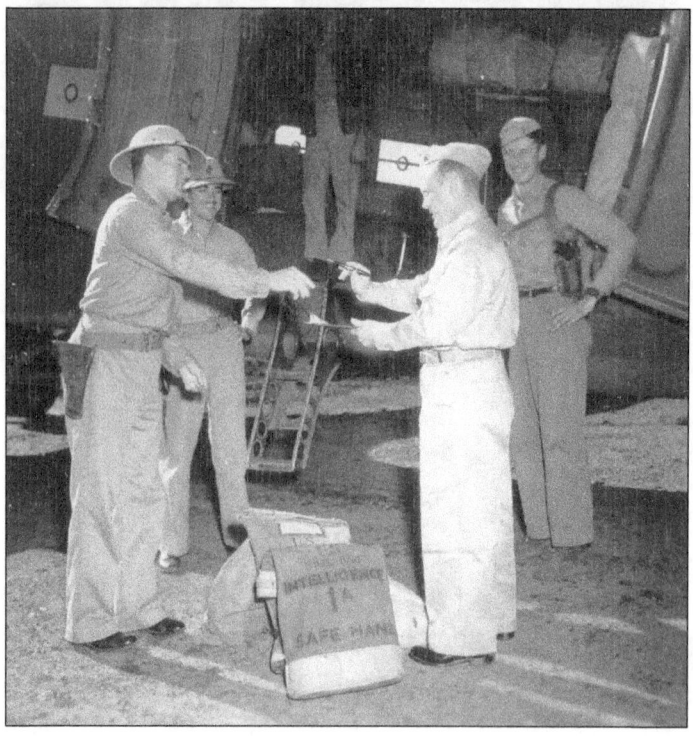

SCAT was the fastest means of transmitting official mail, including secure classified documents. Here, Capt. Peter Wigham (foreground, left) of Headquarters Squadron 25, SCAT's mail officer and a US postal inspector before joining the Marines, transfers official mail sacks to SCAT cargo officer Capt. Cecil Ray (foreground, right). Ray signs for the mail before it is loaded into the waiting R4D. (NARA.)

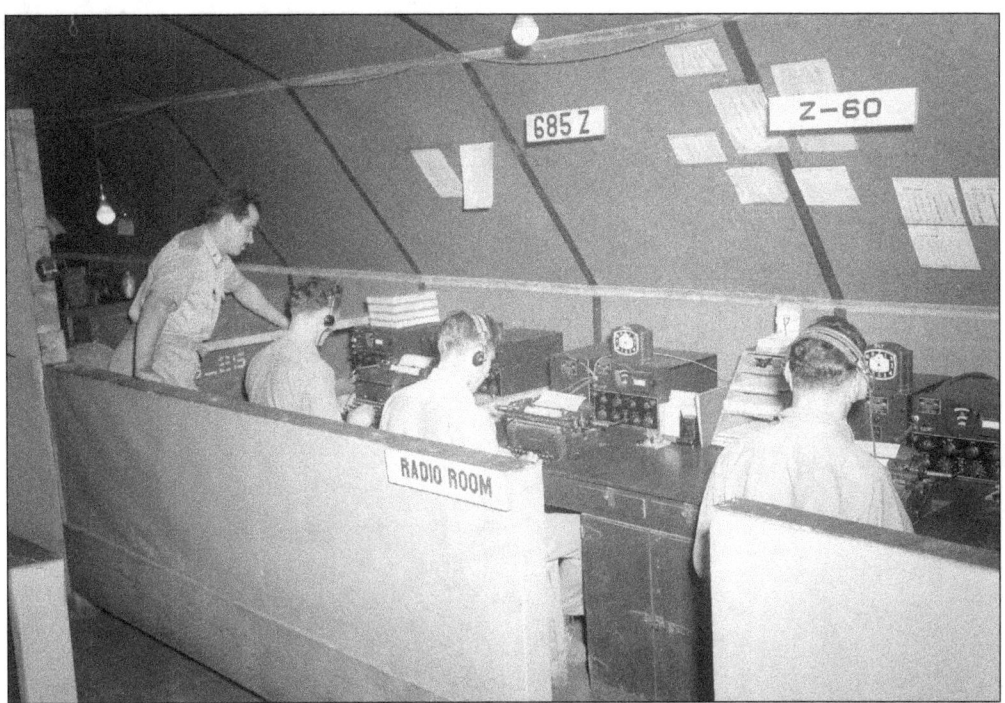

The MAG-25 radio room on Guadalcanal maintained communications with all SCAT aircraft in the Solomons and informed the various island terminals of incoming and departing aircraft. SCAT pilots relied on these men to provide up-to-date weather reports and to receive and transmit their messages to the operations office—including mayday alerts during in-flight emergencies. (NARA.)

On June 28, 1943, 1st Lt. Bernard Nygren, flying R4D-1 01984 from Fiji, suffered fuel exhaustion but successfully ditched off San Cristobal with no serious injuries. The fortunate crew included, from left to right, (first row) crew chief Cpl. Howard Durborow (VMJ-152) and navigator Cpl. Rolf Larson (VMJ-153); (second row) flight corpsman PhM3c. Leon Simmons (Headquarters Squadron 25), copilot 2nd Lt. Dale Stogsdill (VMJ-153), and Lieutenant Nygren (VMJ-153). (MAG-25/SCAT.)

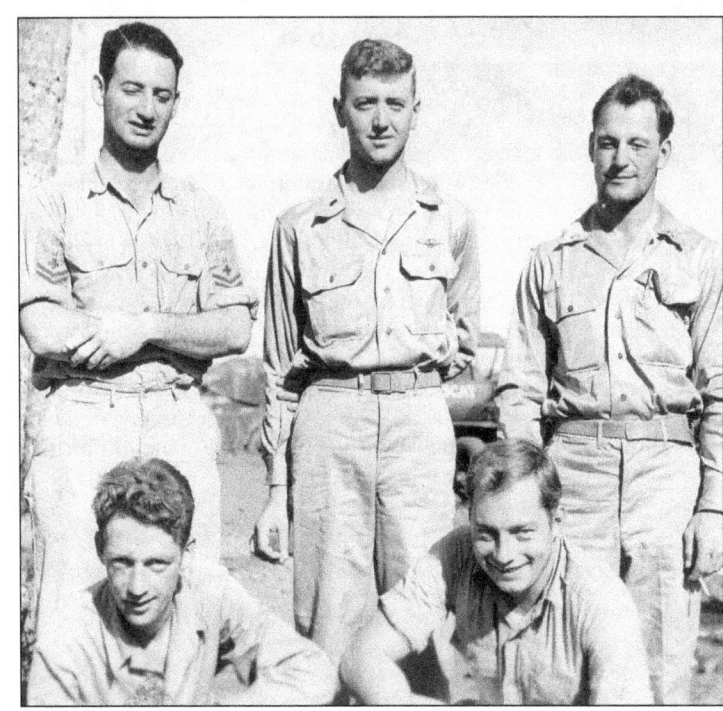

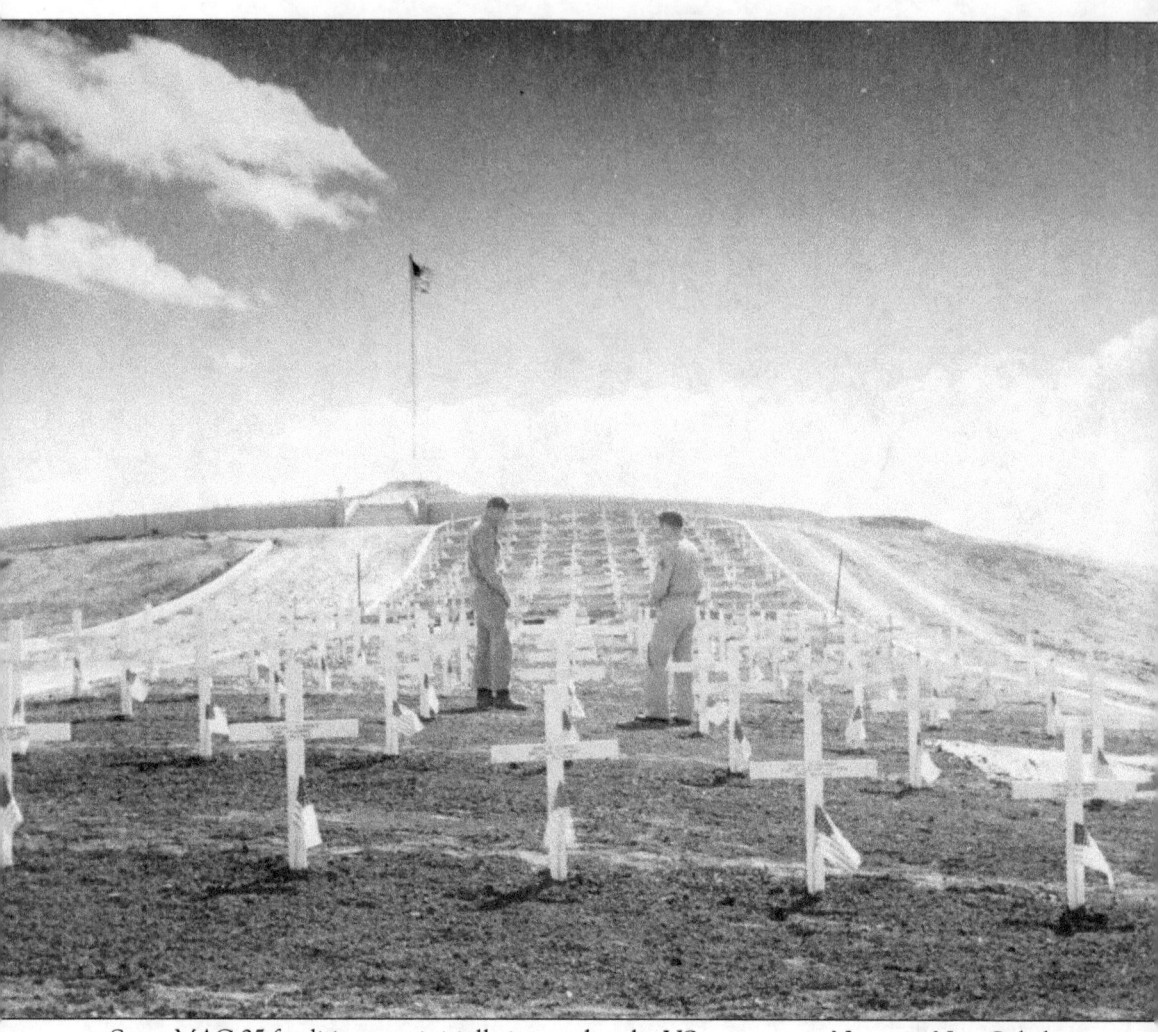

Some MAG-25 fatalities were initially interred at the US cemetery in Nouméa, New Caledonia, including Major Kimball and his crew. Here, the center cross, first row, marks the grave of Sgt. John Clarke of Headquarters Squadron, killed when R4D 12406 crashed on takeoff from Tontouta on June 8, 1943, killing 24. Interred nearby were crewmates PhM2c. Robert Barr, Pfc. Keith Horney, 1st Lt. Robert Kirkpatrick, and 1st Lt. Neal Williams, as well as the flight's passengers, many of whom were torpedo bomber crewmen of VT-11 returning from leave. Also interred at the cemetery was navigator Cpl. John Westaby of VMJ-152, the sole fatality aboard R4D 05055, which ditched in Tontouta Bay during severe weather on April 27, 1943. The odds of a SCAT flight ending in a fatal incident were about one in 2,900. Five aircraft disappeared without a trace somewhere over the vast ocean. Others collided with mountains. At the low altitudes where SCAT pilots often flew, spatial disorientation or mechanical failure could quickly be disastrous. (NARA.)

Four

SIEGE OF RABAUL

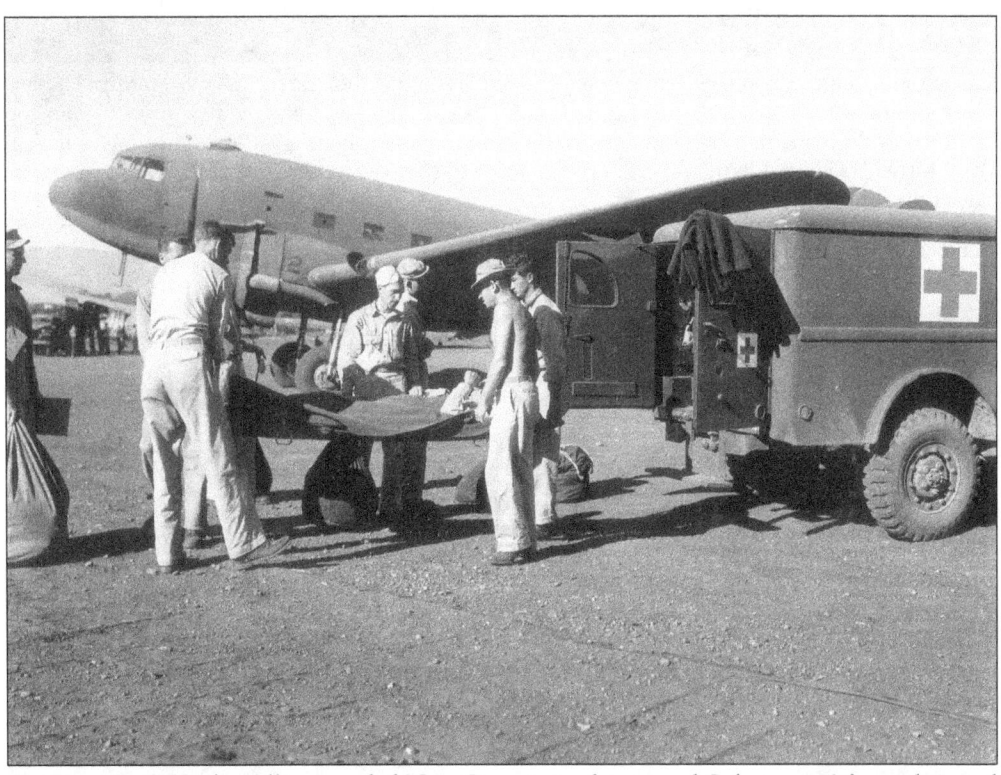

On June 30, 1943, the Allies invaded New Georgia in the central Solomons. After a slow and often frustrating campaign, New Georgia would provide three of the first forward airfields from which the Allies would strangle and neutralize the Japanese base at Rabaul. SCAT again played a critical role in casualty evacuation. Here, medical personnel transfer a patient into a waiting Dodge ambulance on Guadalcanal in July 1943. (NARA.)

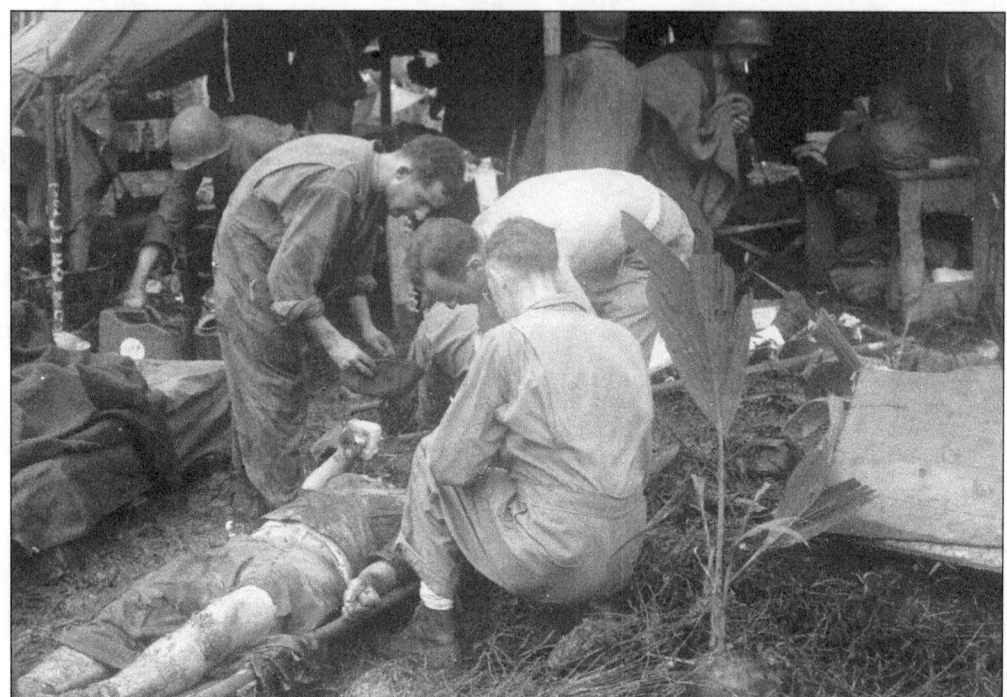

Casualties receive aid on the Rendova beachhead, a staging area for the assault on Munda, New Georgia, and its valuable airfield, on July 1, 1943. SCAT supplied some medical units via airdrop and on July 28 made its first landings on the island, operating an advance detachment at Segi Point airfield on New Georgia's southern tip. Prior to that time, all casualties were evacuated by slower watercraft. (NARA.)

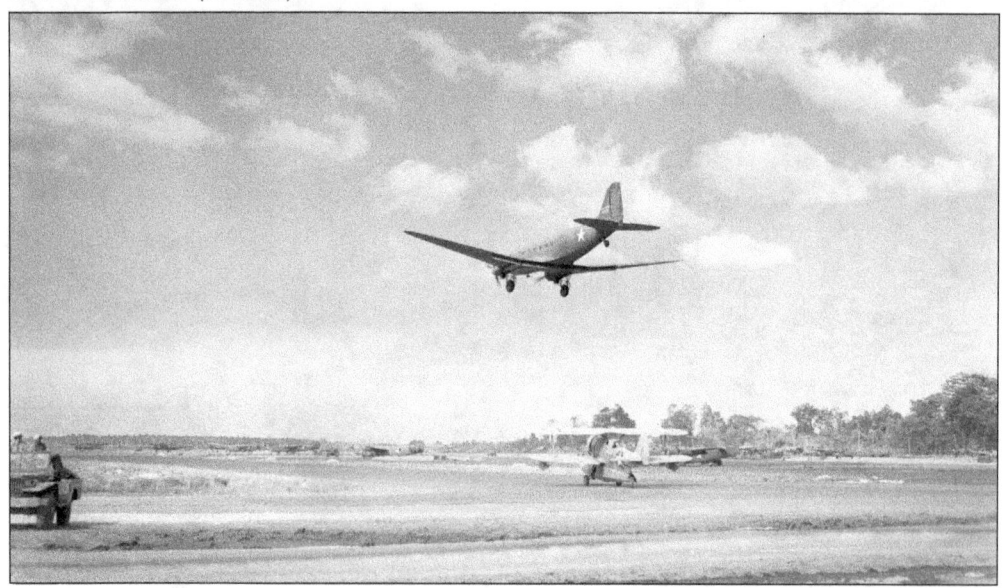

C-47 *Hitler's Hearse/Black Cat 13* (41-18574) comes in for a landing on Guadalcanal during the New Georgia campaign. Guadalcanal's airfields were busy throughout the campaign, and this view includes SCAT transports at left, B-24 Liberator bombers, and P-38 Lightning fighters at right, in addition to the J2F Duck utility amphibian in the foreground. (NARA.)

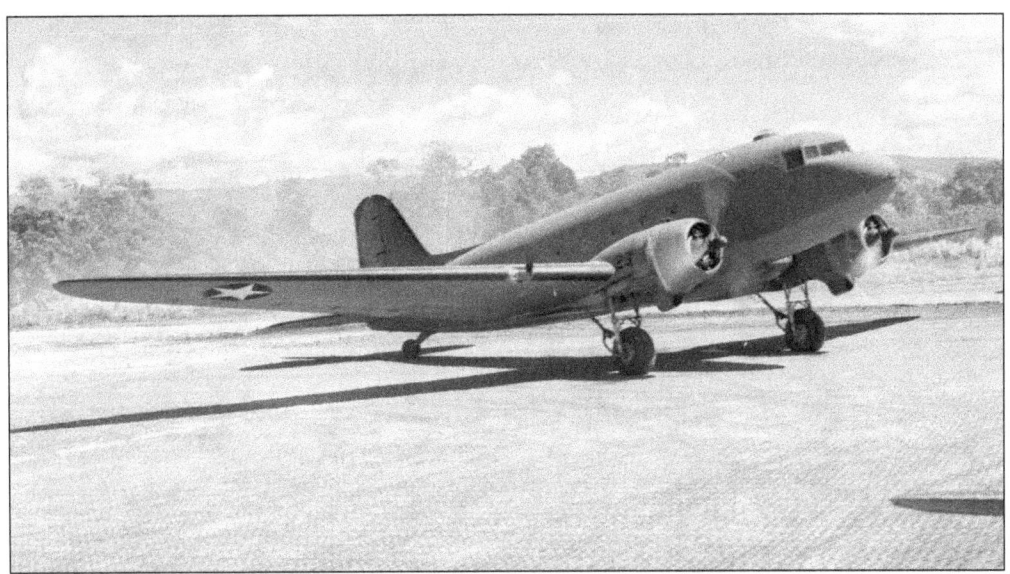

SCAT flew numerous airdrop missions during the New Georgia campaign. Here, R4D "23" (12423) of VMJ-153 prepares to depart Guadalcanal loaded with 5,000 pounds of rations and mortar shells on July 19, 1943. Its crew, who delivered their cargo despite antiaircraft fire, was pilot 1st Lt. Robert Thompson, copilot 1st Lt. Lawrence Buol, navigator 2nd Lt. John Brule, crew chief S.Sgt. Lee Webb, and radio operator Sgt. Edelmiro Rutledge. (NARA.)

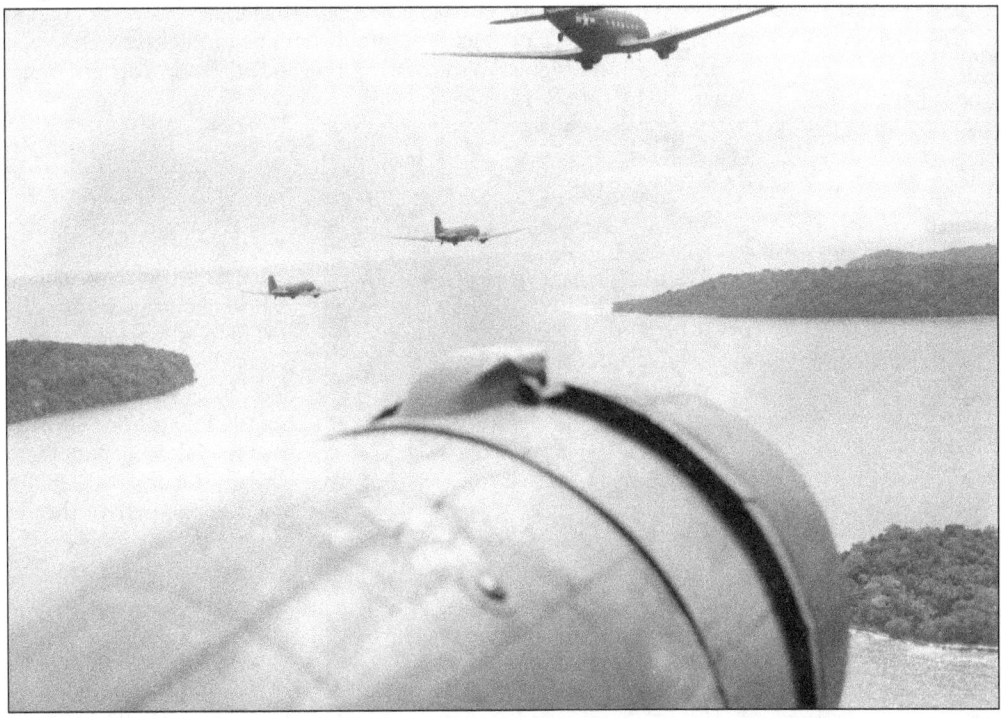

SCAT C-47s (the two aircraft in the distance) and R4Ds are shown en route to New Georgia in this August 1943 photograph taken from an R4D. The C-47 near center, with its white horizontal tail stripe, belonged to the 13th TCS. Units fighting on New Georgia had no good land supply routes, and thus depended largely on SCAT airdrops for food, ammunition, and supplies. (NARA.)

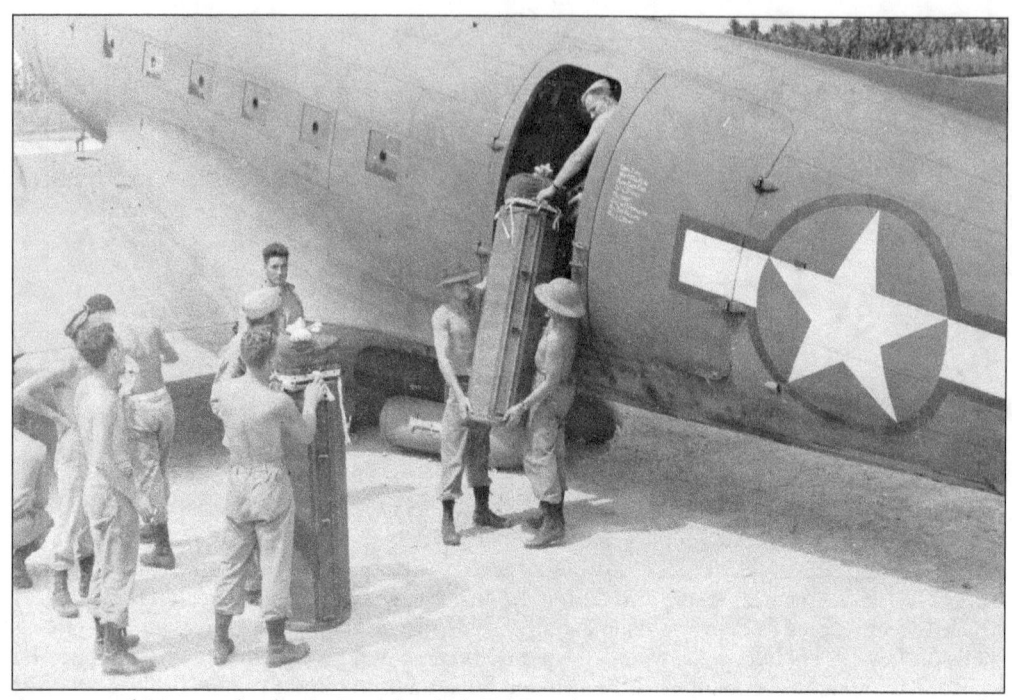

Airmen and Marines load a C-47 of the 64th TCS with "para-packs," parachute containers used to deliver medical and other vital supplies to forces isolated deep in the jungle, prior to a mission to New Georgia. These are rigid type A-8 para-packs, originally designed to deliver rifles. The 64th was the first troop carrier squadron assigned to the newly arrived 403rd Troop Carrier Group, which joined SCAT in August 1943. (NARA.)

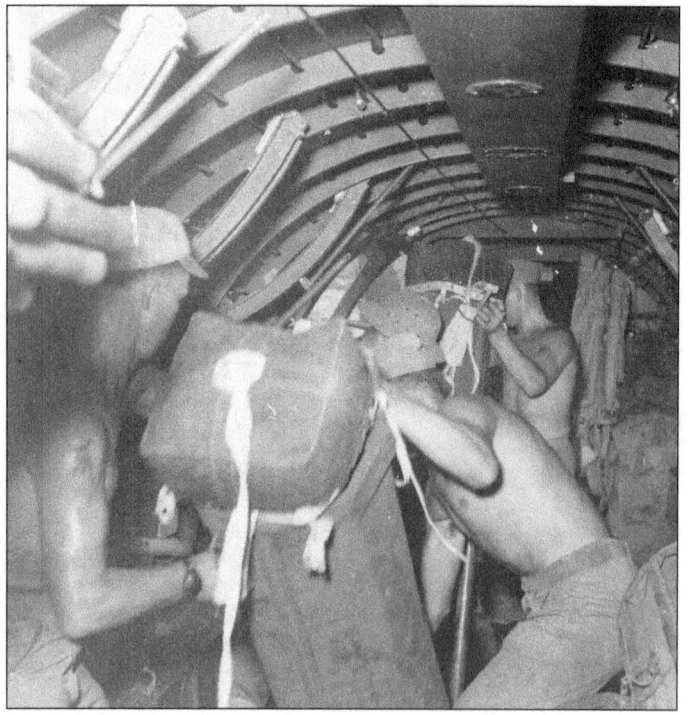

Large para-packs like the A-8 were carried internally and manually thrust out of the open cargo door. SCAT had made occasional airdrops during the Guadalcanal campaign, but New Georgia was its first sustained use of the technique. The aircraft on this page appears to be C-47 42-23722, which 2nd Lt. Kenneth Kidd later successfully ditched off San Cristobal after a double-engine failure on January 26, 1944. (NARA.)

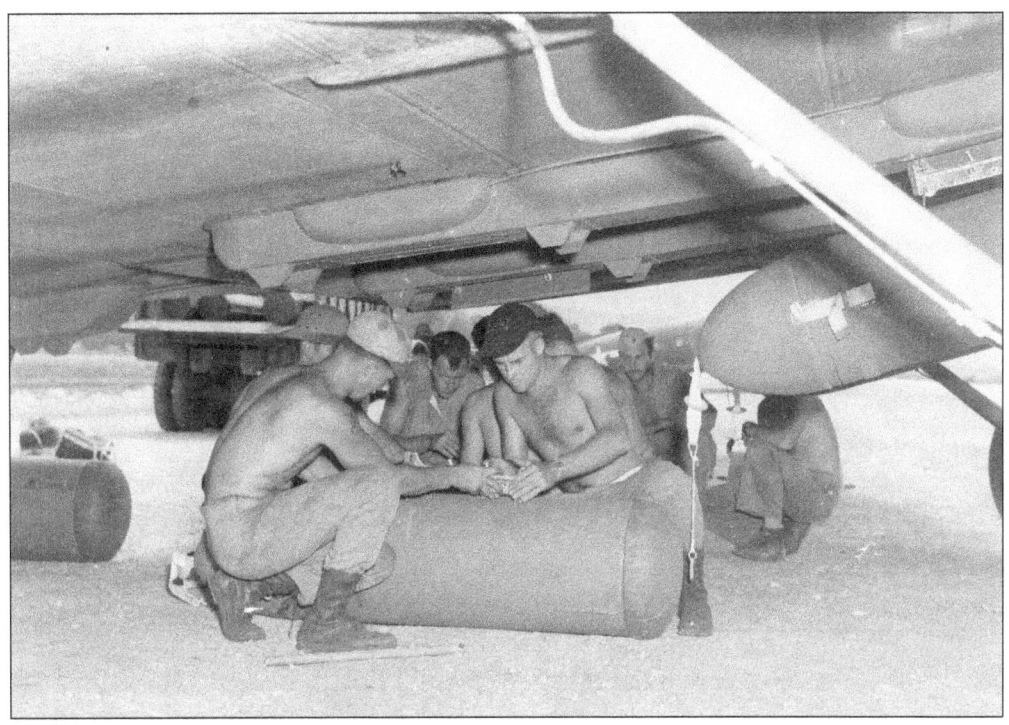

In addition to internal cargo, the C-47/R4D was designed to carry up to six external para-packs. Airmen and Marines, having installed the para-pack racks on the C-47's belly, are shown attaching the shackles to each pack. The entire external para-pack load could be released simultaneously by the pilot via a button in the cockpit. (NARA.)

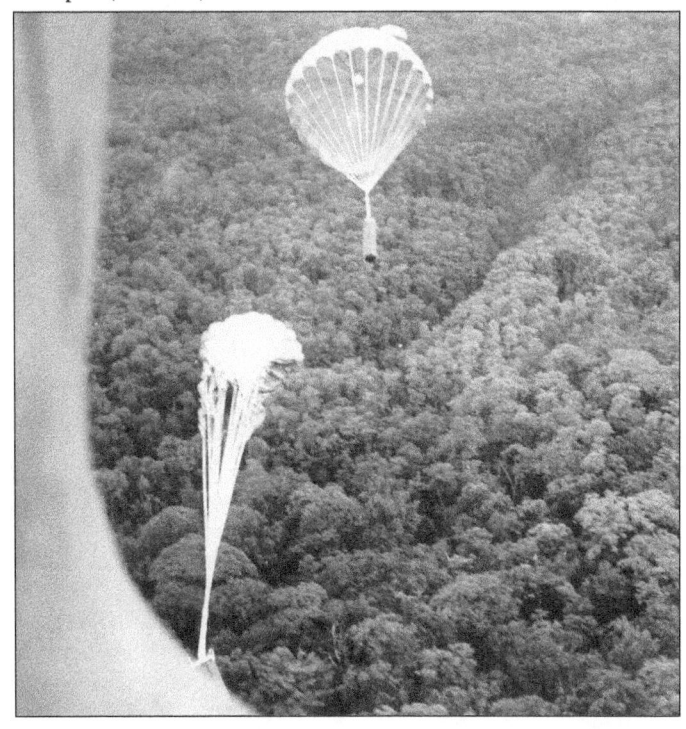

A SCAT transport releases para-packs over New Georgia in August 1943. The para-pack missions were considered particularly dangerous due to ground fire and the threat of enemy fighters, and the transports each had to make numerous passes over the drop zone to unload their full cargo. Still, crews vied for the missions, which were among the few after Guadalcanal for which MAG-25 awarded medals. (NARA.)

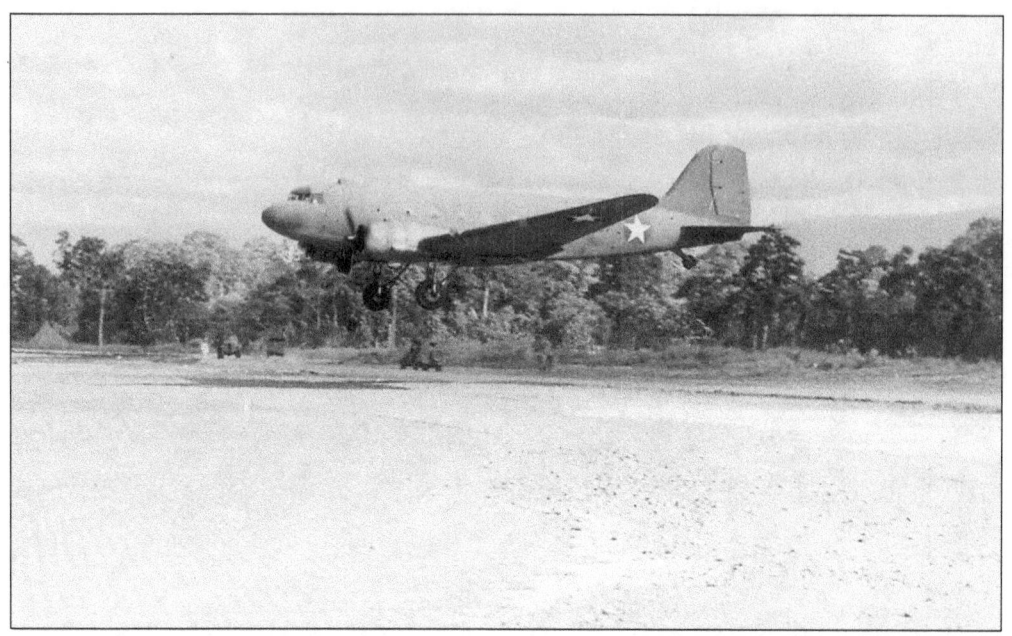

R4D "07" (likely 12407 of VMJ-153) returns to Guadalcanal after a para-pack mission on August 13, 1943. This aircraft still wears the first MAG-25 marking scheme, including six-position national insignia without the recently adopted white "bars" and red outline (the outline would be quickly changed to blue). The following day, SCAT's operations extended northward with the opening of Munda airfield, roughly 45 miles to the northwest of Segi Point. (NARA.)

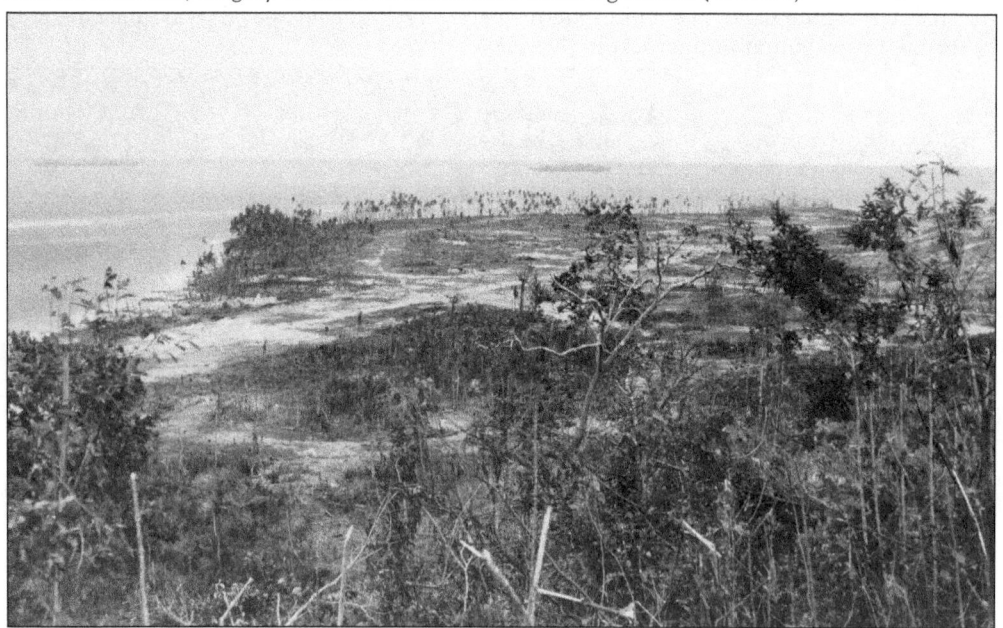

American raids devastated the Japanese airfield at Munda Point, but despite the damage, American engineers had the runway functional again within two weeks of its capture. This is the airfield viewed from newly occupied Bibilo Hill, taken by the 43rd Infantry Division, on August 3, 1943. The 43rd and 37th Infantry Divisions secured the airfield on August 5, but fighting continued on the island into the last week of August. (NARA.)

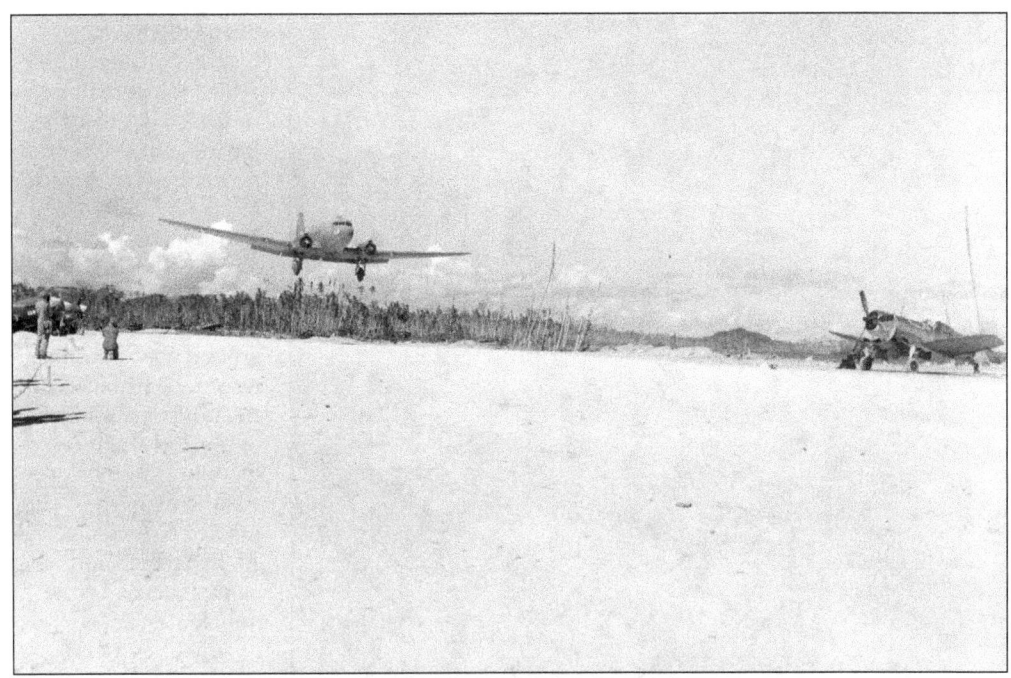

The most noticeable example of interservice rivalry within SCAT was the fight for "first landing" of a transport at new airfields. At Munda, it was C-47 *Snafu* of the 13th TCS that claimed the honor on August 14, 1943 (above). USAAF P-40 Warhawk fighters of the 44th Fighter Squadron (at left) and a Marine F4U Corsair (right) flank the runway. Below, SCAT aircraft share Munda's apron with USAAF P-38 Lightning and Marine F4U Corsair fighters on August 14, the airfield's first day of scheduled operations. The center transport is a C-47, flanked by R4Ds of MAG-25. (Both, NARA.)

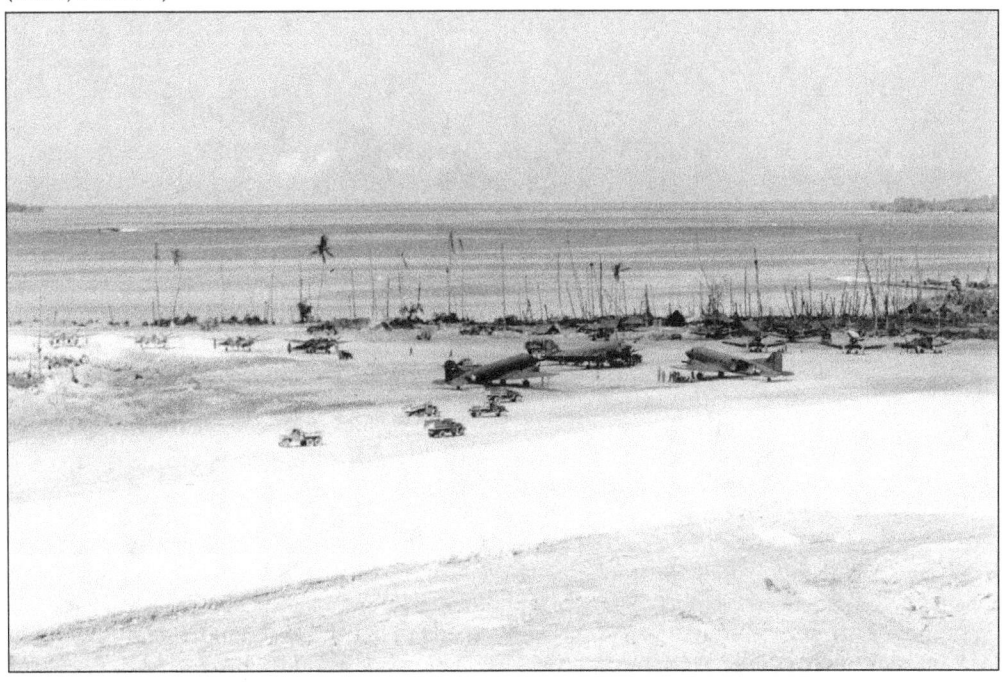

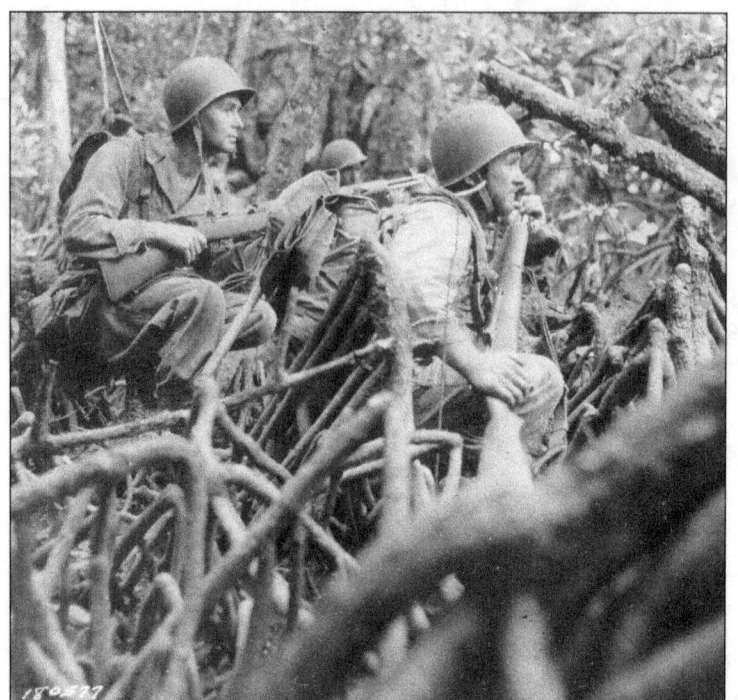

Even before New Georgia was secured, Allied forces struck the next blow against the Japanese in the central Solomons. On August 15, 1943, US Army, Marine, and Navy forces invaded Vella Lavella. They initially encountered little ground opposition, but resistance stiffened inland. Here, soldiers of the 25th Infantry Division pause before advancing in the jungle on September 13, five days before being relieved by the 3rd New Zealand Division. (NARA.)

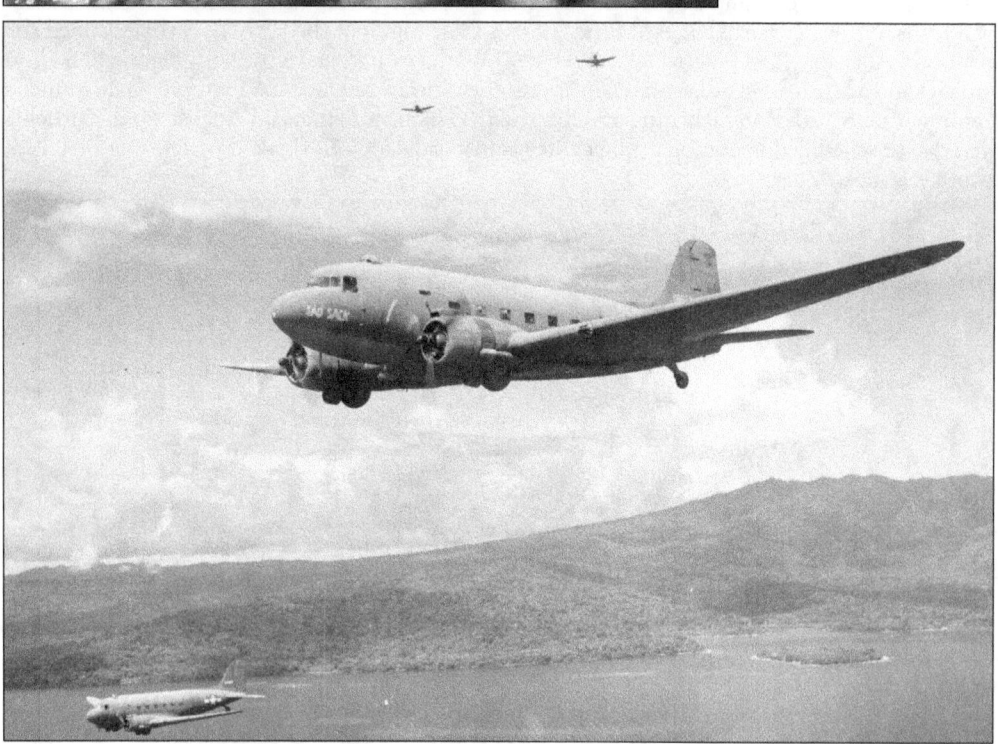

C-47 *Sad Sack* (41-18572) and squadron mate 41-19499 of the 13th TCS are shown on a mission in the central Solomons in October 1943, likely photographed from a MAG-25 R4D. *Sad Sack* was an original 13th TCS aircraft, and the star on its nose reflects the Distinguished Unit Citation for Guadalcanal. Four P-40 Warhawks of the 44th Fighter Squadron fly cover. (NARA.)

Even crew members vied for "first" at new airfields. Second Lt. Dorothy Shikoski of the 801st MAETS became the first nurse on New Georgia, arriving at Munda aboard a SCAT R4D on August 25, 1943. Upon her arrival, Lieutenant Shikoski was greeted by SCAT's commanding officer, Col. Fiske Marshall (left), and 2nd Marine Aircraft Wing commanding officer Brig. Gen. Francis Mulcahy, outside the latter's headquarters by Kokengola Hill. (NARA.)

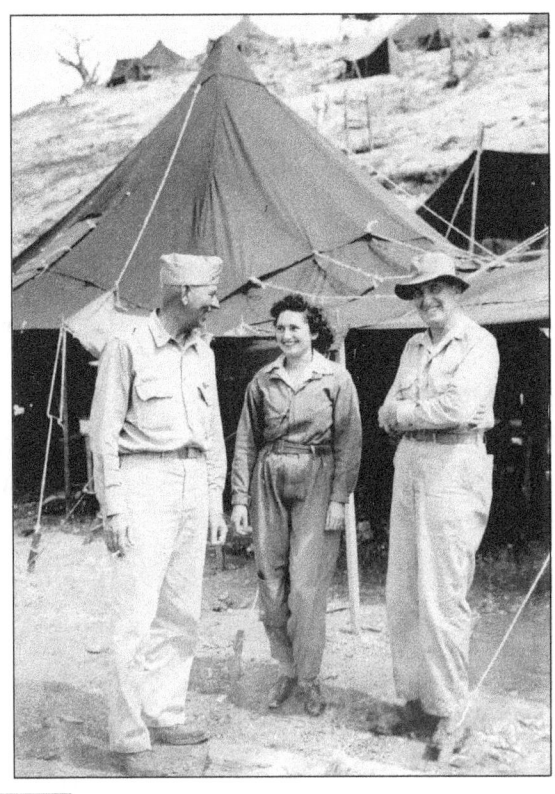

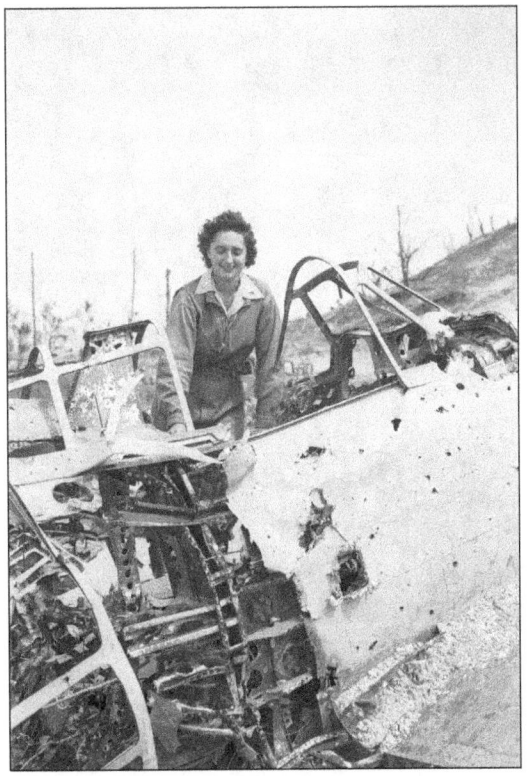

Near Kokengola Hill, Lieutenant Shikoski inspects the wreckage of a Mitsubishi A6M Type 0 naval fighter, one of many aircraft destroyed during the Allied air campaign against the former Japanese air base. Kokengola Hill had been the last Japanese stronghold on the island, but by this time it was the nerve center of American air operations at Munda. (NARA.)

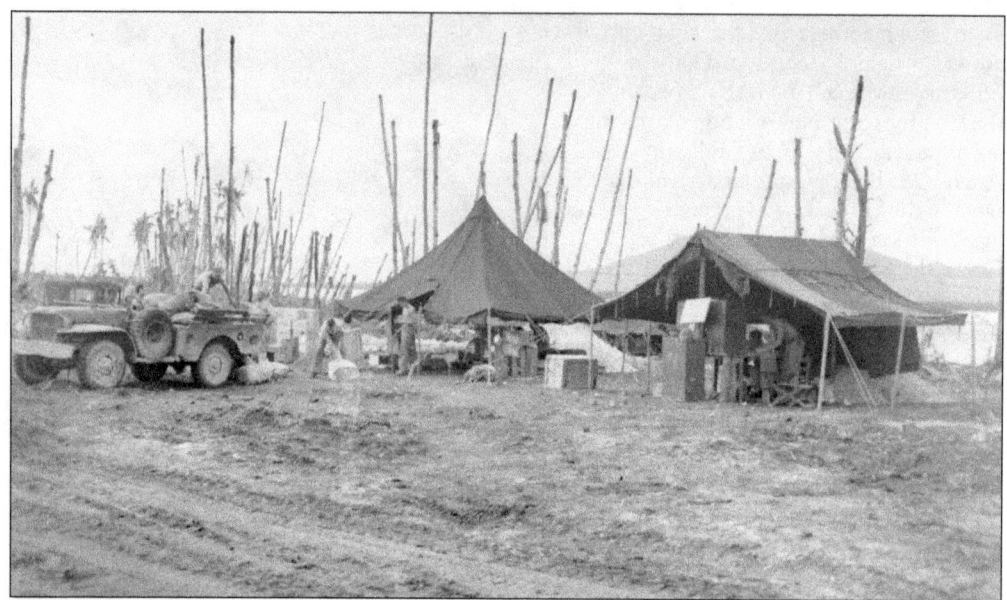

SCAT's first operations office at Munda, shown shortly after the airfield opened, was typical of its bare-bones facilities at advanced bases. Here, men load one of the Dodge weapons carriers that conveyed cargo to the aircraft. The SCAT forward detachment at Munda was then overseen by officer-in-charge Lt. Andrieus Jones, US Naval Reserve, of Headquarters Squadron 25. (NARA.)

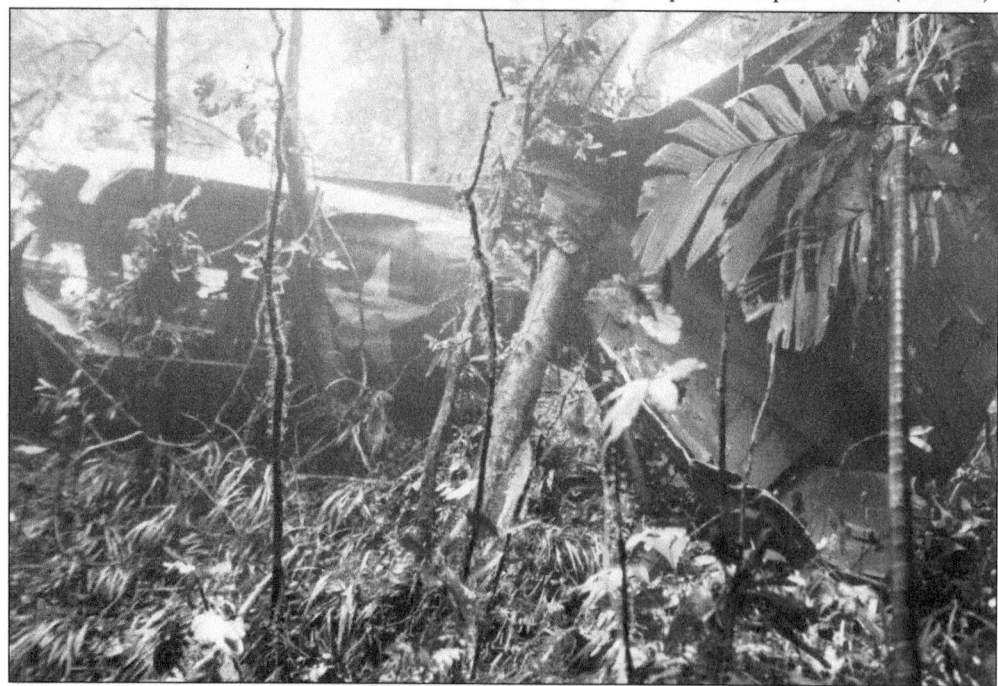

The torn rear fuselage of R4D 12411 sits tangled in the jungle on northern San Cristobal. Piloted by Capt. William Spence and 1st Lt. Charles Brush of VMJ-152, the aircraft struck a mountainside during severe weather on July 29, 1943, while evacuating patients from Munda. Of the 28 aboard, 8 were killed and all sustained injuries. From September 1942 to July 1944, SCAT's squadrons suffered 14 fatal aircraft losses. (NARA.)

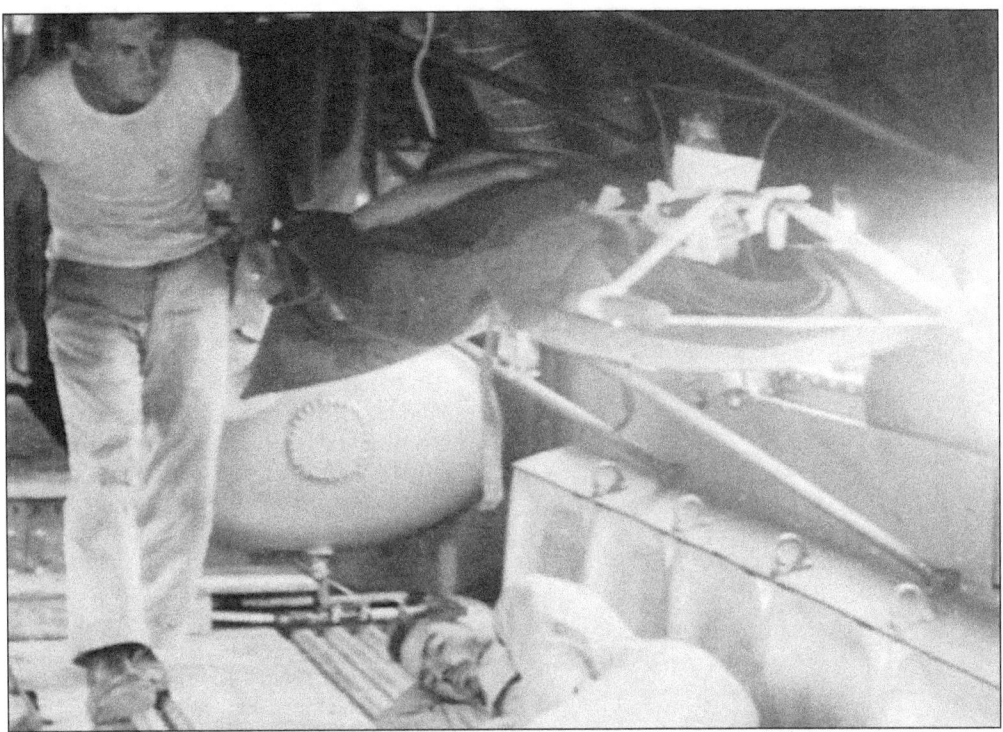

Although the 801st MAETS nurses received most photographers' attention, SCAT flights were just as likely to include one of the squadron's medical corpsmen. Here, a corpsman tends to patients just evacuated from Munda, including two with severe wounds. This was likely an emergency mission, given the small number of patients and litters aboard the R4D. Above, a sick or less severely wounded man is relegated to the floor under a man with a severe leg wound. Note the ovular long-range fuel tank in the background. Below, the corpsman gives water to one of the severely wounded men. These evacuees were destined for one of the hospitals on Guadalcanal. (Both, NARA.)

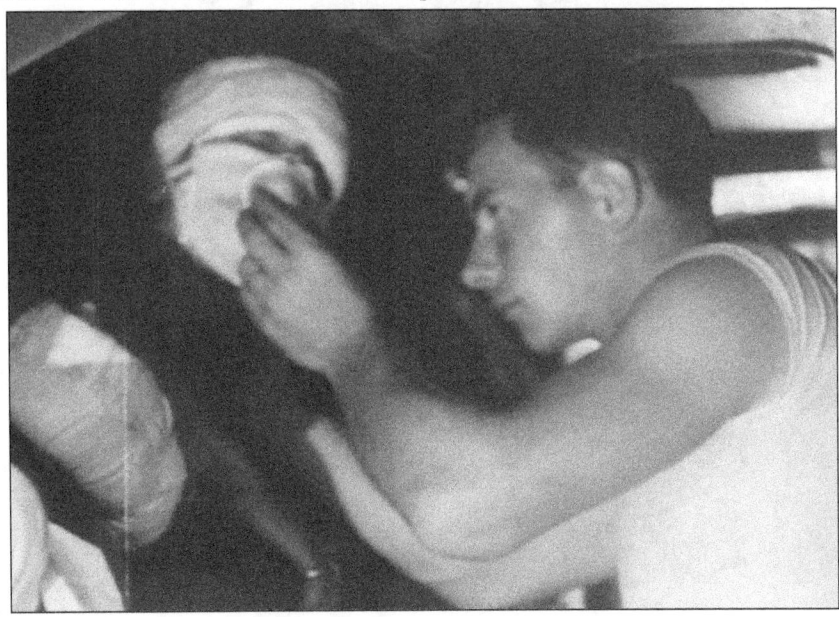

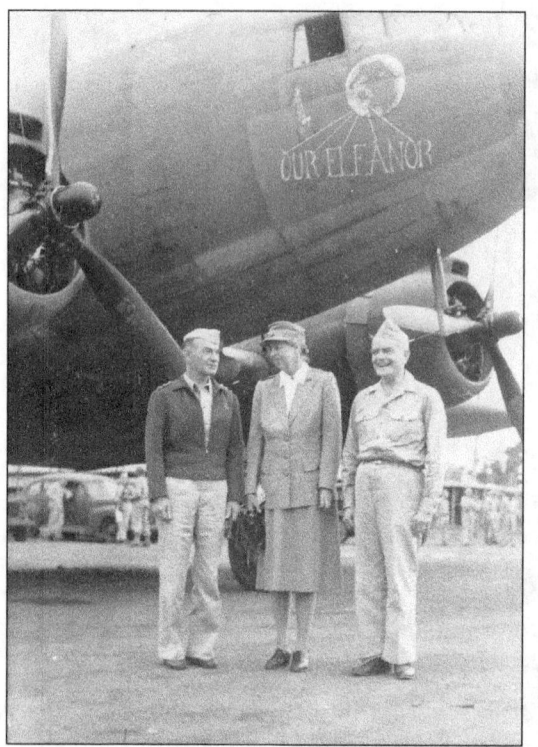

In 1943, the 13th TCS flew First Lady Eleanor Roosevelt to several destinations during her Red Cross goodwill tour of the South Pacific. Her first flights were aboard *Snafu* on August 25, and she was made an honorary squadron member. Here, she poses with Lt. Gen. Millard Harmon (left), Adm. William Halsey, and her honorary C-47, *Our Eleanor*, on September 15. (Courtesy of the Franklin D. Roosevelt Library.)

After *Snafu's* triumphant landing at Munda, 13th TCS ground crewmen—organized by their home states—posed proudly with the trailblazing aircraft. These men represented Massachusetts. From left to right are (first row) Cpl. William Bond, S.Sgt. William Eaton, Cpl. George Granger, Cpl. Norman LeBlanc, T.Sgt. Leonard Lindahl, and Cpl. Frederick Lord; (second row) 1st Sgt. Gaetano Mazzone, Sgt. Francis McAllister, Cpl. J.P. McNulty, Pfc. Robert Morin, and Pfc. Lawrence Walsh. (NARA.)

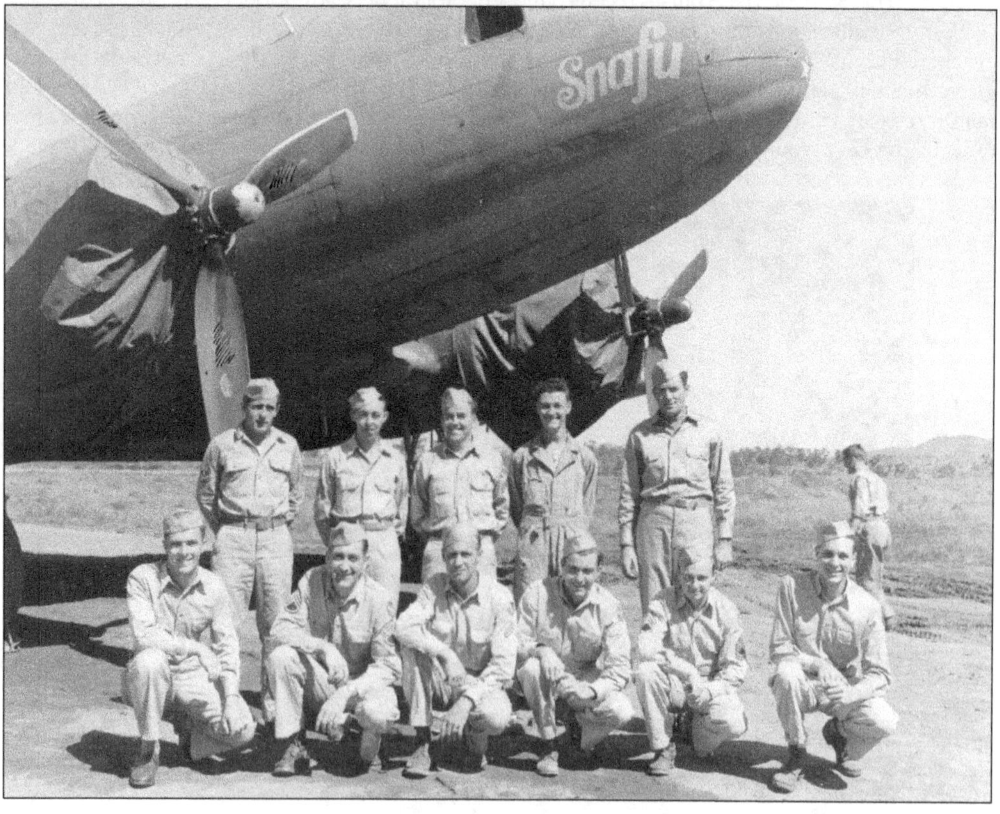

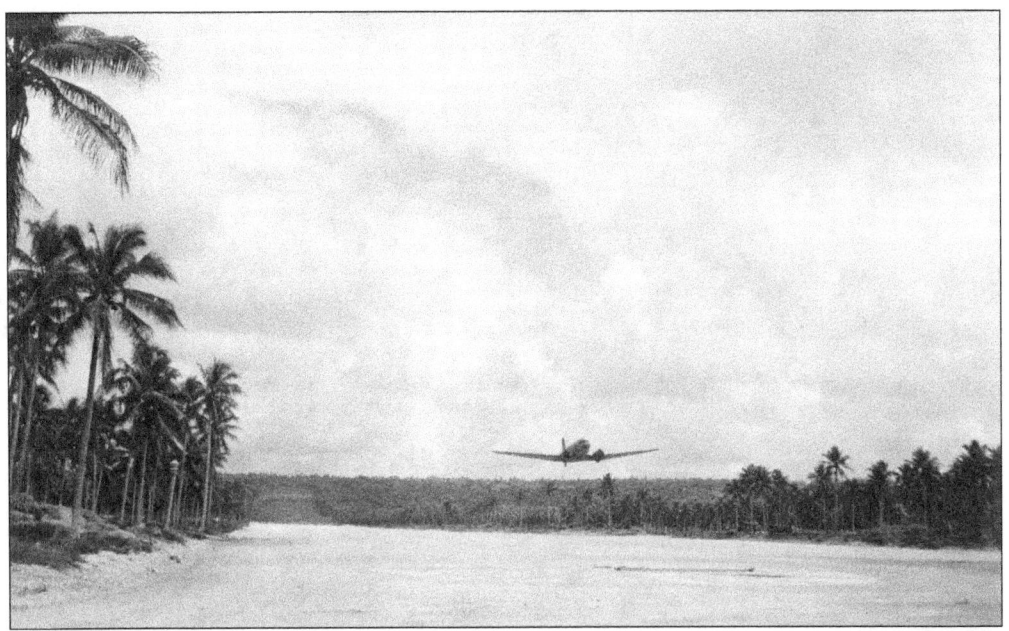

A 13th TCS C-47 departs from Fighter 1 (Turtle Bay) airstrip on Espiritu Santo on September 26, 1943. On October 23, the air echelon of the 13th TCS completed the squadron's relocation to nearby Pekoa. The 403rd Troop Carrier Group at Pekoa became the immediate parent unit of the 13th TCS in October 1943. Many personnel of the "Thirsty Thirteenth" disliked losing their long-held "orphan" status. (NARA.)

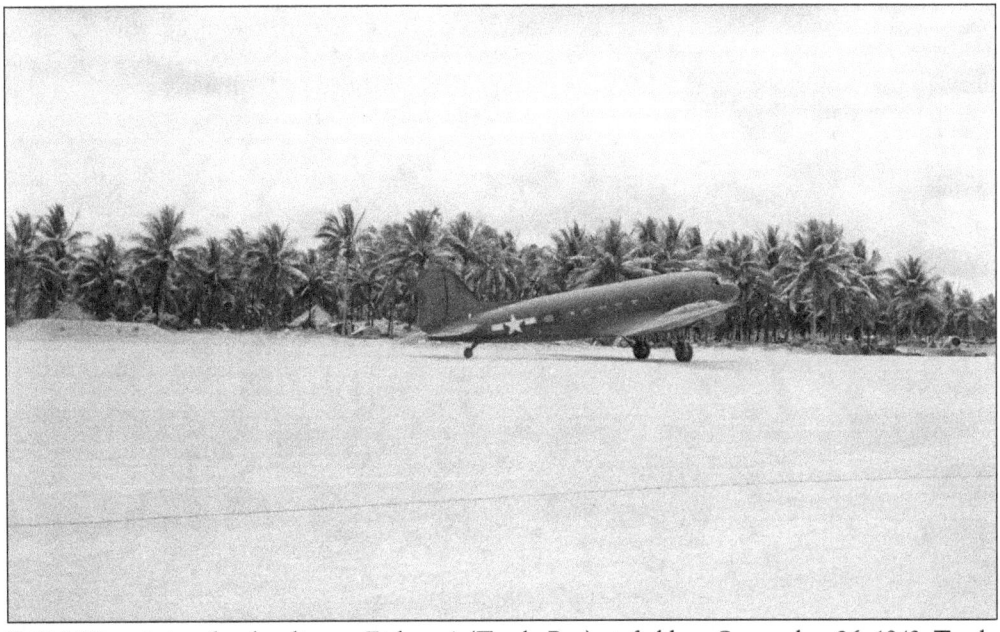

R4D "42" taxis in after landing at Fighter 1 (Turtle Bay) airfield on September 26, 1943. Turtle Bay was home to MAG-11, which included fighter, dive-bomber, and torpedo bomber squadrons, and like other air groups in the region, relied on SCAT for logistical support. SCAT had recently relocated its headquarters to nearby Bomber 2 (Pekoa) airfield, less than nine miles away by air. (NARA.)

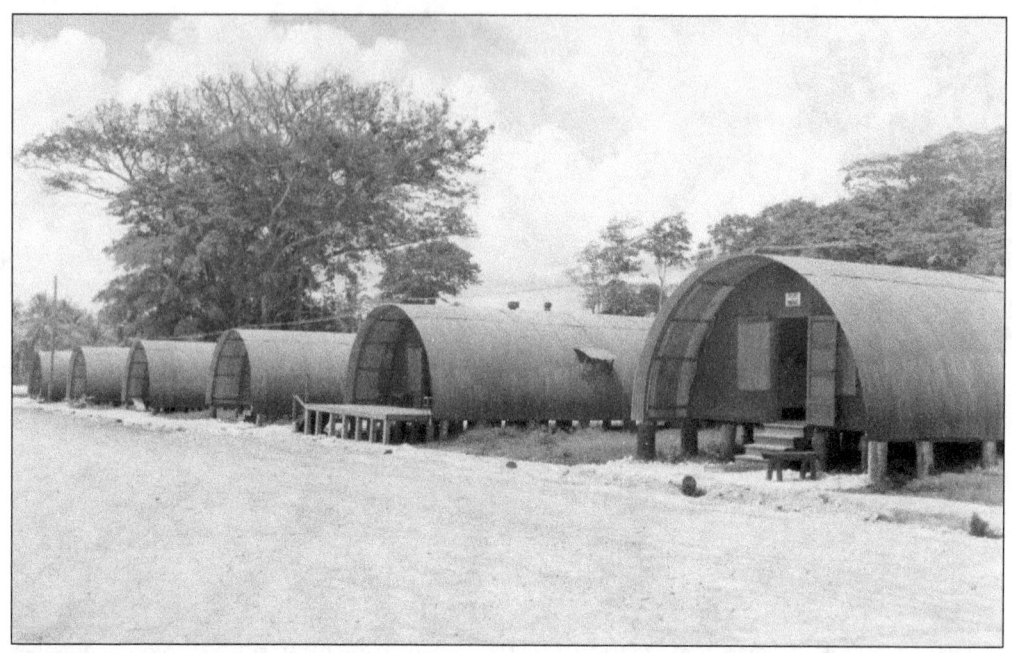

SCAT's complex at Pekoa airfield, formerly known as Bomber 2 until November 1943, was located near the center of the airfield. Above, the local SCAT operations offices and cargo warehouse were similar to those established at each of the unit's island outposts; the SCAT mail office is in the foreground. Other huts included the SCAT Medical Department office and dispensary, cargo office, passenger terminal, and flight operations office. Below, SCAT had moved its headquarters operations to Bomber 2 shortly after the 403rd Troop Carrier Group arrived, allowing for more effective administrative control of SCAT's assets. The 801st MAETS relocated to Pekoa from Guadalcanal in October 1943. MAG-25's headquarters remained at Tontouta. Pekoa airfield is still in use as Santo-Pekoa International Airport. (Both, NARA.)

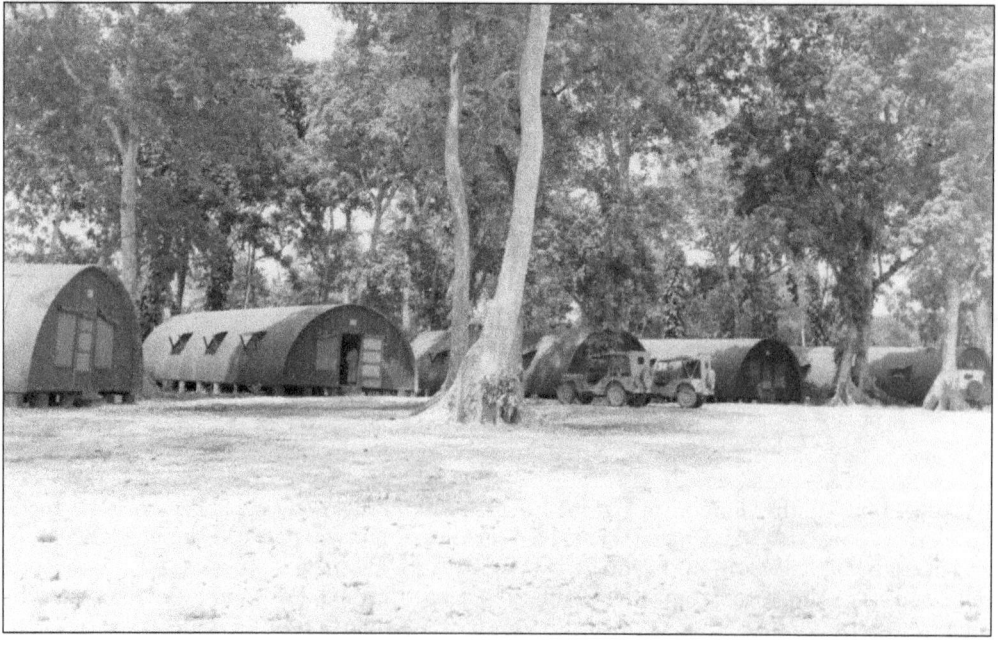

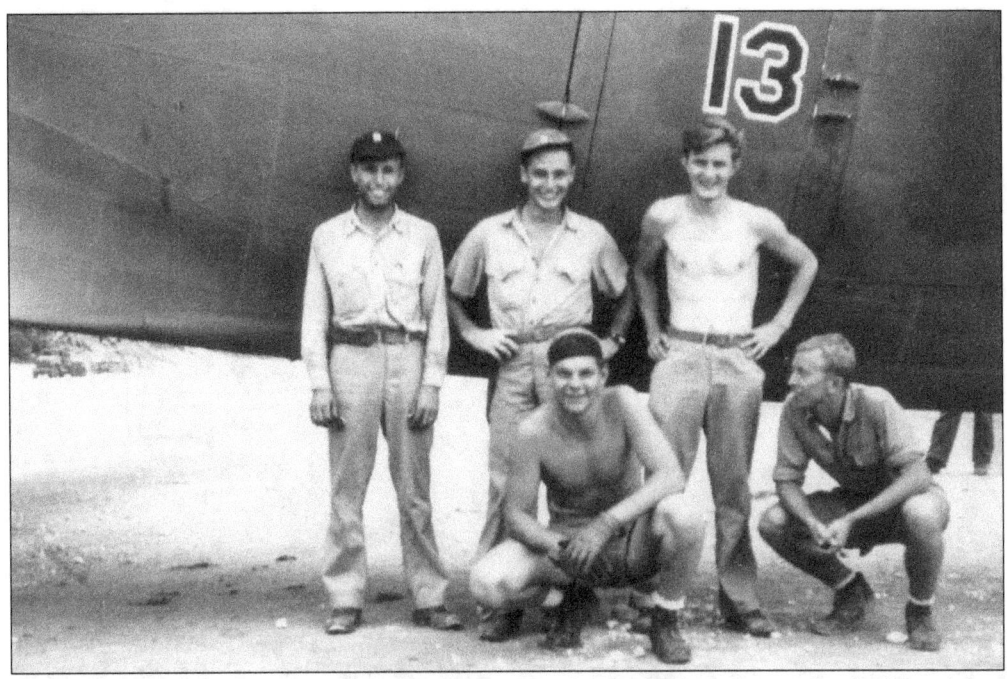

A Seabee took these photographs of VMJ-152's "Lucky 13" and crew at unfinished Barakoma airfield on Vella Lavella on September 27, 1943. They likely were the first SCAT crew to land on the embattled island. Above, from left to right, are pilots Capt. William Dukes and Capt. Dale Hupe, crew chief T.Sgt. Bernard Schwartz (kneeling), navigator S.Sgt. Roland Hutchings, and radio operator Sgt. Robert Peppey. By the end of their MAG-25 tours, Dukes, Hupe, Peppey, and Schwartz had all earned the Distinguished Flying Cross. Hupe gained a moment of fame in 1970 while flying for Trans World Airlines (TWA), after surviving a gunshot wound during a failed hijacking attempt. Note the new MAG-25 aircraft number style, black with a white surround. (Both, courtesy of Ted Schwartz.)

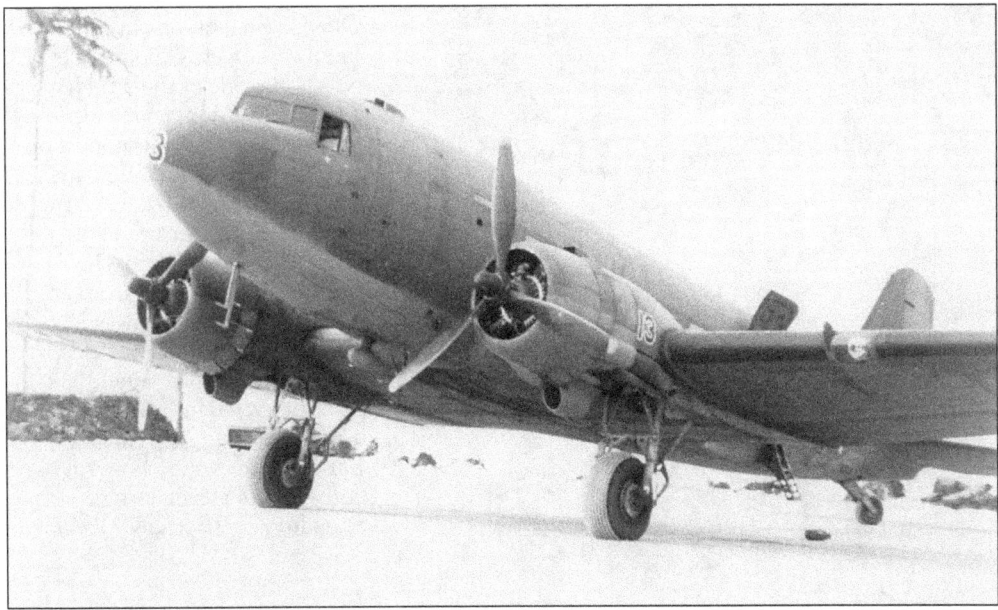

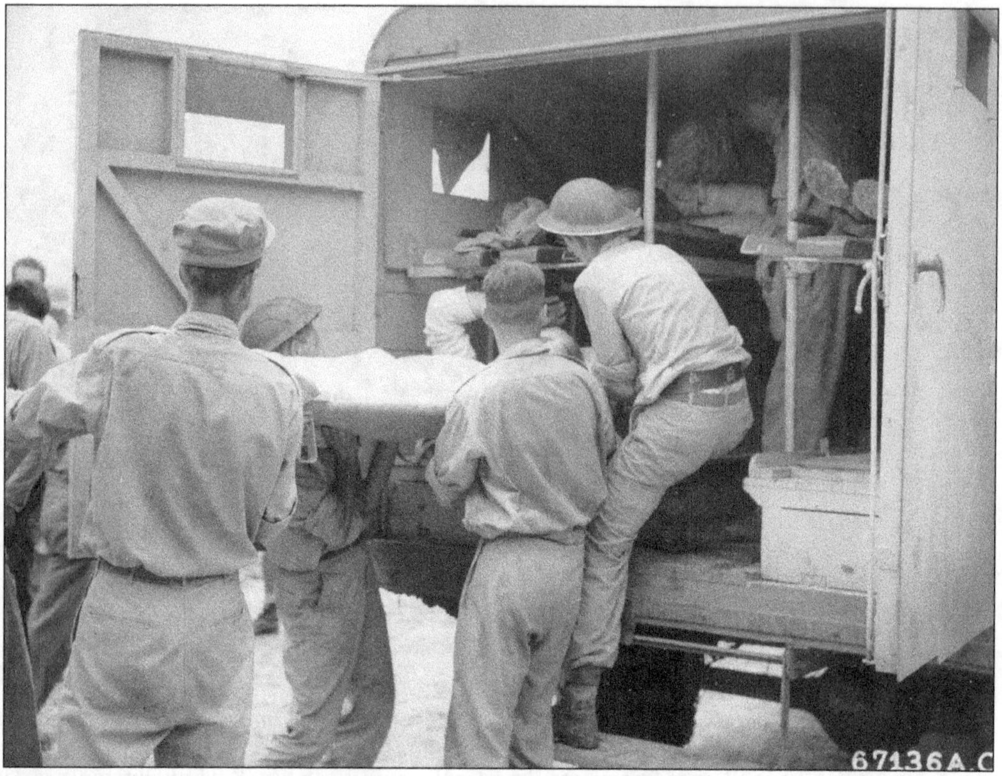

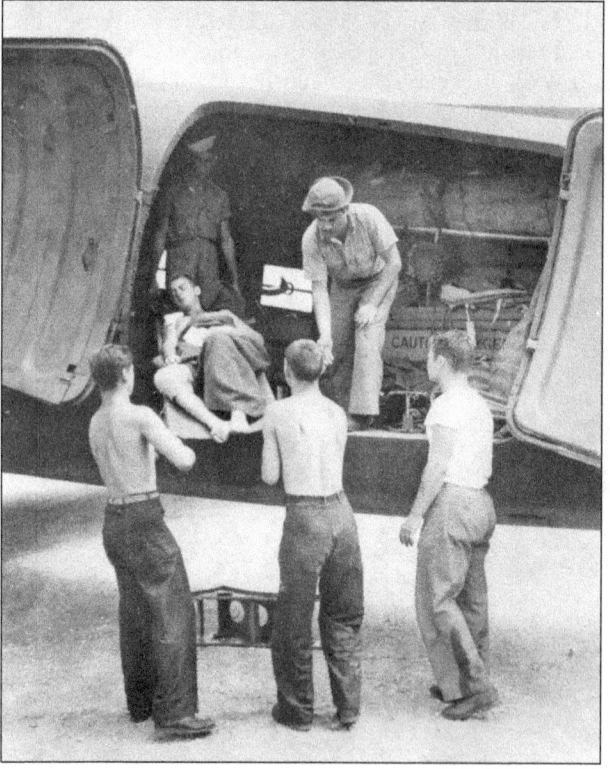

The fighting on Vella Lavella was light compared to New Georgia, but deadly air attacks and occasional ground skirmishes continued through the first week of October 1943. Offensive operations in the final weeks were conducted by No. 14 Brigade of the 3rd New Zealand Division, which also provided the medical support on the island. Above, Americans assist Royal New Zealand Army Medical Corps personnel of No. 22 Field Ambulance in transferring casualties from an ambulance to a waiting SCAT aircraft at Barakoma airfield. At left, ground personnel transfer a stretcher patient to a SCAT R4D crew. The sailor in the white cap is a hospital corpsman of Headquarters Squadron 25. (Both, NARA.)

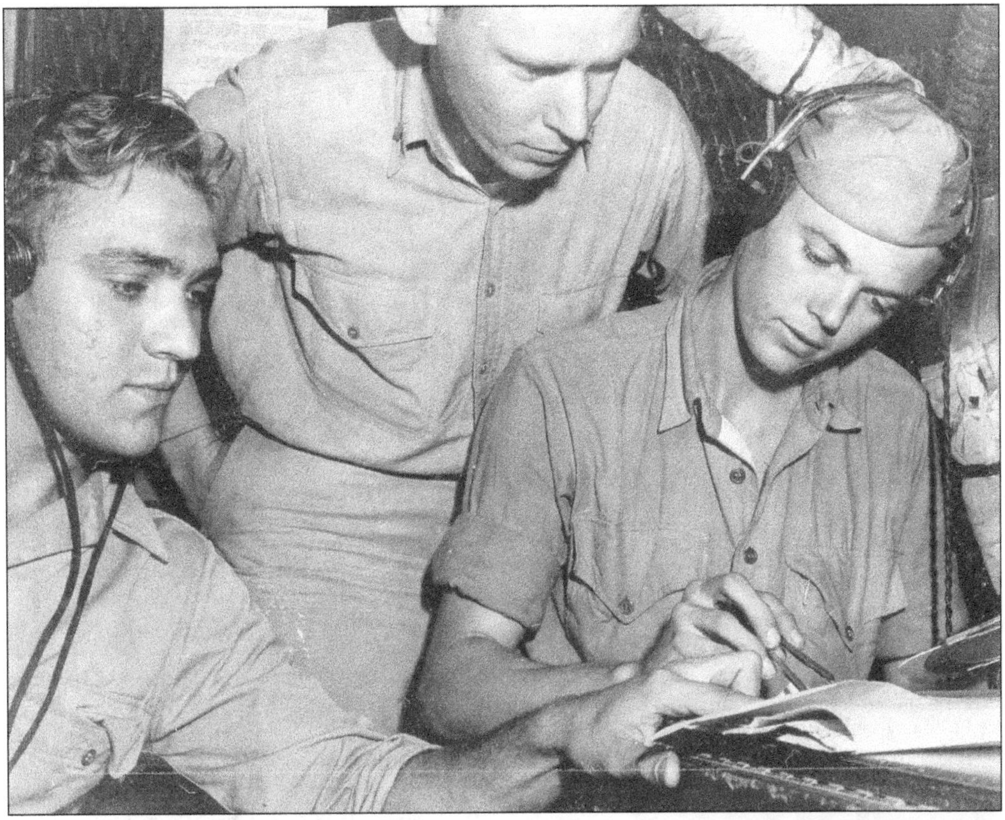

Prior to a photographic mission, a radio operator, photographer, and navigator confer aboard an R4D of VMJ-152. Most photographers aboard SCAT aircraft were there to document the unit itself. However, one pilot recalled a photographer causing incredulous chuckles when he asked his R4D crew if they could fly inverted, permitting him to take photographs through the navigator's astrodome. (Author's collection.)

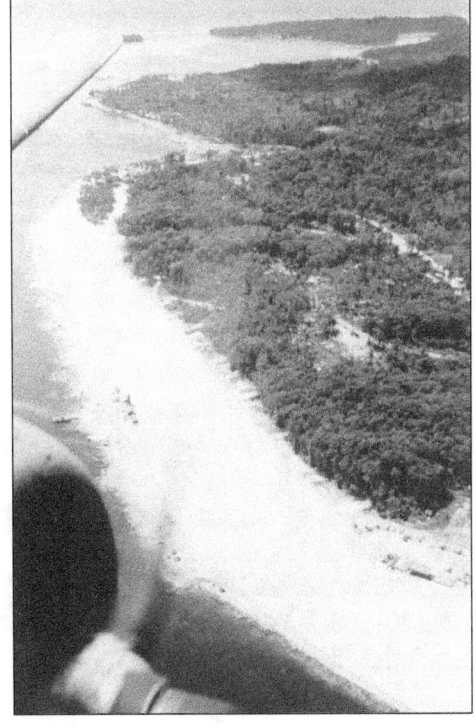

Although not designed for the task and not ideal because of its window configuration, when needed, the Douglas transport could provide a slow and stable platform for oblique aerial photography. This photograph of Barakoma airfield on Vella Lavella was taken through the pilot's window of a SCAT transport. (NARA.)

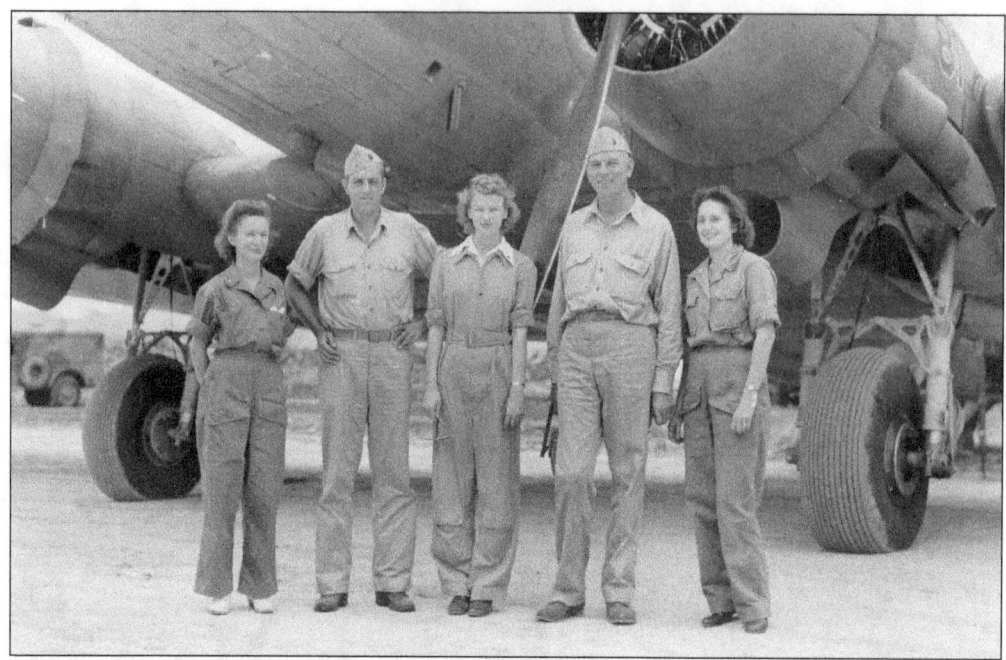

Nurses of the 801st MAETS pose with R4D "81" on Guadalcanal prior to their first flight to Vella Lavella. From left to right are 2nd Lt. Cora Conerly; Col. Perry Parmelee, commanding officer of MAG-14; 2nd Lt. Burnette Stensrud; SCAT commanding officer Col. Fiske Marshall; and 2nd Lt. Dorothy Shikoski. MAG-14 and SCAT had a close working relationship. (NARA.)

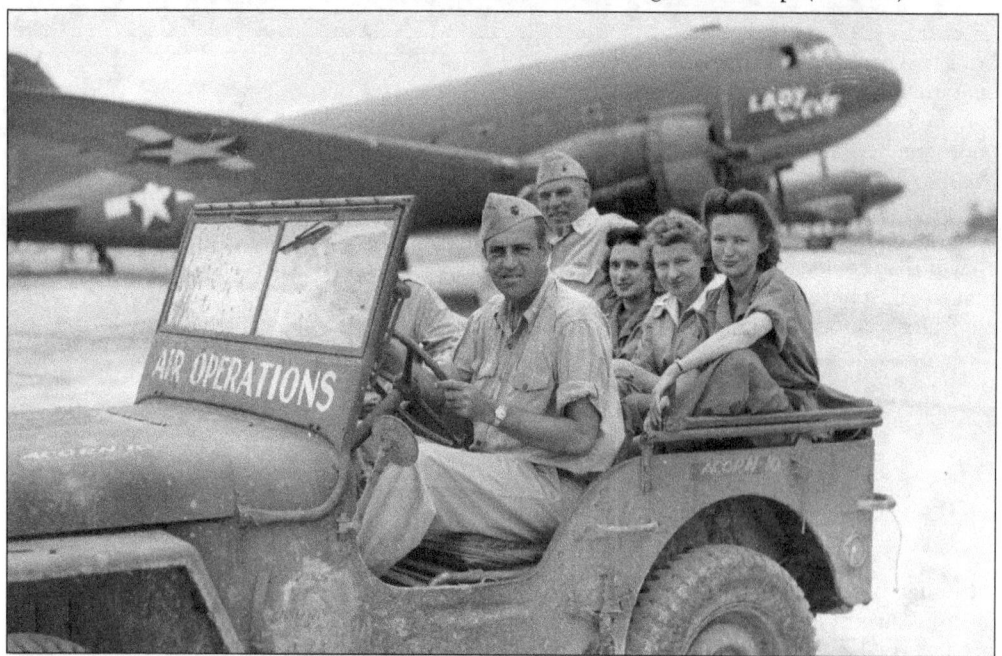

After arriving on Vella Lavella, Colonel Parmelee leads the group on a tour of the newly completed Barakoma airfield. In the background is *Lady Eve* (C-47 41-18580) of the 13th TCS and an unidentified R4D. The jeep belonged to the US Navy's ACORN-10, the logistics unit that oversaw flight operations at Barakoma. (NARA.)

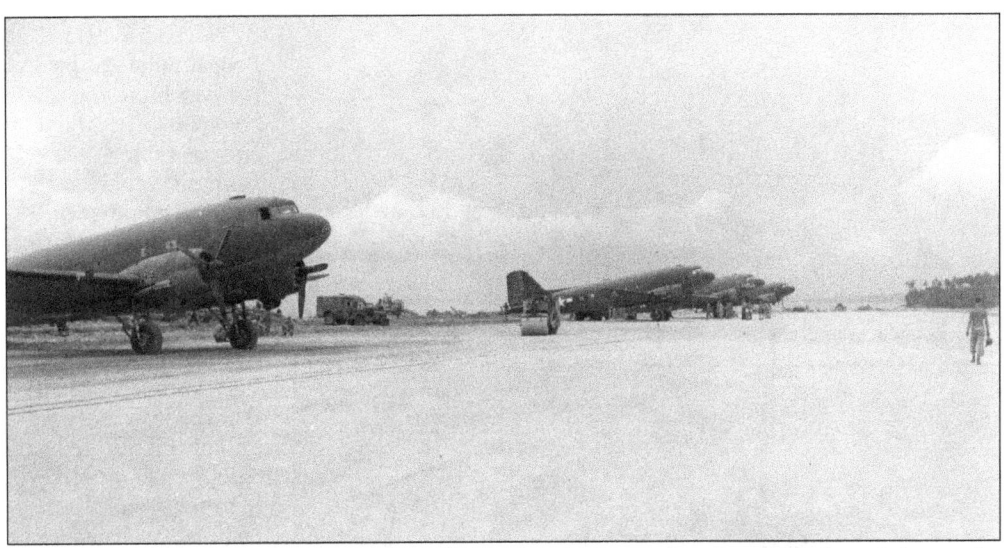

The flight of SCAT aircraft is shown parked at Barakoma in October 1943. From left to right are R4Ds "43" and "81," C-47 *Lady Eve*, and an unidentified R4D. R4D "81" appears to have been assigned to Headquarters Squadron 25, and was probably flown by Colonel Marshall. Aircraft based at Barakoma would soon play a major role supporting the next Allied assaults to the northwest: the Treasury Islands and Bougainville. (NARA.)

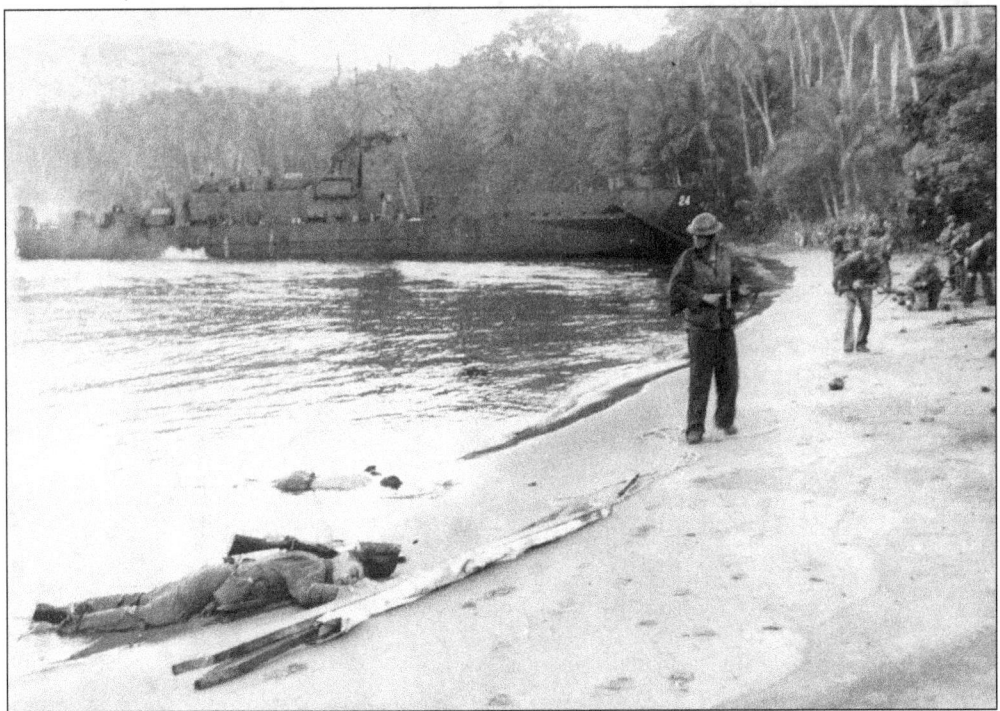

Soldiers of No. 8 New Zealand Brigade Group of the 3rd New Zealand Division and the US 198th Coast Artillery, just disembarked from USS *LCI(L)-24*, look for a camouflaged Japanese pillbox that had gunned down two soldiers of the first wave on Orange Beach, Mono, during the invasion of the Treasury Islands on October 27, 1943. Elements of both units also landed on neighboring Stirling, future site of an important airfield. (NHHC.)

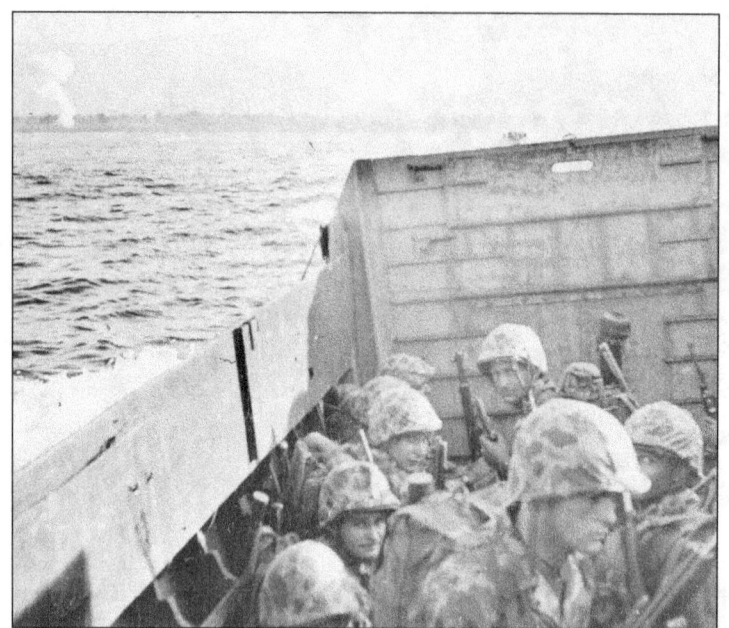

By November 1943, Bougainville was Japan's last bastion in the Solomons. An Allied air base there would put fighter aircraft well within range of Rabaul. The 3rd Marine Division went ashore at Empress Augusta Bay near Torokina Point on November 1, 1943, a surprise assault that the Japanese were initially unprepared to repulse in force. Here, Marines approach Empress Augusta Bay in an LCVP (landing craft, vehicles and personnel). (NARA.)

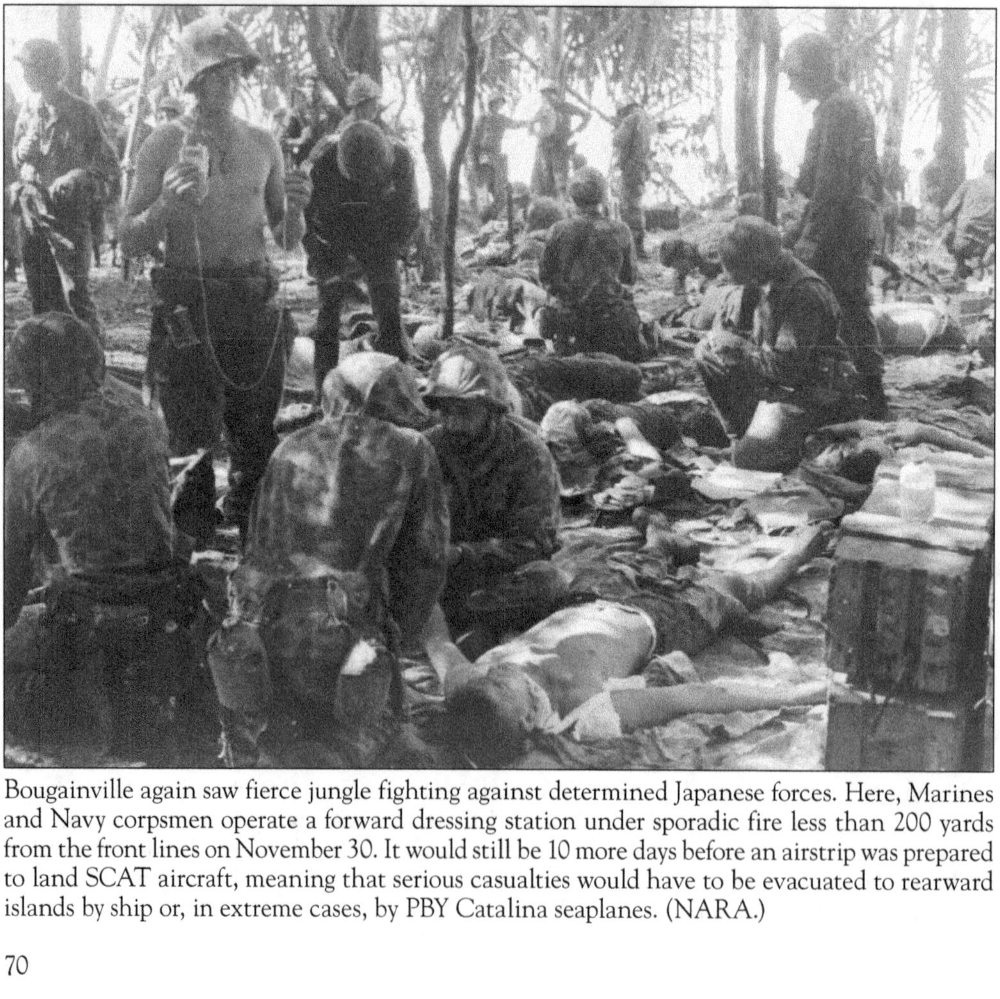

Bougainville again saw fierce jungle fighting against determined Japanese forces. Here, Marines and Navy corpsmen operate a forward dressing station under sporadic fire less than 200 yards from the front lines on November 30. It would still be 10 more days before an airstrip was prepared to land SCAT aircraft, meaning that serious casualties would have to be evacuated to rearward islands by ship or, in extreme cases, by PBY Catalina seaplanes. (NARA.)

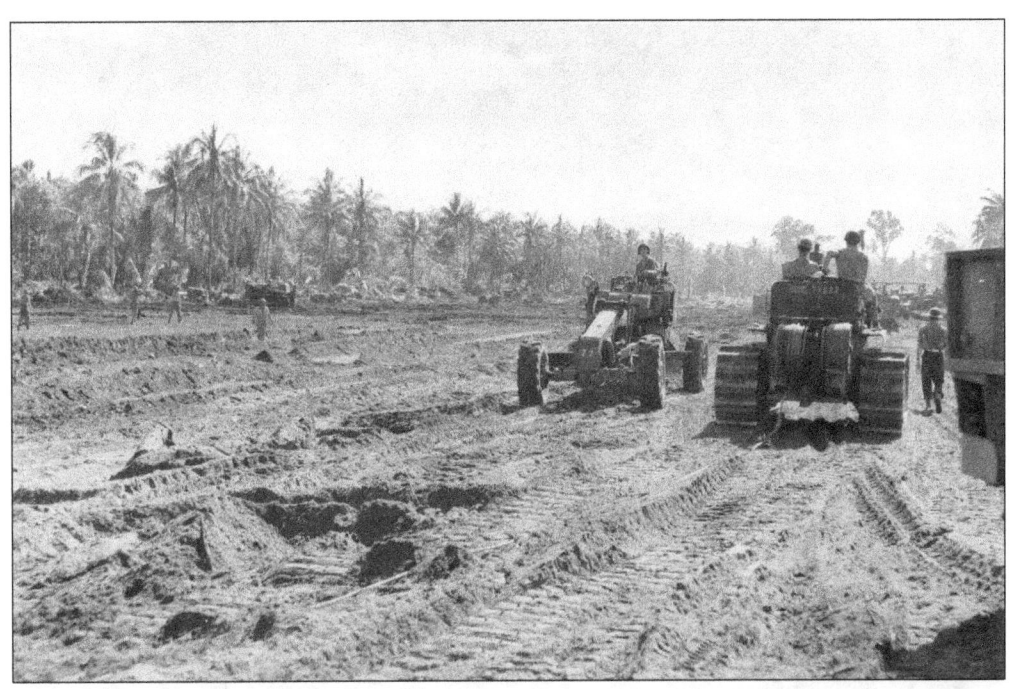

Rather than attempt to capture one of the existing Japanese airstrips on Bougainville, American forces built three new ones near Torokina Point. Construction of the first airstrip, along the beach at Torokina, began shortly after the initial landing, with construction crews often working under enemy fire. Long before the airfields were open to aircraft, SCAT was supporting the invasion force. Above, Seabees begin grading a runway after clearing away the dense jungle foliage. Below, a SCAT transport airdrops supplies as Seabees lay pierced steel planking ("PSP" or "Marston mat") to surface a runway on November 30, 1943. (Both, NARA.)

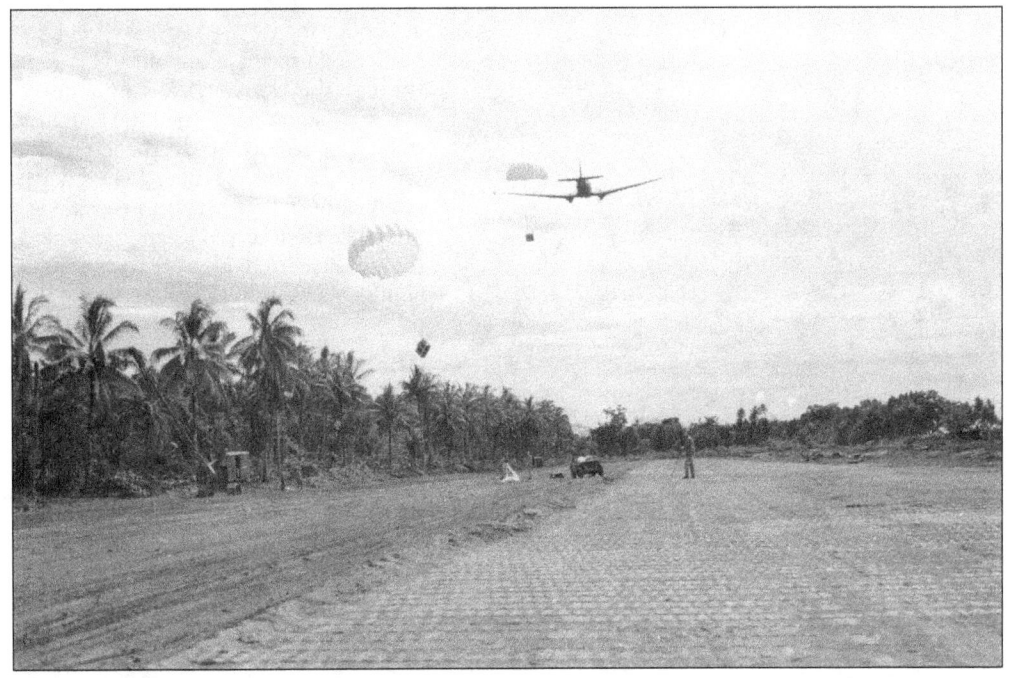

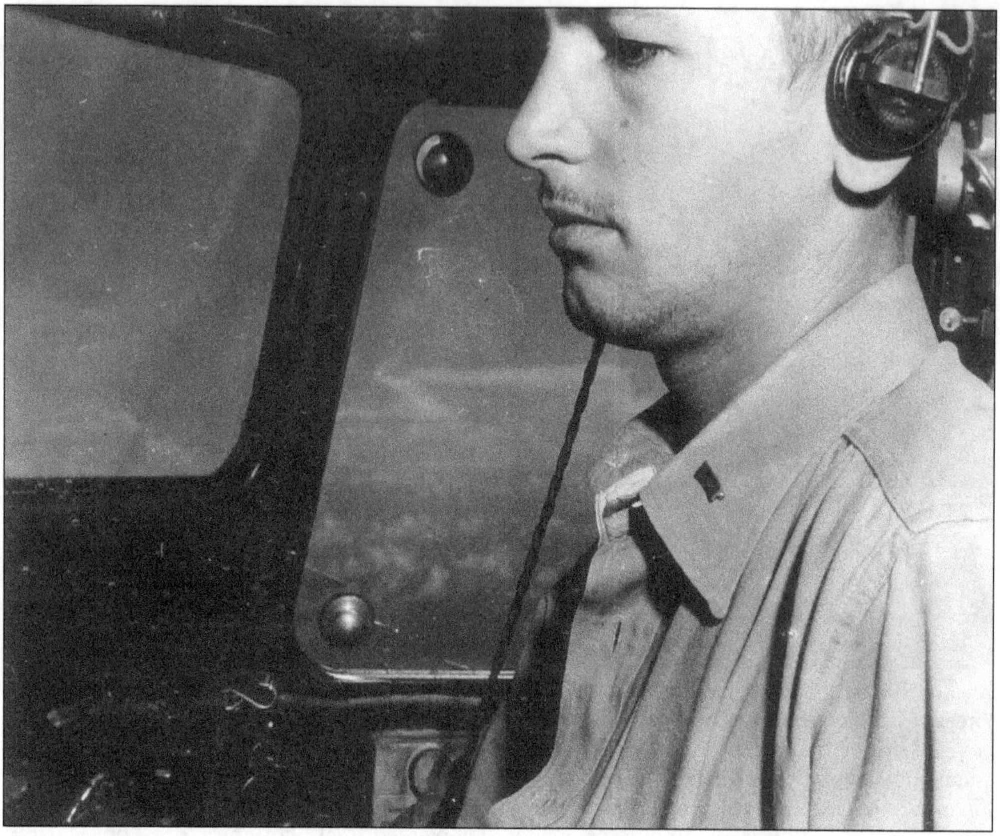

This rare cockpit view shows 1st Lt. William DuRoss of VMJ-152 flying as copilot in late 1943 or early 1944. DuRoss, a private pilot, enlisted through the US Navy's V-5 Aviation Cadet program. He joined the squadron in September 1943 and returned to the United States in February 1945. Like many of his fellow MAG-25 veteran pilots, he then served as an instrument flight instructor with MAG-35 in California. (Author's collection.)

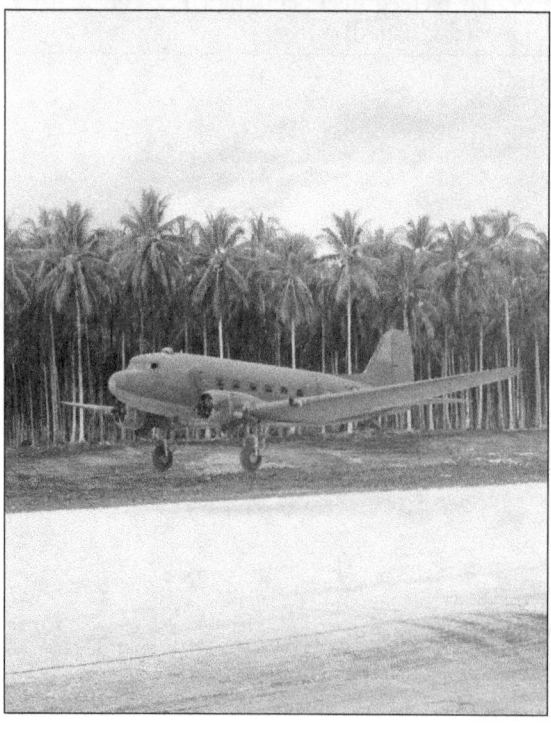

R4D "73" comes in for a landing on Banika in the Russell Islands on November 10, 1943. US Army and Marine units occupied the Russells unopposed on February 21, 1943, and the islands were used as a staging area for the New Georgia campaign. By this time, BuAer numbers were no longer universally used in assigning MAG-25 aircraft numbers, and the identity of "73" is currently unknown. (NARA.)

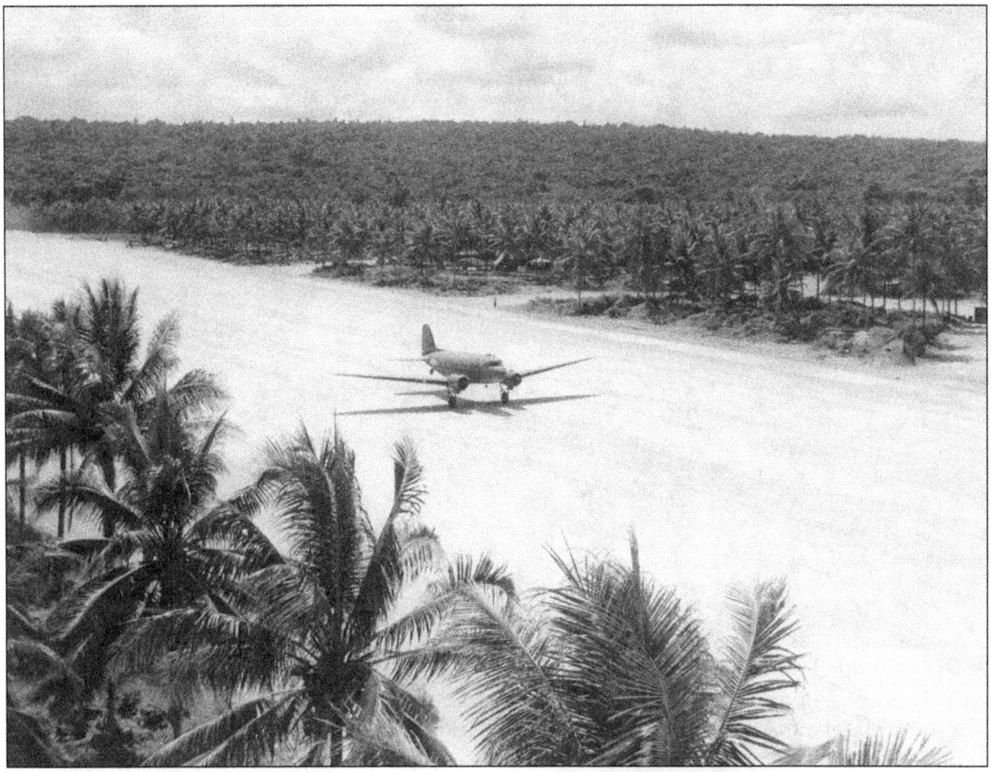

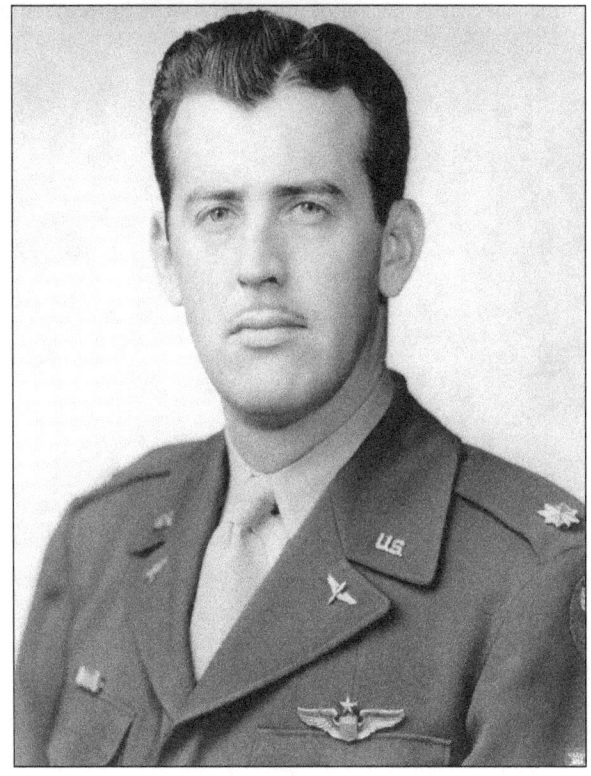

An R4D takes off from Turtle Bay airfield on Espiritu Santo on November 9, 1943. In the background are F4U Corsair fighters of MAG-11. The runway, taxiways, and revetments were carved out of a coconut plantation. SCAT aircraft often escorted short-range aircraft northward on ferry flights from Turtle Bay, which served as a depot to receive Marine Corps replacement aircraft from the United States. (NARA.)

Col. Harry J. Sands commanded the 403rd Troop Carrier Group, and from August 1943 to July 1944 also served as SCAT's executive officer. He was in direct command of roughly half of SCAT's air assets during much of that time. Sands had a distinguished career, retiring from the US Air Force as a major general in 1968 following duty as commandant of the Air Command and Staff College. (NARA.)

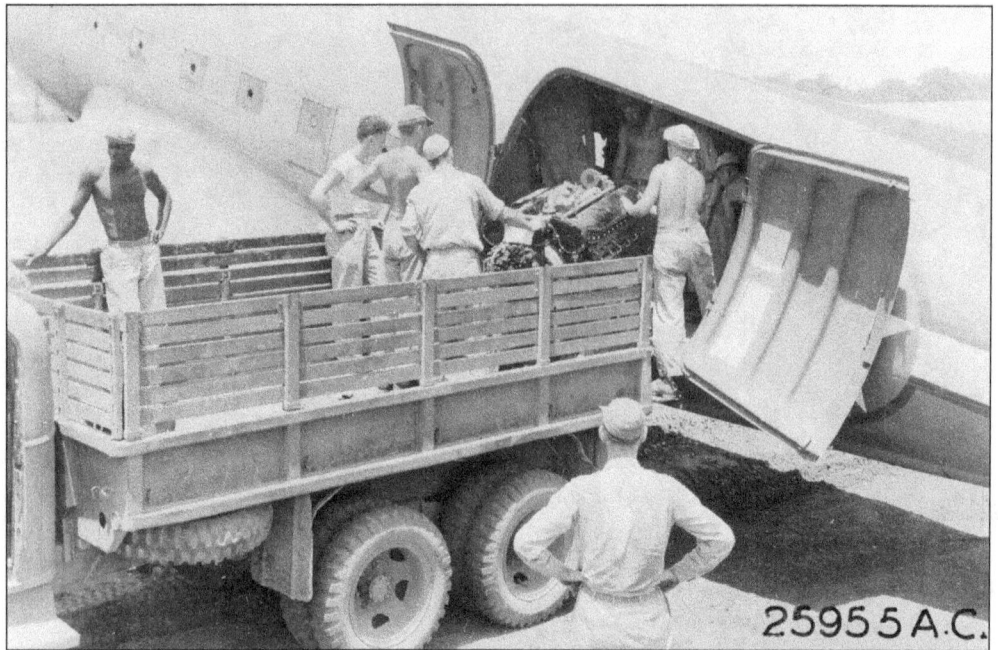

SCAT personnel on Guadalcanal load an urgent shipment of Allison V-1710 engines destined for P-39 Airacobra or P-40 Warhawk fighters based at Munda in November 1943. USAAF and Royal New Zealand Air Force fighters based at Munda and Ondonga on New Georgia provided fighter cover for naval, air, and ground units taking part in the Bougainville operation, including numerous SCAT para-pack missions during November and December. (NARA.)

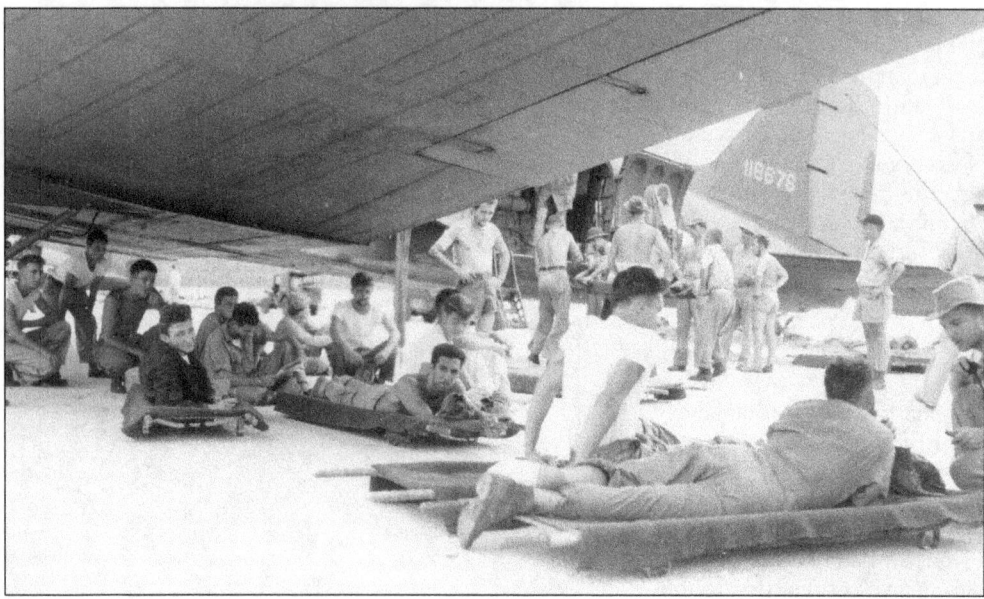

On Vella Lavella, severely wounded men from Bougainville are loaded aboard C-47 41-18676 of the 63rd TCS on November 29, 1943, while less-severely wounded patients are tended to under the wings. The men had been evacuated from Bougainville by sea. The 63rd TCS, 403rd Troop Carrier Group, began flying SCAT missions in October 1943, having spent August and September flying rear area routes for the 13th Air Depot. (NARA.)

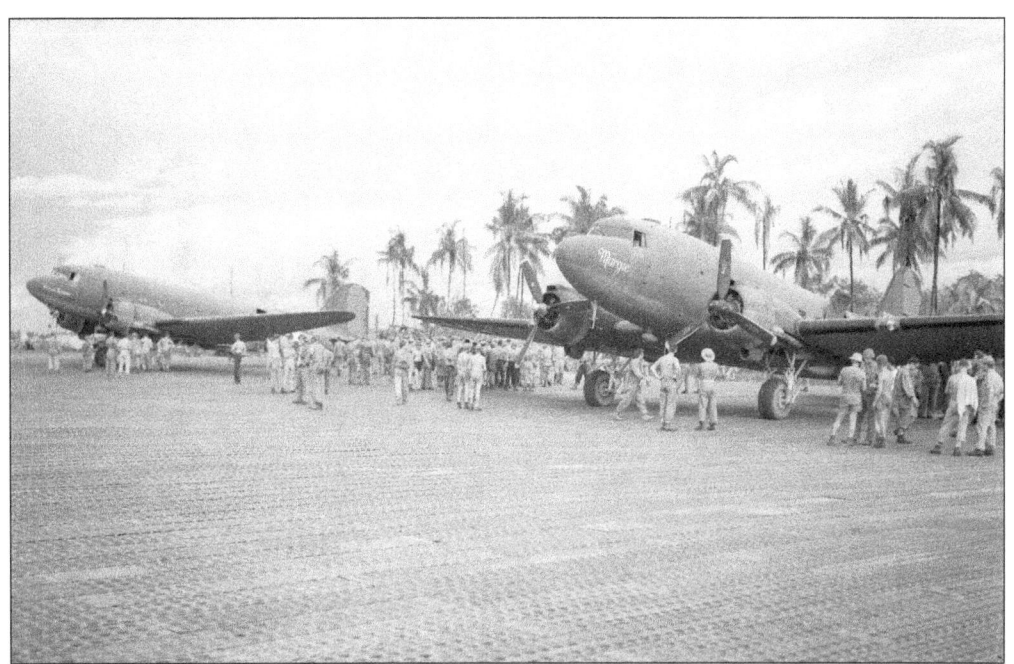

Bougainville was the next "first landing" prize, and records indicate that the 64th TCS grabbed the honors unbeknownst to their 403rd Troop Carrier Group and MAG-25 peers. Here the first and second arrivals, C-47s *Margie* (right) and *Texas Tramp* (left), attract a crowd after landing on December 10. The aircraft had just completed a para-pack mission to supply Marine paratroopers on Hill 1000, on the perimeter's outer edge. (NARA.)

Honoring an old aeronautical tradition, Brig. Gen. Field Harris (right), commanding general of the 1st Marine Aircraft Wing, signs "short snorter" bills for some of the first USAAF SCAT crewmen to arrive on Bougainville. Popular among South Pacific crews, the bills were souvenir currency signed by crewmates, particularly on memorable missions. Harris was another veteran of VJ-6M, as well as the 1st Marine Aircraft Group at Quantico. (NARA.)

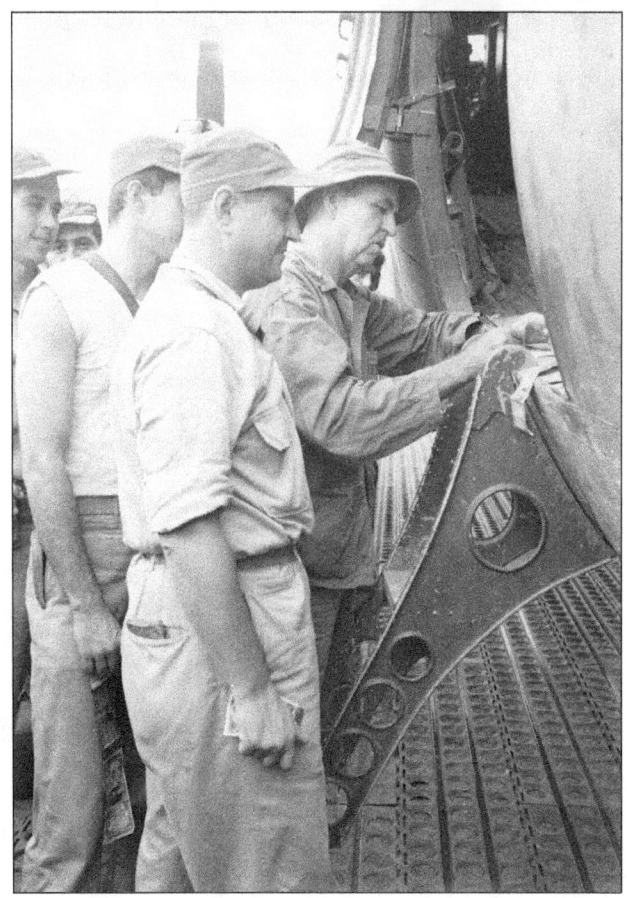

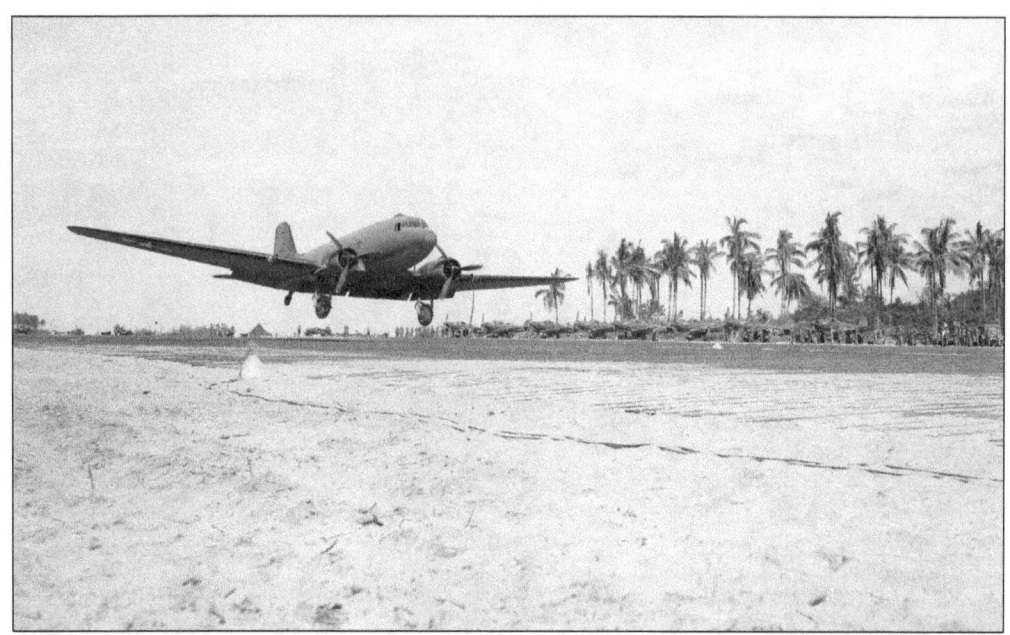

Reportedly the first scheduled SCAT transport on Bougainville, R4D "43" lands on the new Torokina airstrip. P-39 Airacobras of the 70th Fighter Squadron, based at Munda, line the runway. This aircraft was likely flown by 1st Lt. Paul "Hookie" Wynn of VMJ-152. Apparently, nobody in the flight was then aware that the 64th TCS had already claimed the "first landing" honor. (NARA.)

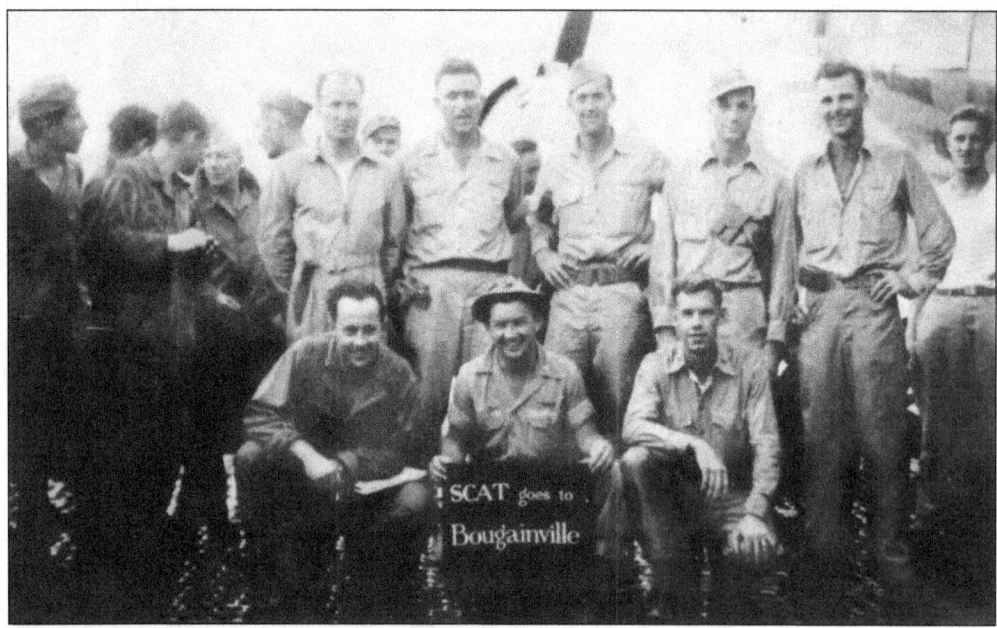

The first scheduled SCAT crews on Bougainville pose for a commemorative photograph. Holding the sign is Lieutenant Wynn, the first to land. Behind him, fourth from right, is Col. Harry Sands of the 403rd Troop Carrier Group, victim of friendly rivalry, who had been first in line to land but received an underhanded wave-off from the Marine ground controller. (Author's collection, courtesy of Maj. Paul E. Wynn.)

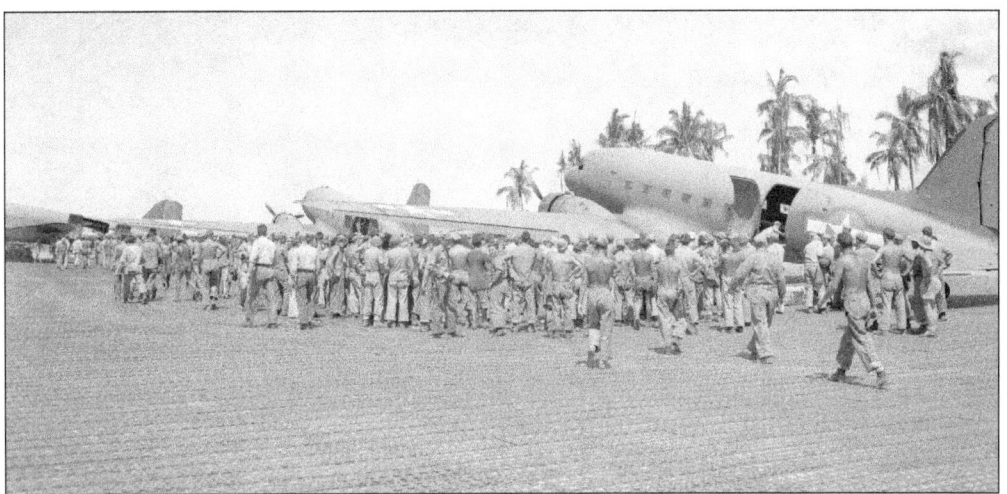

Crowds swarm the first MAG-25 arrivals at Torokina Point, with three R4Ds visible in this view ("78" at left, "54" or "64" in the center, and "43" at right). R4D "78" is packed with aircraft drop tanks. The initial transport flights into Torokina were escorted by P-40 Kittyhawks of the Royal New Zealand Air Force and F4U Corsairs of VMF-223. (NARA.)

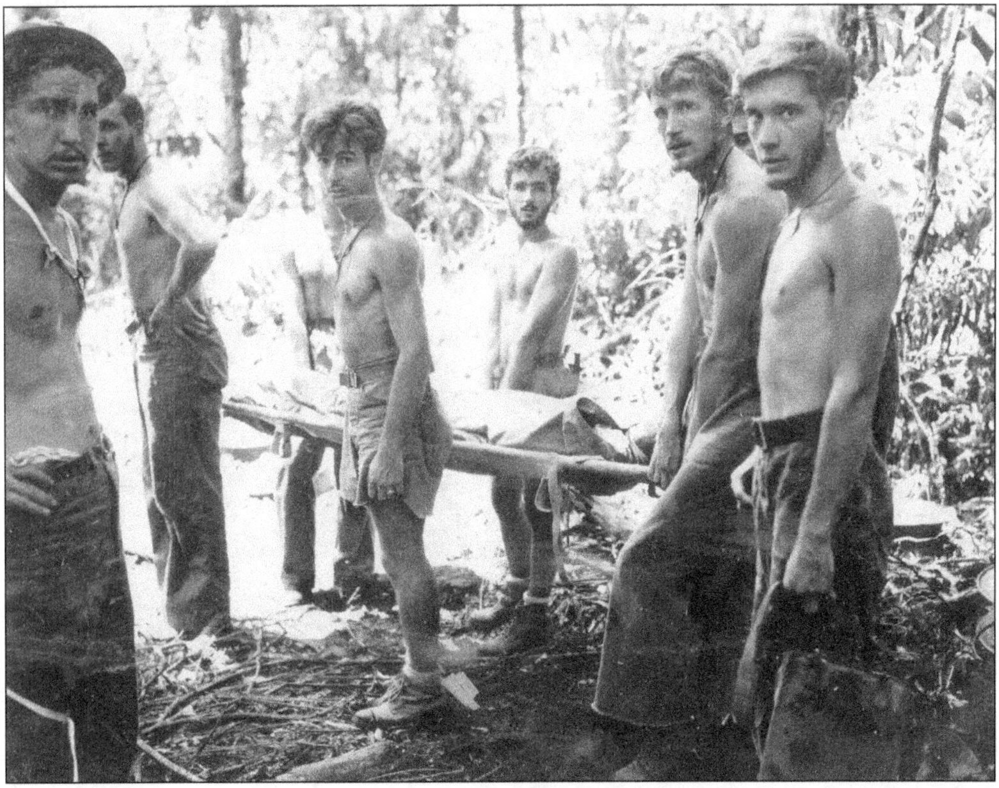

Marines evacuate a casualty from the front on December 10, likely among the first to be evacuated by SCAT. Although the runway was open, the Americans still only held a defensive perimeter around it. Tens of thousands of Japanese soldiers and naval personnel, estimated at 60,000 or more, still occupied the island. The Marines and soldiers along the perimeter braced for a counterattack that they considered inevitable. (NARA.)

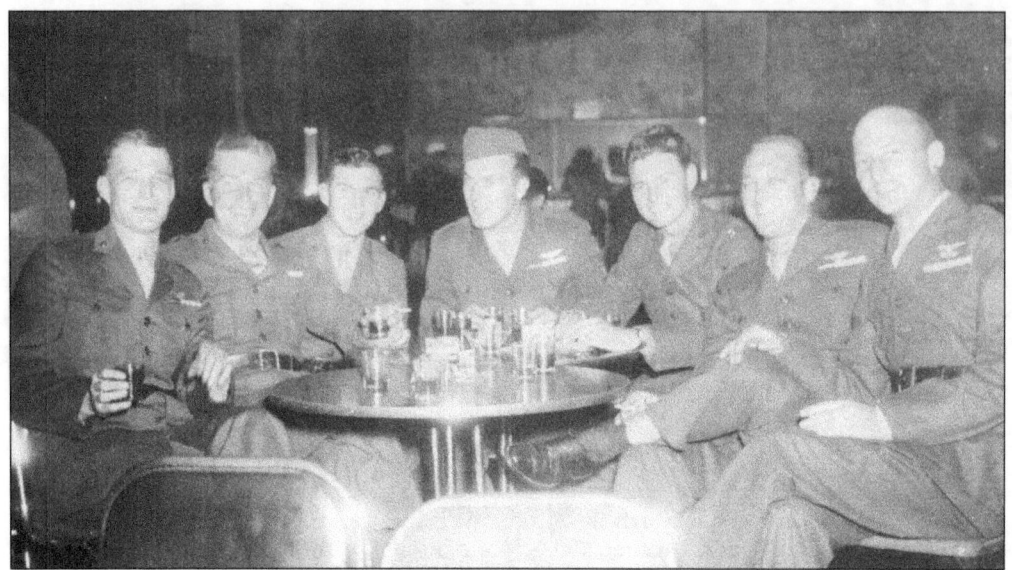

Original personnel of VMJ-253, all navigators, relax at popular Sherman's Bar in San Diego in December 1943 after returning from the South Pacific. Pictured from left to right are T.Sgt. Walter McColm, Sgt. Jack Steele, an unidentified first sergeant, S.Sgt. Jerome Eoff, S.Sgt. Gheral Taylor, Sgt. C. Frank "Poncho" Wood, and T.Sgt. Paul Asher (also a veteran of VMJ-153). Most wear the Distinguished (Presidential) Unit Citation ribbon awarded for Guadalcanal. (MAG-25/SCAT)

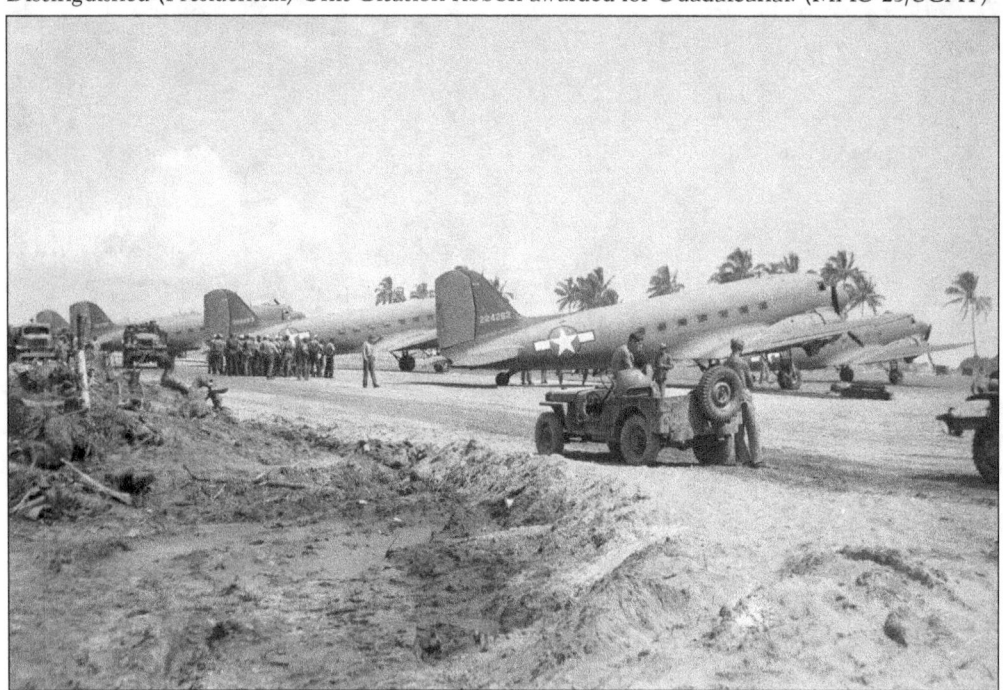

C-47s of the 64th TCS line the Torokina airstrip on December 23, 1943. Through the end of the Bougainville campaign, the 64th flew missions under SCAT operational control as needed, although the squadron also appears to have flown occasional non-SCAT flights during that time. The aircraft nearest the foreground, 42-24262, was destroyed in a nonfatal landing accident at Cape Gloucester, New Britain, on June 20, 1944. (NARA.)

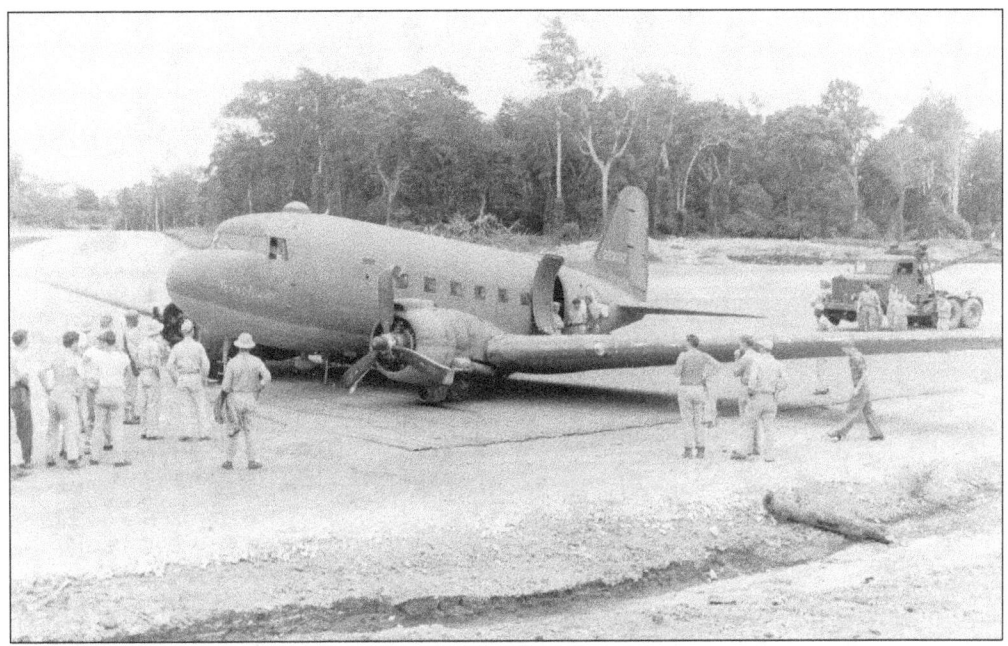

C-47A *Texas Tramp* of the 64th TCS (42-23722) suffered a landing gear retraction on takeoff at Pekoa airfield, Espiritu Santo, on January 13, 1944, and as with all such accidents drew a curious crowd of onlookers. While the damage appears minor—the DC airliner series was initially designed with only partially retracting main gear to enable belly landings—*Texas Tramp* was stricken and salvaged for parts. (NARA.)

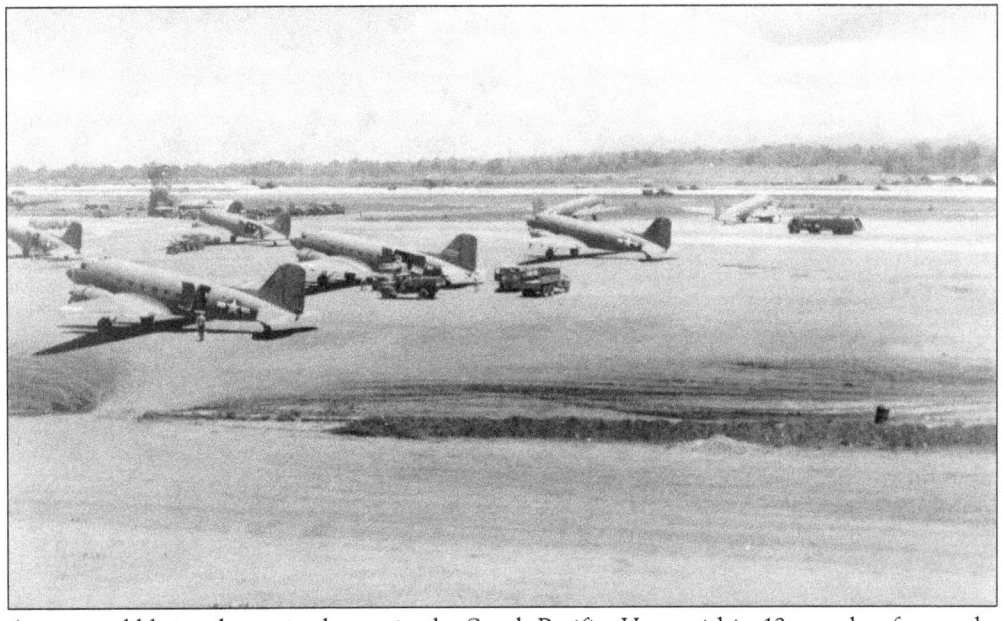

A year could bring dramatic change in the South Pacific. Here, within 12 months after crude, muddy Henderson Field was still being periodically blasted by Japanese bombs and shells, a fleet of SCAT aircraft sits close together in safety next to a well-maintained runway on Guadalcanal. By this time, Guadalcanal had become a major American base supporting operations in the Northern Solomons. (NARA.)

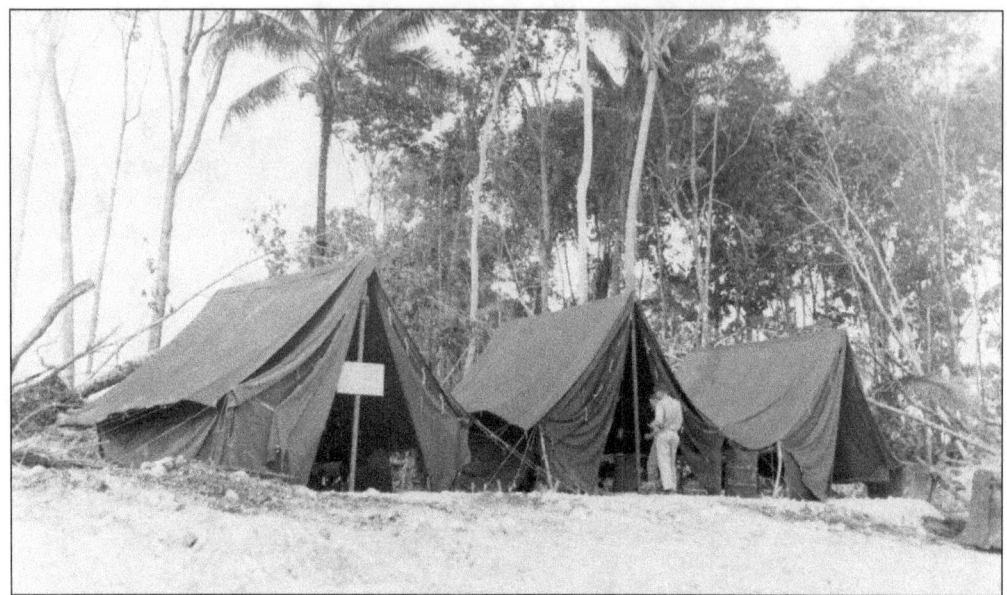

The airstrip on Stirling Island in the Treasuries began receiving aircraft in late November 1943, within a month of the Allied invasion. Naval Advance Base, Treasury Islands, supported combat operations on Bougainville and subsequent operations to the north. In January 1944, SCAT's primitive quarters were in keeping with the base's status as an advance facility. (NARA.)

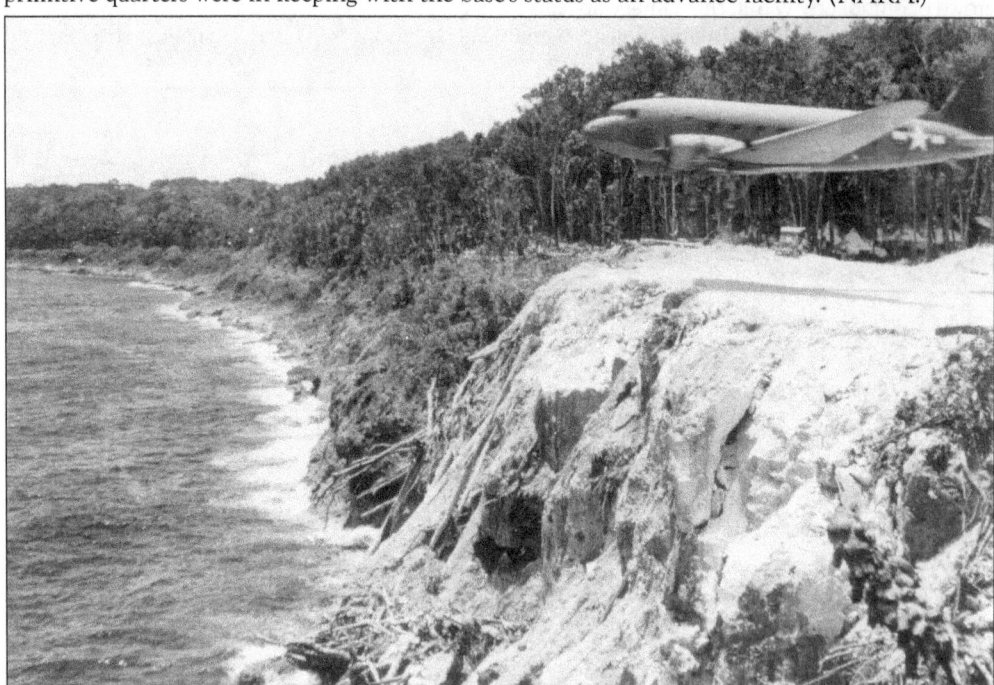

An R4D lifts off from Stirling's newly extended 6,000-foot airstrip, famous for its sudden termination at the island's edge, in this March 1944 photograph by David Douglas Duncan. Despite the respectable runway length, the cliffside dropoff could make departures a hair-raising experience in an overloaded transport. The margin of error for SCAT pilots was thin, but mission requirements made heavy loads the norm. (NARA.)

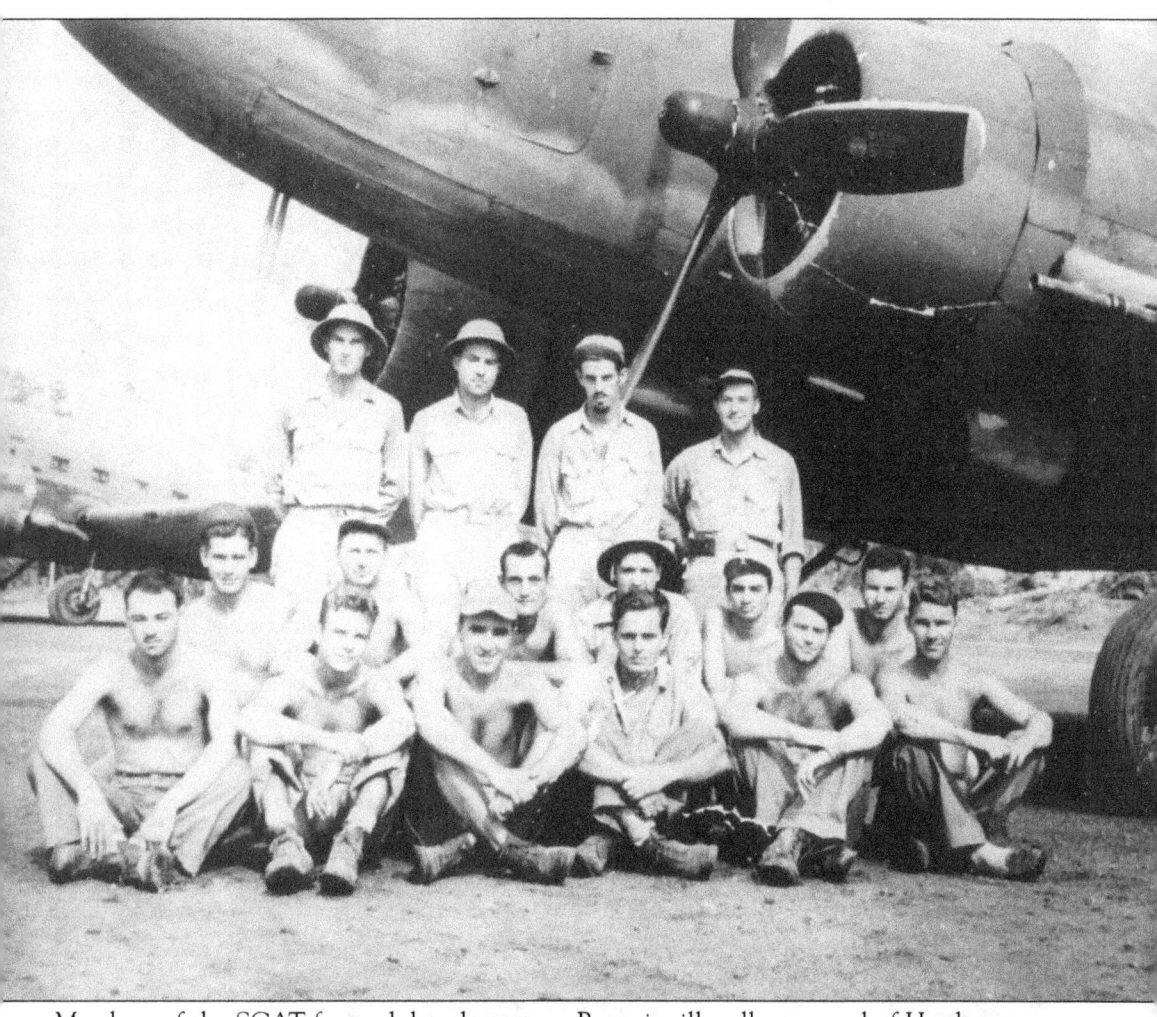

Members of the SCAT forward detachment on Bougainville, all personnel of Headquarters Squadron 25, pose by an R4D in January 1944. From left to right are (first row) unidentified, Pfc. Ross Offenstine Jr., Pfc. Elbert Yezzi, unidentified, Cpl. John Morrow, and Pfc. Joseph Whitmore; (second row) AMM3c. Fred Ulrich, Sgt. Thomas Massingill, FCR3c. Thomas McIntyre, Pfc. Daniel Throneburg, PhM3c. Alfred Nelson, and AOM3c. Donald Meyer; (third row) Lt. (j.g.) Hollis Dole, Lt. Richard M. Nixon (officer-in-charge), 1st Lt. Martin Dupree Jr., and Lt. Paul Peterson. Decades before the future 37th president of the United States became a politically infamous figure, Lieutenant Nixon was a well-respected MAG-25 Naval Reserve officer. After requesting an overseas assignment, Nixon joined Headquarters Squadron 25 on July 2, 1943, serving briefly as an assistant SCAT passenger officer and assistant SCAT operations officer, before serving as officer-in-charge of a series of SCAT forward detachments at newly established bases. The detachment on Green Island was his last SCAT assignment, from March 5 to 17, 1944. Nixon received a Navy Letter of Commendation in recognition of his performance. (MAG-25/SCAT.)

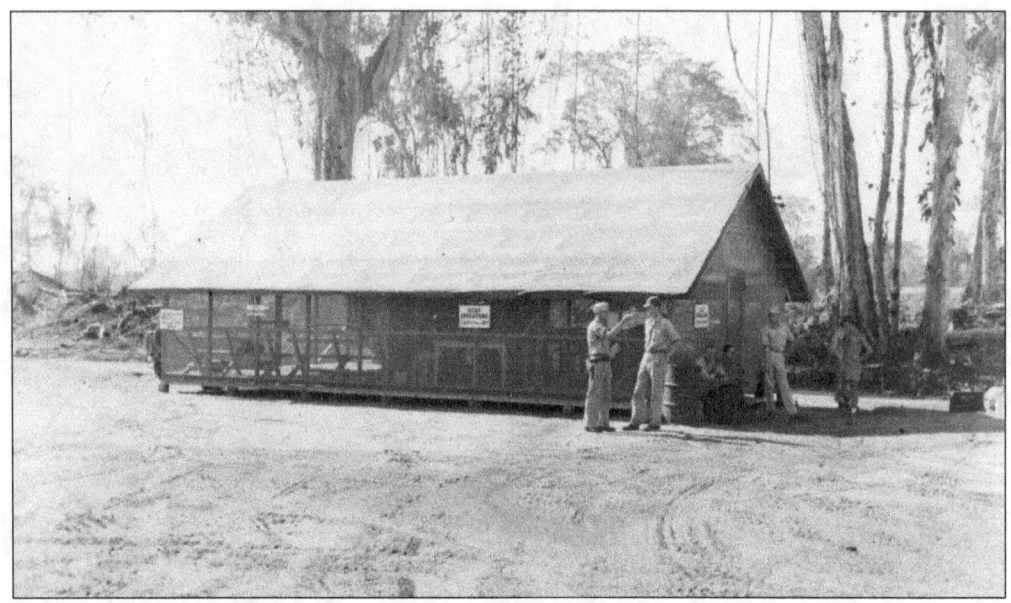

By February 1944, SCAT's facilities on Bougainville were rustic but comfortable. By the end of 1943, the original Torokina airstrip was joined by another complex, a parallel set of runways at Piva, further inland to the north. Here, pilots and other personnel relax outside of the SCAT Operations Office at Piva Uncle airstrip. (NARA.)

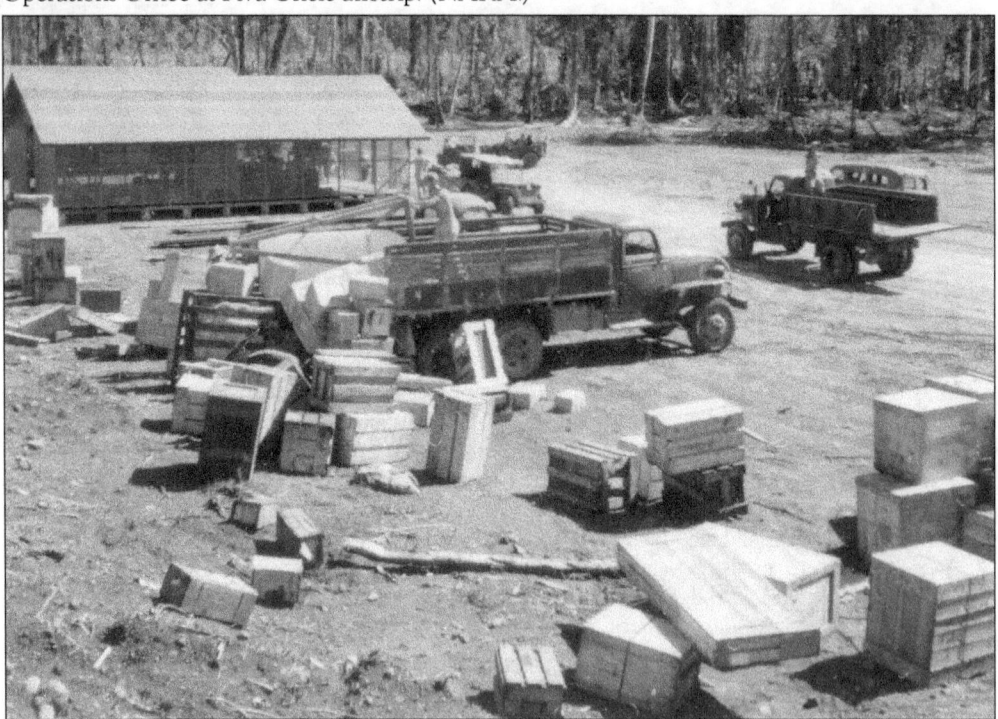

Cargo stacks up outside of SCAT's freight office at Piva Uncle. Piva Uncle (also "Piva North" or "Piva Bomber") was a bomber strip, while Piva Yoke ("Piva South" or "Piva Fighter") was a shorter fighter strip. SCAT could operate from either with a moderate load but typically operated from Piva Uncle due to its longer runway. (NARA.)

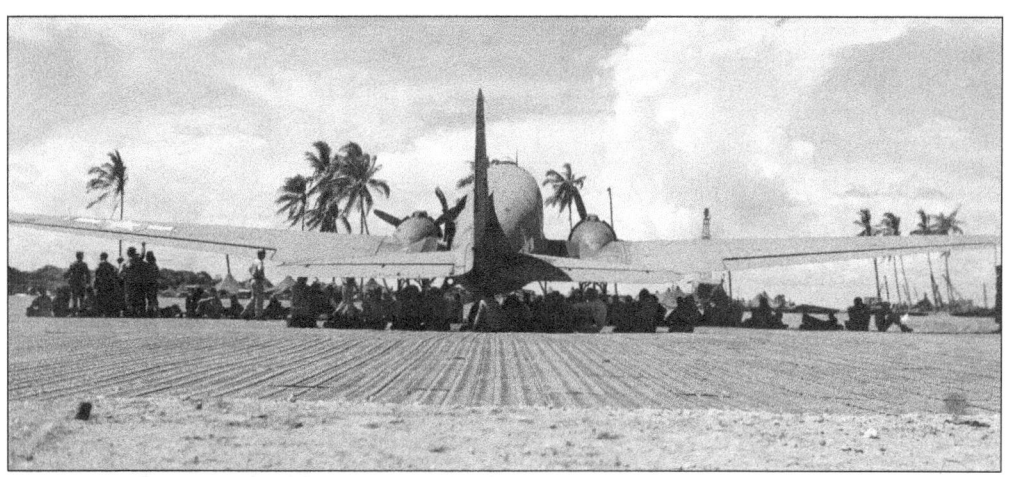

Passengers awaiting transport crowd under the shade of a SCAT C-47 at Torokina on a hot summer day in January 1944. On flights within the Solomons, SCAT aircraft typically flew a varied mix of passengers and cargo. However, longer flights were also routine, flying full loads of passengers on leave to rest and recreation ("R&R") in Auckland, Brisbane, or Sydney, and back. (NARA.)

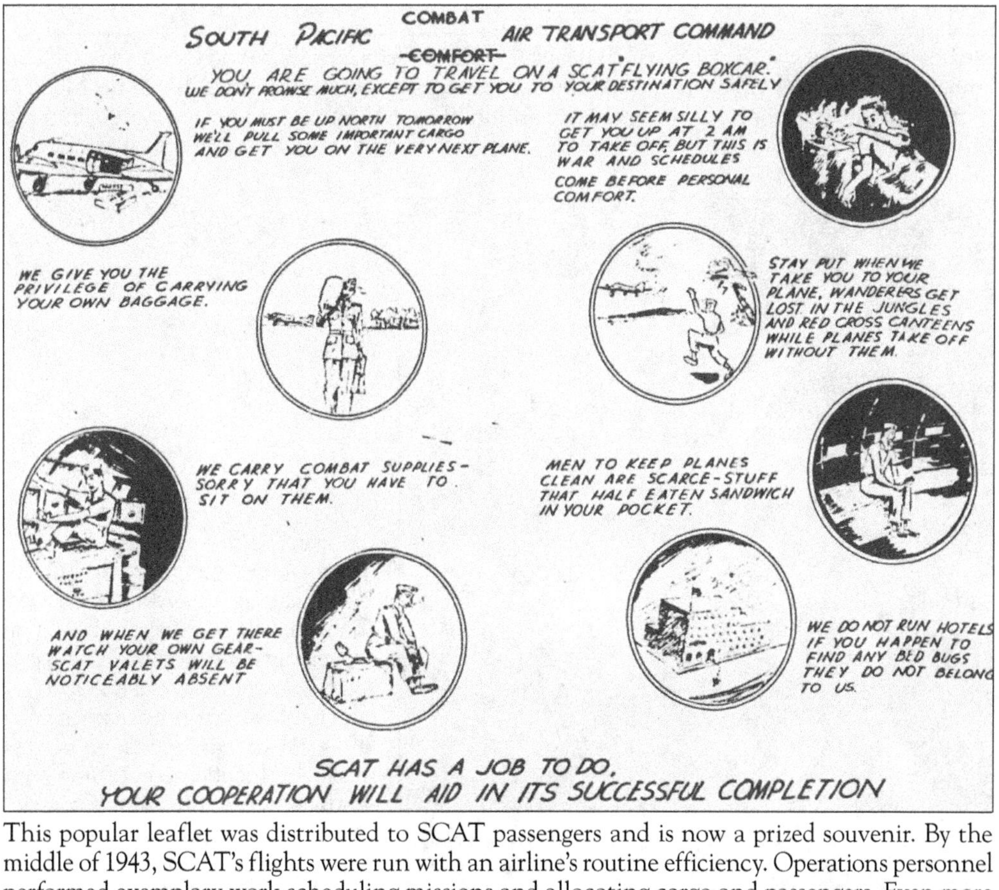

SOUTH PACIFIC COMBAT AIR TRANSPORT COMMAND
~~COMFORT~~
YOU ARE GOING TO TRAVEL ON A SCAT FLYING BOXCAR.
WE DON'T PROMISE MUCH, EXCEPT TO GET YOU TO YOUR DESTINATION SAFELY

IF YOU MUST BE UP NORTH TOMORROW WE'LL PULL SOME IMPORTANT CARGO AND GET YOU ON THE VERY NEXT PLANE.

IT MAY SEEM SILLY TO GET YOU UP AT 2 AM TO TAKE OFF, BUT THIS IS WAR AND SCHEDULES COME BEFORE PERSONAL COMFORT.

WE GIVE YOU THE PRIVILEGE OF CARRYING YOUR OWN BAGGAGE.

STAY PUT WHEN WE TAKE YOU TO YOUR PLANE, WANDERERS GET LOST IN THE JUNGLES AND RED CROSS CANTEENS WHILE PLANES TAKE OFF WITHOUT THEM.

WE CARRY COMBAT SUPPLIES — SORRY THAT YOU HAVE TO SIT ON THEM.

MEN TO KEEP PLANES CLEAN ARE SCARCE — STUFF THAT HALF EATEN SANDWICH IN YOUR POCKET.

AND WHEN WE GET THERE WATCH YOUR OWN GEAR — SCAT VALETS WILL BE NOTICEABLY ABSENT

WE DO NOT RUN HOTELS IF YOU HAPPEN TO FIND ANY BED BUGS THEY DO NOT BELONG TO US.

SCAT HAS A JOB TO DO.
YOUR COOPERATION WILL AID IN ITS SUCCESSFUL COMPLETION

This popular leaflet was distributed to SCAT passengers and is now a prized souvenir. By the middle of 1943, SCAT's flights were run with an airline's routine efficiency. Operations personnel performed exemplary work scheduling missions and allocating cargo and passengers. Even more impressive, however, was SCAT's ability to quickly adapt to meet emergency requirements, providing aircraft at a moment's notice. (Courtesy of Ted Schwartz.)

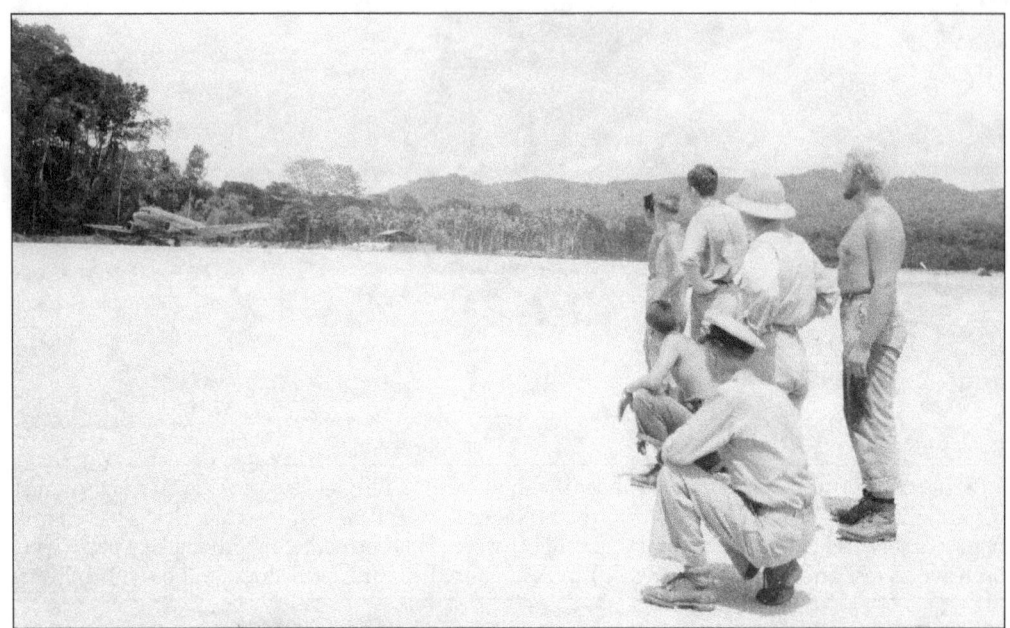

Medical personnel watch as a SCAT R4D takes off from Vella Lavella bound for Guadalcanal on January 18, 1944. Vella Lavella housed the hospital facilities of the Marines' 1st Corps Medical Battalion, which supported the 1st Marine Amphibious Corps throughout the Bougainville campaign. Patients stabilized there were routinely transferred to larger hospital facilities farther to the rear. (NARA.)

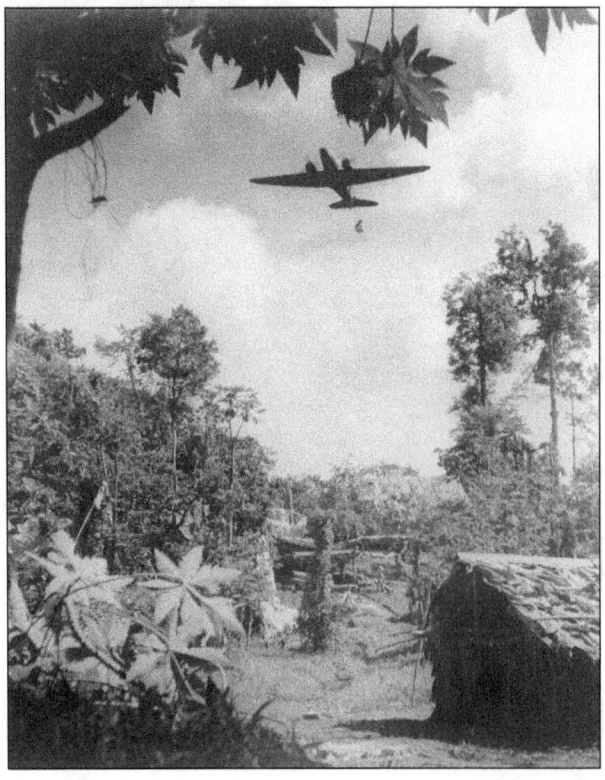

Second Lt. David Douglas Duncan photographed this SCAT C-47 making an airdrop over Bougainville in February 1944. For Americans, most ground combat on Bougainville would end in April. However, in December 1944, Australian and Fijian troops resumed the offensive, relying on both SCAT and Royal Australian Air Force transports to airdrop supplies to remote locations. The last Japanese forces on Bougainville did not surrender until August 21, 1945. (NARA.)

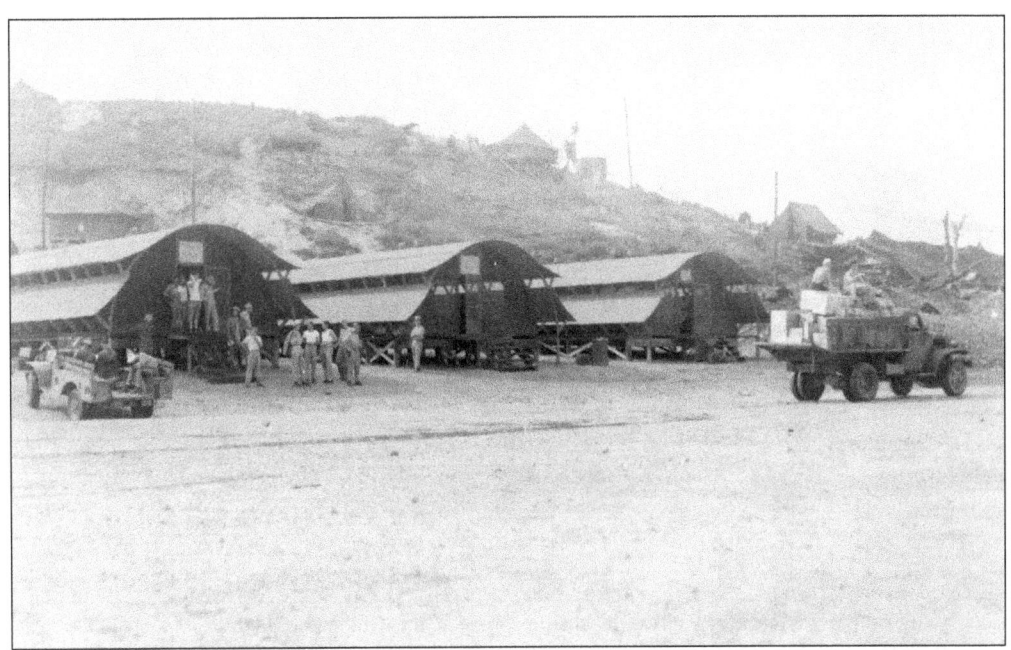

By January 1944, SCAT's facilities at Munda had improved considerably, set beneath Kokengola Hill. As at most forward bases, the enemy threat did not entirely disappear once New Georgia was secured. Japanese bombers struck the island as late as January 15, exploding a fuel dump and damaging a number of aircraft, including VMJ-152's 17095. Above, passengers and crews await an incoming aircraft at the operations offices while a truck loaded with cargo heads for the apron. Below, a C-47 (left) and two R4Ds prepare for their next flights in the SCAT operations area as a C-47 takes off in the background. (Both, NARA.)

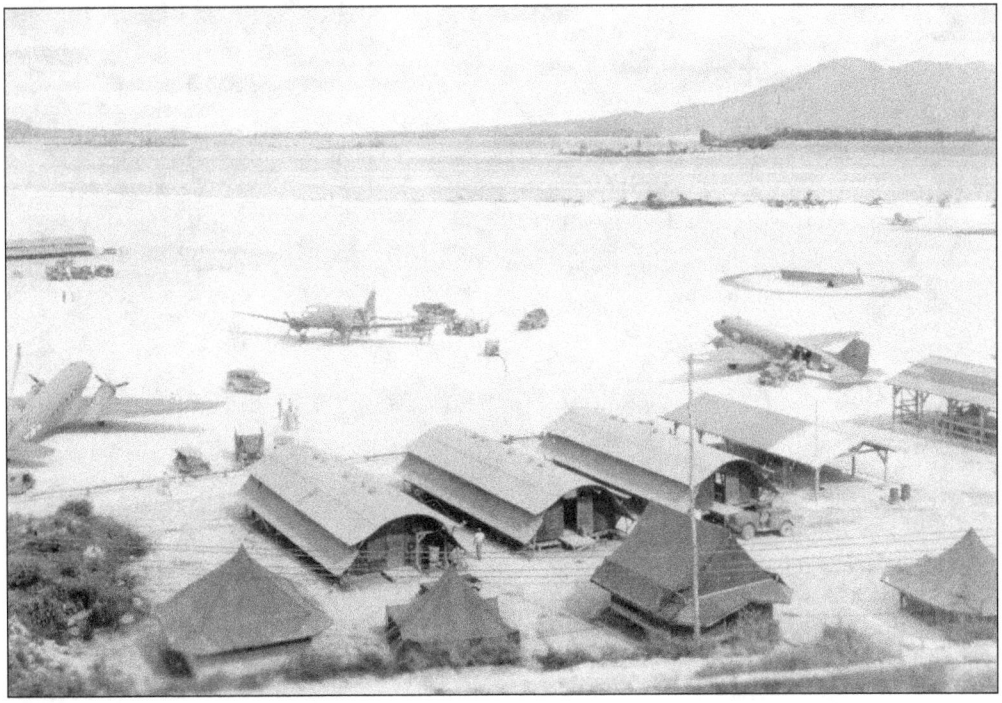

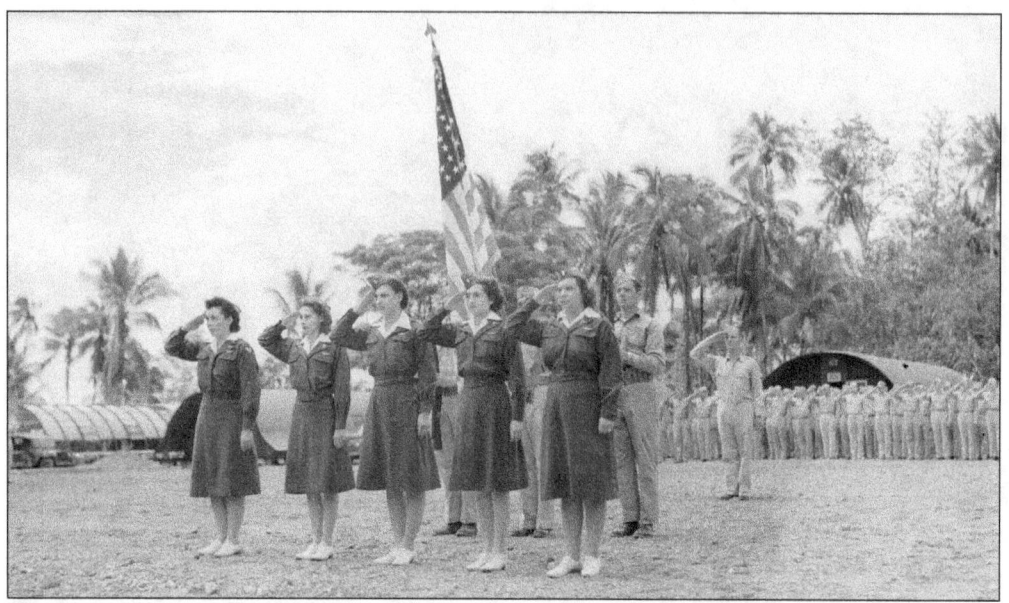

Second lieutenants Margaret Richey, Jeraldine Jones, Mary Muckerheide, Dorothy Shikoski, and Joyce Boisvert of the 801st MAETS salute during an award ceremony on Guadalcanal on February 17, 1944. They each received the Air Medal with Oak Leaf Cluster from Maj. Gen. Hubert R. Harmon, commanding officer of the 13th Air Force. (NARA.)

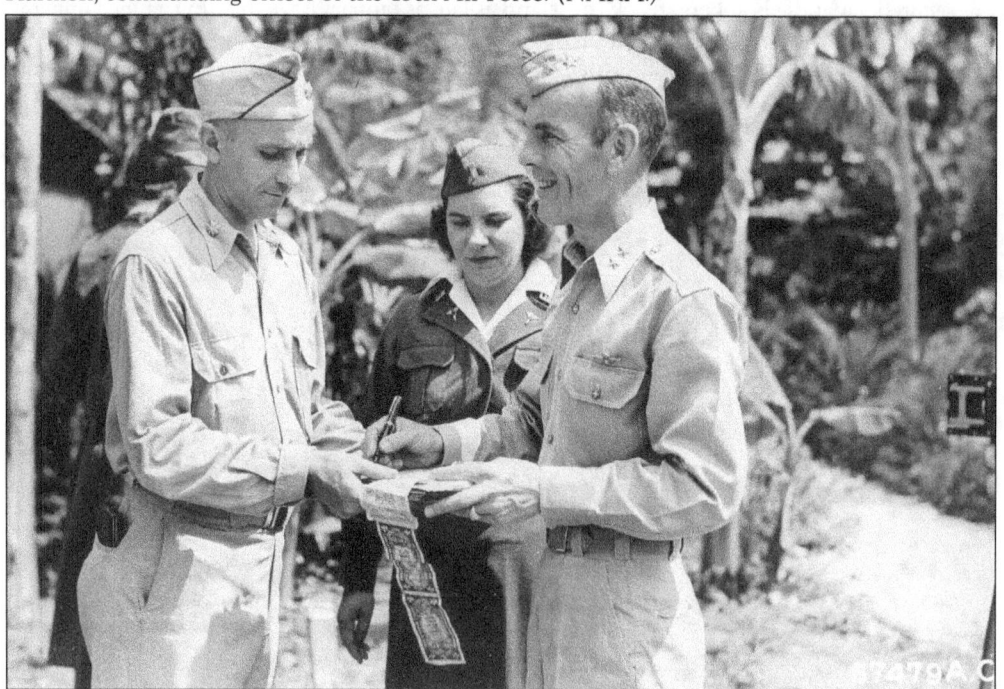

Maj. Gen. Hubert Harmon (right), signs a "short snorter" bill for 2nd Lt. Joyce Boisvert of the 801st MAETS. Assisting is Lt. Col. Charles Worthington (left). Harmon would later become the first superintendent of the United States Air Force Academy. He was the younger brother of Lt. Gen. Millard Harmon, who had commanded US Army forces in the South Pacific and did not survive the war. (NARA.)

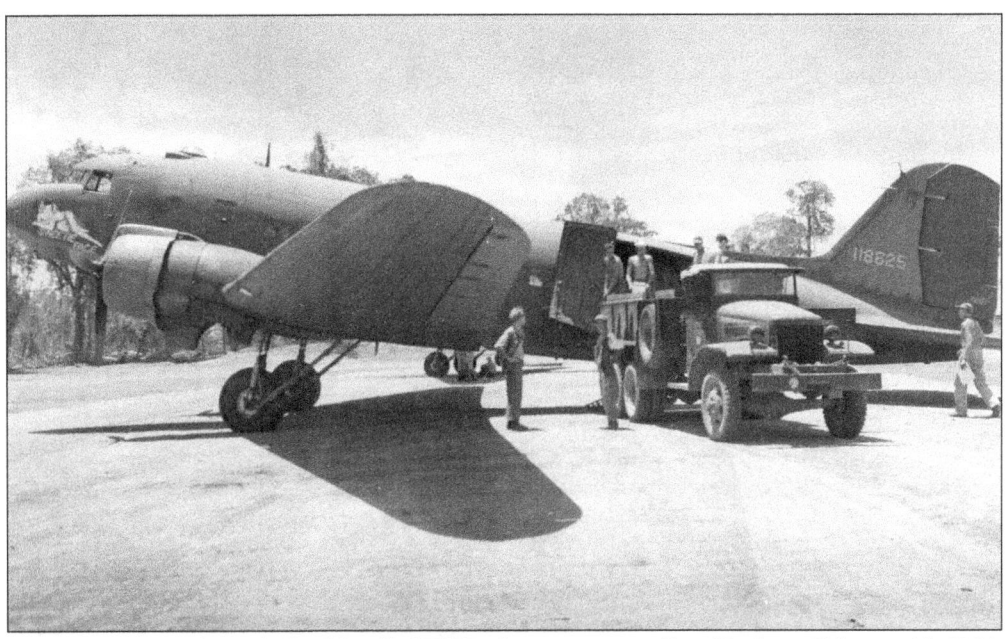

C-47 *Sweetie Face* (41-18625) of the 63rd TCS takes on cargo at Piva Uncle on February 15, 1944, loaded by a Navy and Marine crew. In order to ensure mission readiness, aircraft of the 13th, 63rd, and 64th TCS were sometimes shared between the three squadrons. MAG-25's squadrons also occasionally lent each other R4Ds, and on rare occasions, SCAT aircraft were even shared between the USAAF and Marines. (NARA.)

David Douglas Duncan captured this image of Vice Adm. Aubrey W. Fitch, COMAIRSOPAC, sharing a moment of amusement with Lt. Col. Harry Van Liew, SCAT's operations officer, on Bougainville in March 1944. Van Liew had previously commanded VMJ-153, joining Headquarters Squadron 25 in April 1943. Before the war, he was a United Air Lines pilot and reserve officer attached to the East Coast Expeditionary Force at Quantico. (NARA.)

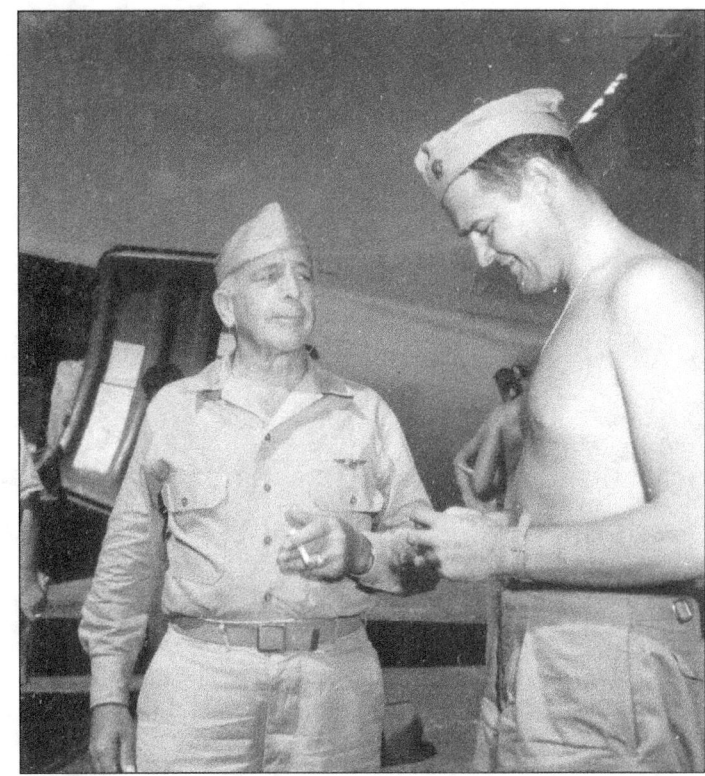

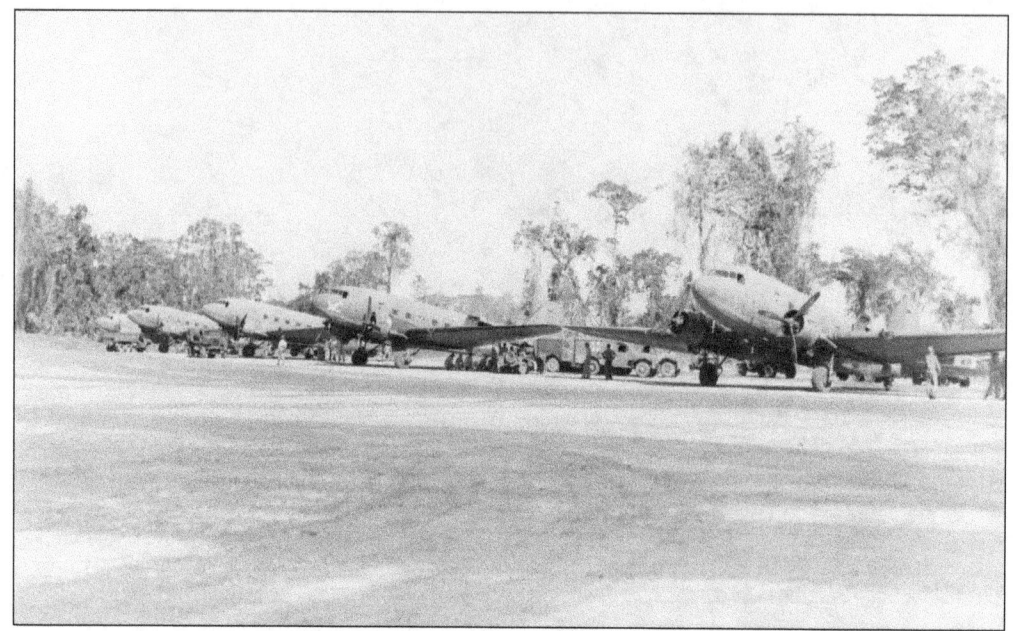

SCAT's most intense period of casualty evacuation was in March 1944, during the Battle of the Bougainville Perimeter, the long-awaited Japanese counterattack against the American air base that lasted from March 9 to March 27. In one 10-day period, SCAT evacuated over 1,600 casualties to hospitals in the rear. Here, four MAG-25 R4Ds and C-47 *Pluto* of the 13th TCS (fourth from left) receive evacuees at Piva on March 15. (NARA.)

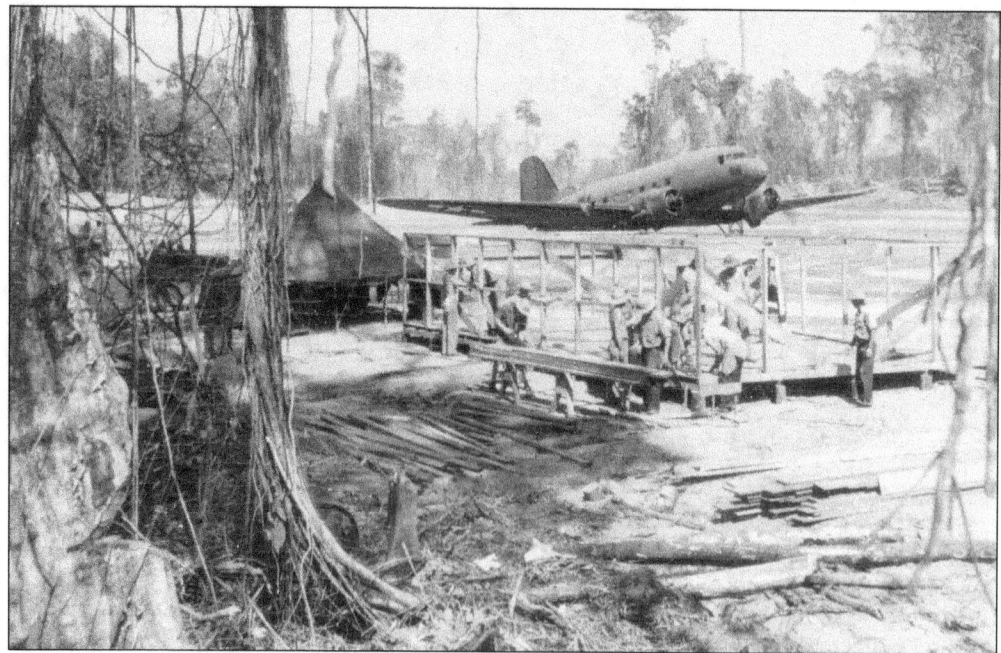

R4D "85" taxis past SCAT's passenger office at Piva on Bougainville in March 1944. Seabees are hard at work constructing a new passenger terminal at the jungle's edge, to take the place of the original tent visible at center left. In the distance, just before the tree line, is the SCAT loading area. (NARA.)

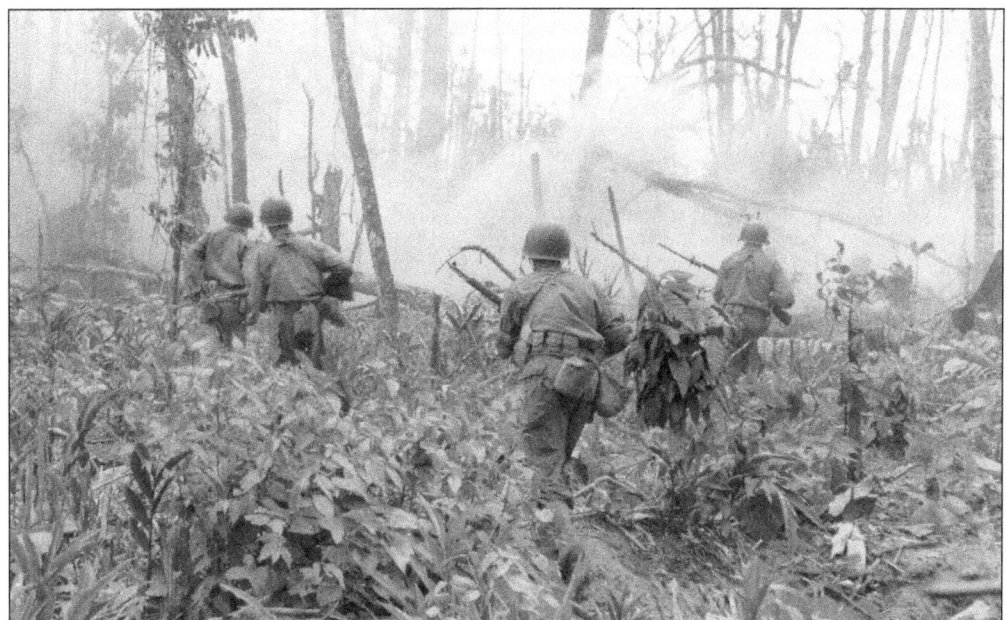

Soldiers of the 132nd Infantry Regiment, Americal (23rd Infantry) Division, patrol beyond the Bougainville perimeter in 1944, using flamethrowers and Bangalore torpedoes to destroy Japanese strongpoints. The US Army took over command of Bougainville operations on December 15, 1943, and the Americal Division replaced the 3rd Marine Division on December 28. The 37th Infantry Division had arrived during November. (NARA.)

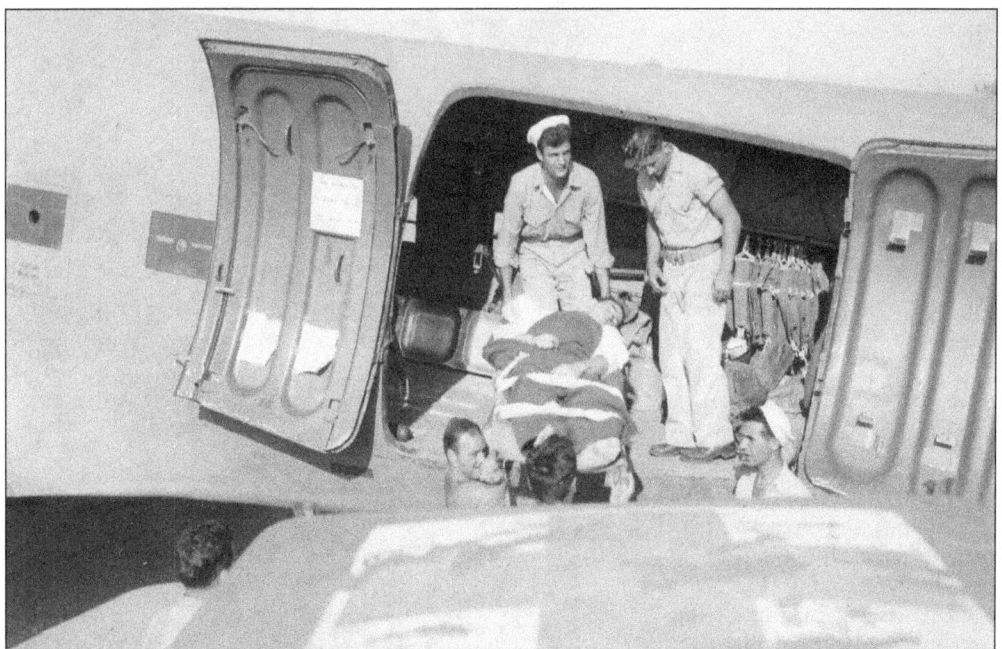

A joint-service team including a corpsman from Headquarters Squadron 25 (in the aircraft, holding the stretcher) loads patients from an ambulance into a SCAT C-47 during the Battle of the Bougainville Perimeter on March 17, 1944. During the battle, Japanese shelling frequently rendered the Piva complex unusable, forcing the transports to load at more distant Torokina. (NARA.)

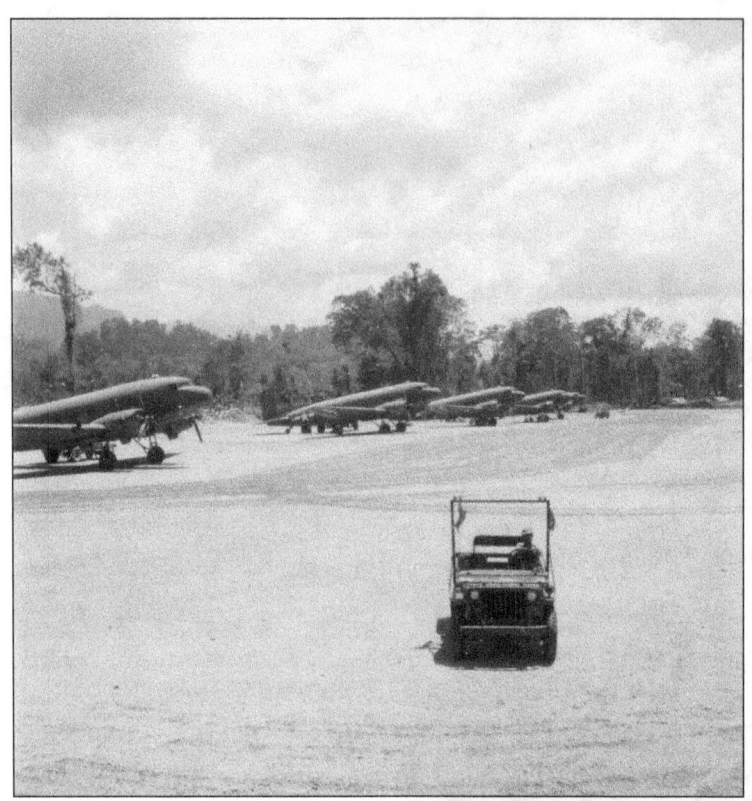

One of Bougainville's brightly flagged "follow me" jeeps prepares to lead transports to the runway at the Piva complex, with R4D "24" and four C-47s in the background. Wingtips were occasionally damaged while maneuvering on crowded airstrips. Piva's two runways were connected by taxiways and were a hive of activity as fighters and bombers carried out missions against Rabaul. (NARA.)

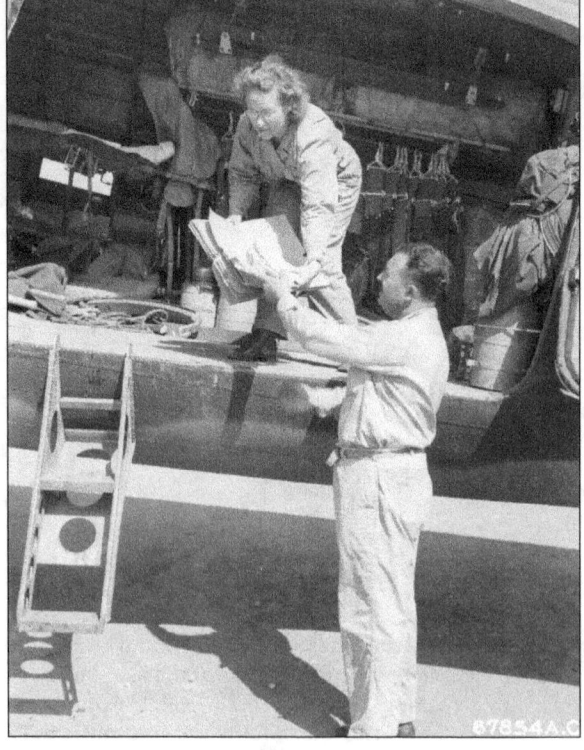

Just prior to departure from Bougainville on March 17, 1944, 2nd Lt. Evelyn Ordway of the 801st MAETS receives her patients' medical files from Capt. Jesse Lieberman. On this day, the Japanese again attempted to overrun the northern edge of the American perimeter, making small gains before being repulsed by the 37th Infantry Division's 129th Infantry Regiment. (NARA.)

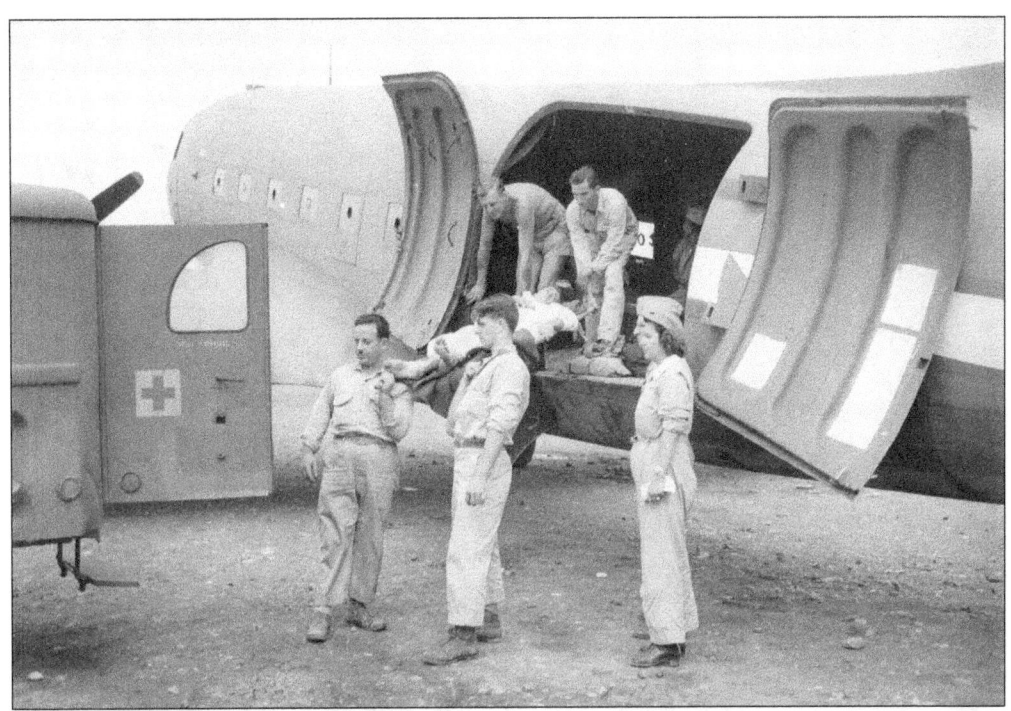

Above, flight crew, including 2nd Lt. Joyce Boisvert of the 801st MAETS (right), supervise the transfer of a patient into a SCAT Medical Department Dodge WC54 ambulance on Guadalcanal in early 1944. These patients are probably casualties from the Bougainville perimeter and are destined for Guadalcanal's well-equipped 20th Station Hospital (below). It took three hours to fly nonstop from Bougainville to Guadalcanal. Before SCAT began operations on Bougainville, the trip could take over 40 hours aboard an LST, which was the typical method of medical evacuation from the island for six weeks after the invasion. (Both, NARA.)

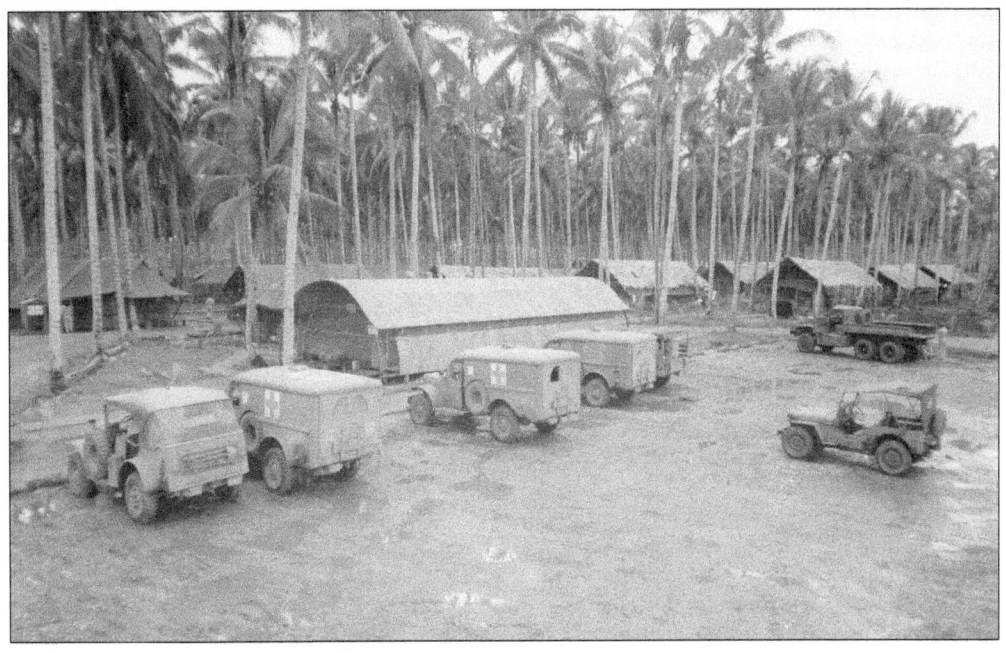

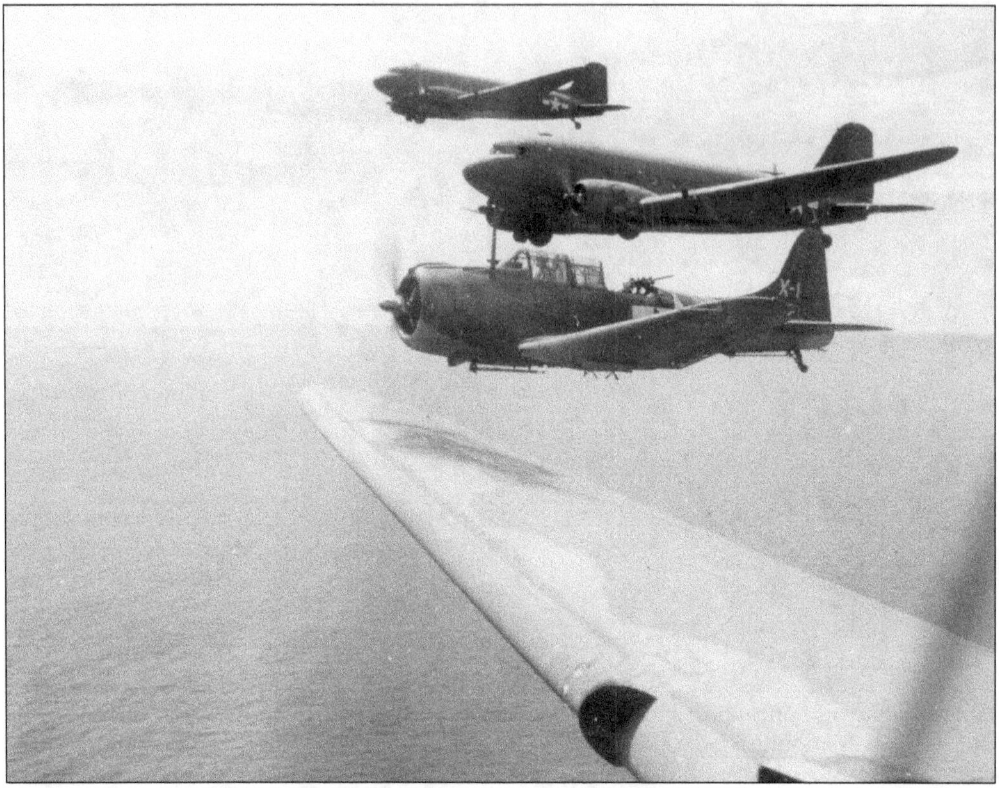

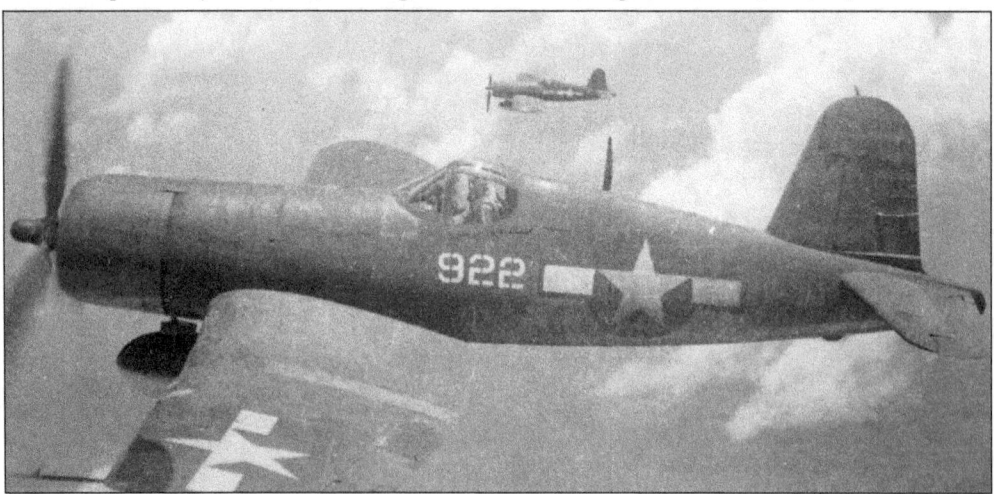

A flight of SCAT R4Ds headed to Green Island provides navigational escort to an SBD-5 Dauntless dive-bomber, a common practice. This image may have been taken from R4D "35." The others are "69" and, in the distance, "81," flown by SCAT's commanding officer, Col. Allen Koonce. Due to its proximity to Rabaul, this flight also had a P-40 fighter escort. (NARA.)

Only on occasion did SCAT aircraft receive fighter escort, most frequently in the forward areas closest to Rabaul. This photograph shows a far more common occurrence: an R4D of VMJ-152 escorting a ferry flight of F4U Corsairs. Single-engine pilots, trained to operate within radio range of a land base or aircraft carrier, rarely received the intense navigational and instrument flying training required of their SCAT counterparts. (Author's collection.)

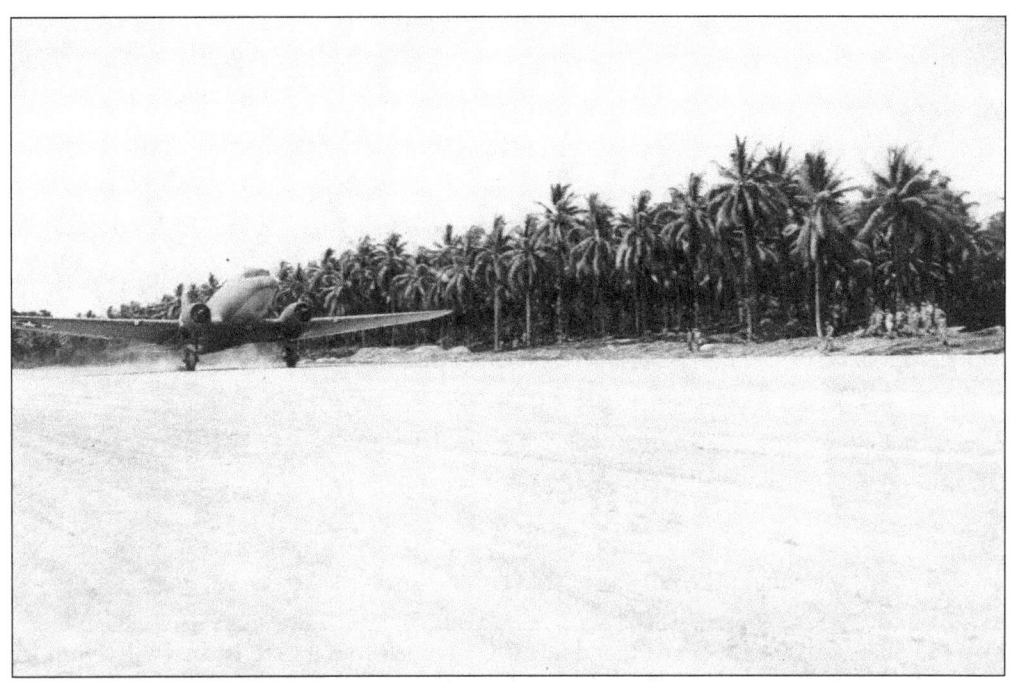

Records are unclear as to which transport landed first on Green Island, but here R4D "35" reportedly claims the honor as it touches down on March 6, 1944, ironically captured and noted by a USAAF photographer (above). An R4D from VMJ-153 may have arrived the day before, and Colonel Koonce in "81" claimed the first March 6 landing on paper. Tales of the "first landing" rivalry became legendary, with some pilots determined to claim bragging rights by hook or by crook, and crews took any opportunity to get a landing in before the first officially scheduled flight. Below, R4Ds "69" (left) and "35" prepare to depart. (Both, NARA.)

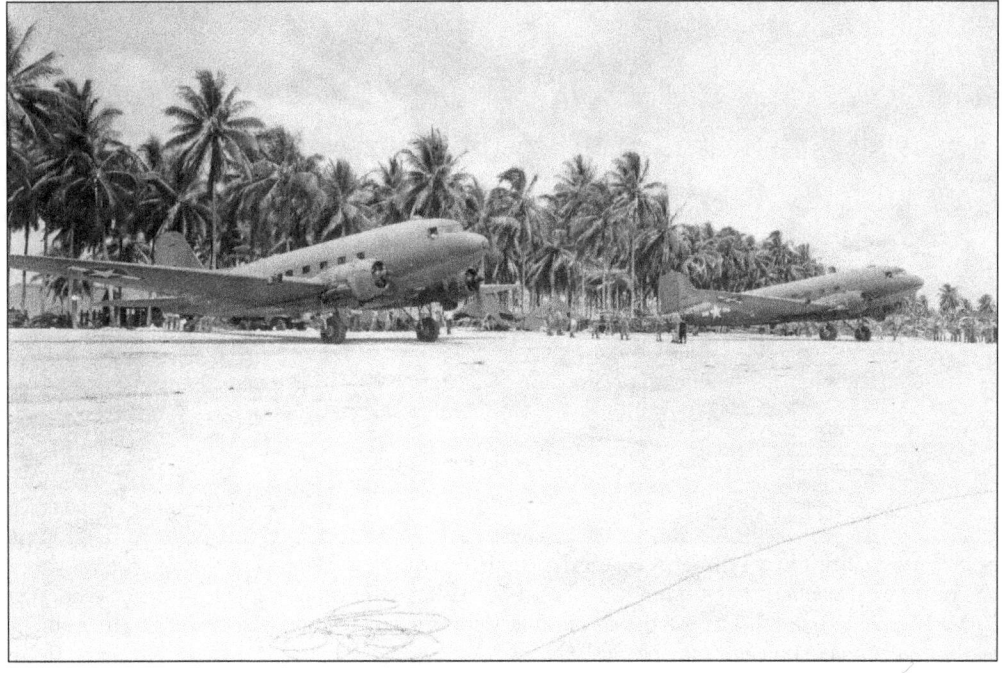

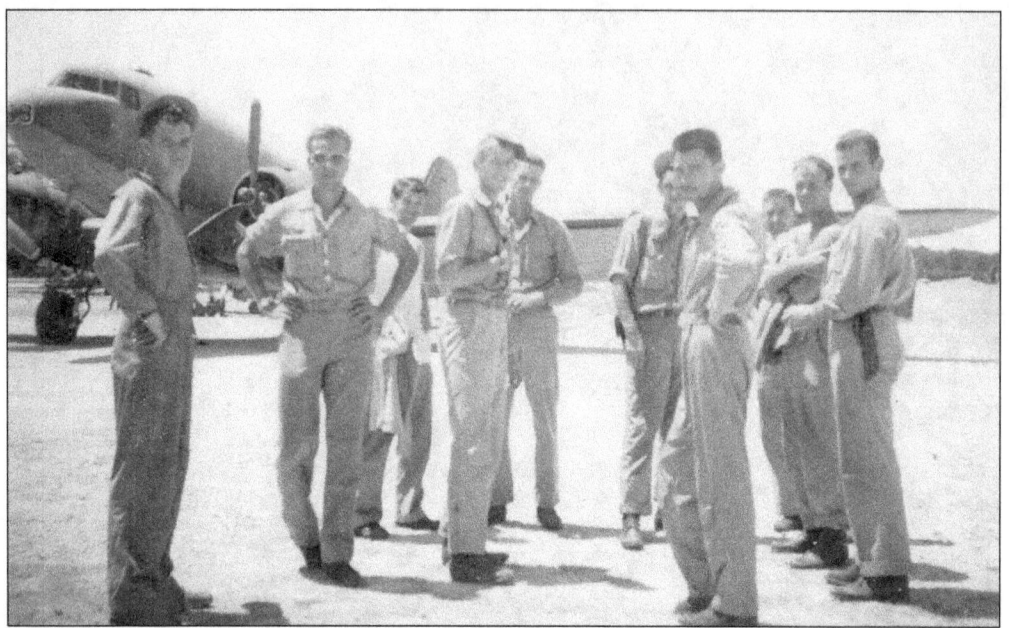

MAG-25 pilots convene on Green Island in 1944. From left to right are 1st Lt. Paul Wynn, 1st Lt. Charles Johnson, 1st Lt. Jack Froehlich, 1st Lt. Arthur Duboise, 1st Lt. Ingram Rader, 1st Lt. William DuRoss, Maj. William Addington, 1st Lt. Homer Stokes, Capt. Lawrence Davis, and 1st Lt. Franklin Potter. Johnson and Froehlich were with VMJ-253, Duboise and Rader were with VMJ-153, and the rest were with VMJ-152. (Author's collection.)

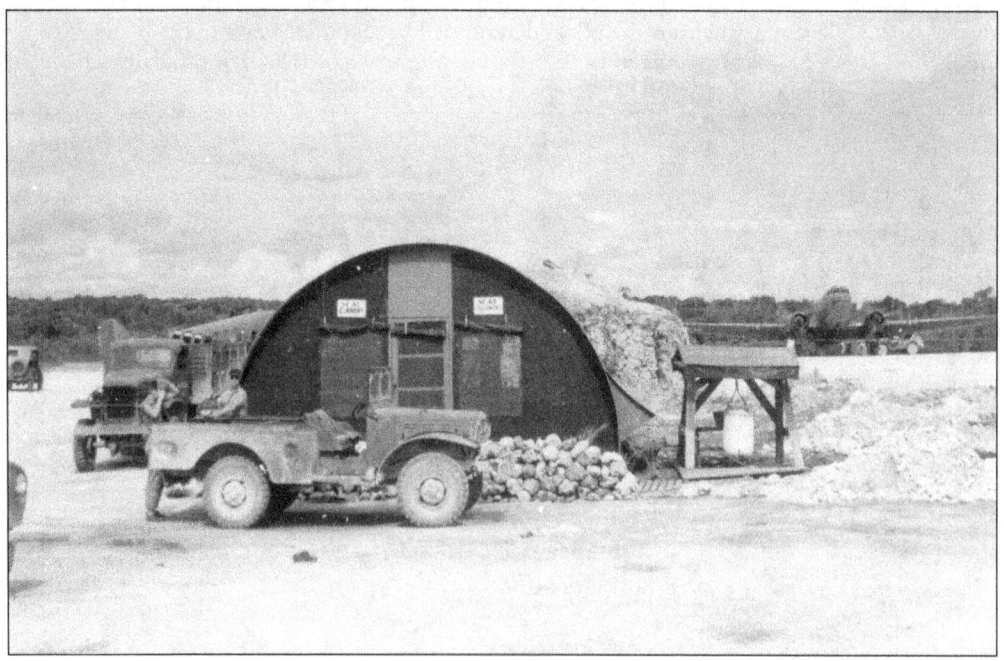

SCAT also maintained a presence at Ondonga airfield on New Georgia, a fighter base to which the unit made frequent trips. This is a view of SCAT's cargo and passenger offices at Ondonga in March 1944. The R4D in the background at right appears to have just taxied in. Its number is difficult to make out, but may be "53." (NARA.)

This picturesque view shows SCAT's operations offices on Banika in the Russell Islands in March 1944, along with a C-47 of the 403rd Troop Carrier Group. Banika, with its hospital facilities, was separated by narrow Sunlight Channel from neighboring Pavuvu, an important rest and training camp for the 1st Marine Division, and remained a SCAT waypoint throughout the unit's existence. (NARA.)

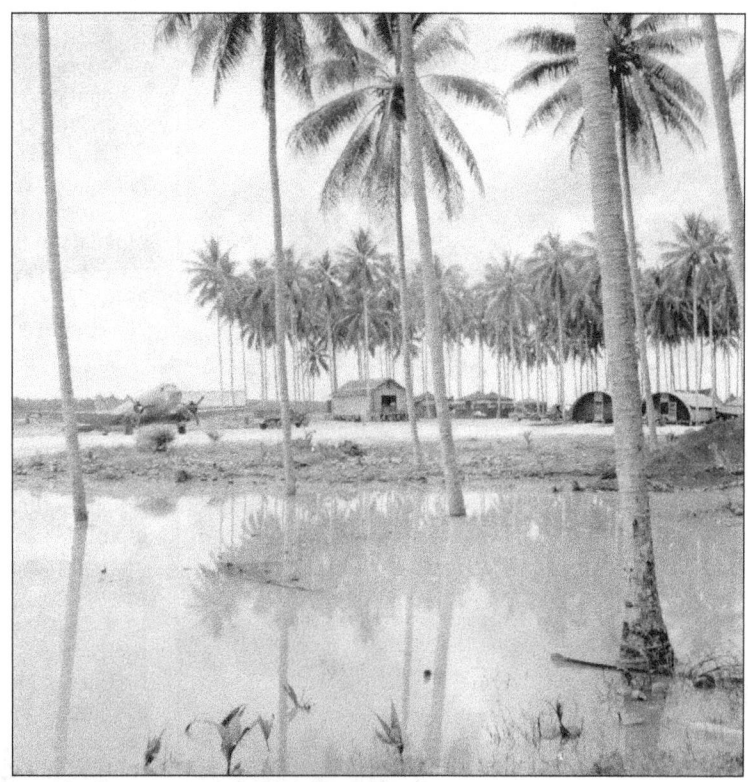

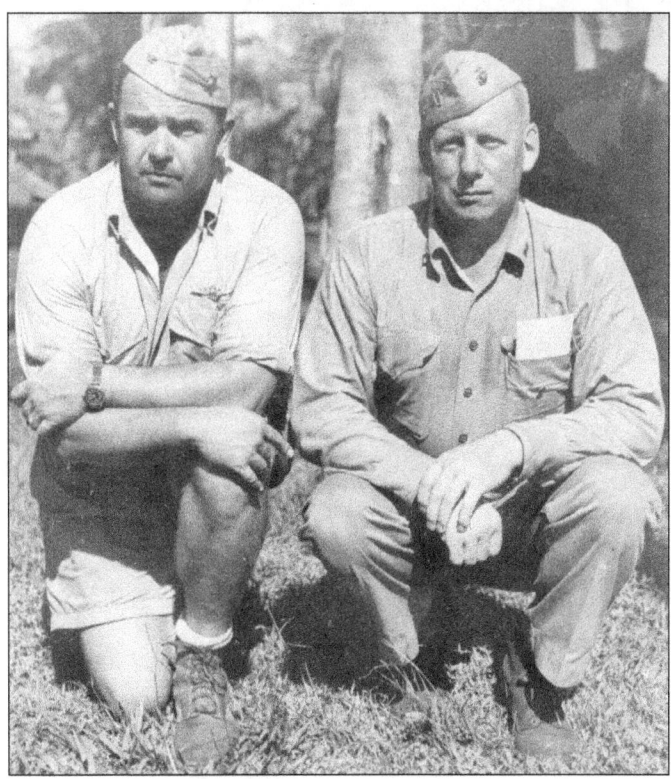

Col. Allen C. "Augie" Koonce, who commanded SCAT from December 1943 until its dissolution in February 1945 (left), poses with Capt. Robert J. Allen at Espiritu Santo in mid-1944. Koonce, a Naval Academy graduate, entered the Marine Corps in 1927. His many flying assignments included VJ-6M in 1936–1937 and VMJ-1 in 1938–1939. Allen was assigned executive officer of Headquarters Squadron 25 in February 1944 and transferred to VMJ-152 in July. (MAG-25/SCAT.)

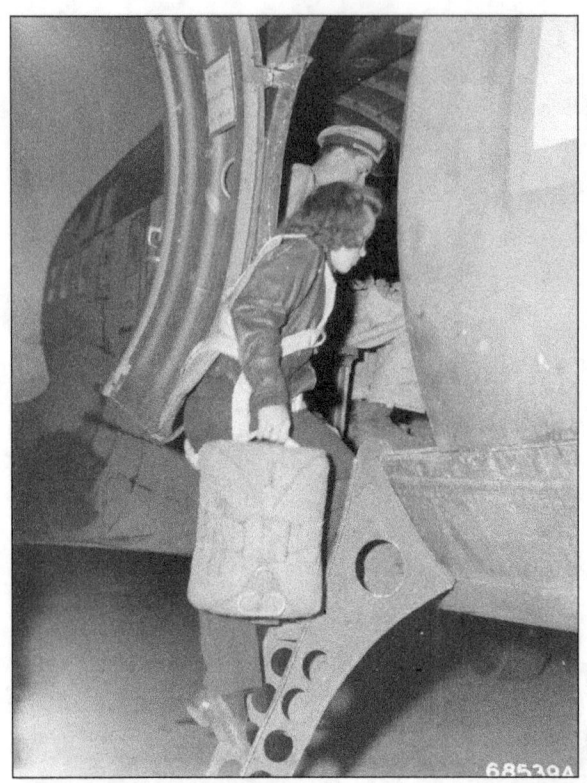

In April 1944, a USAAF photographer chronicled a casualty evacuation mission flown by 2nd Lt. Bernice Harrington of the 801st MAETS. Here, carrying her parachute, Harrington enters her R4D in the predawn darkness on Guadalcanal, headed for a forward airstrip. This aircraft likely belonged to VMJ-152, which is stenciled on Harrington's parachute. (NARA.)

Lieutenant Harrington's destination was likely Piva Uncle on Bougainville, where casualties were mounting during the US Army's mop-up patrols and engagements against entrenched Japanese forces in the surrounding jungle following the Battle of the Bougainville Perimeter. Here, upon their return to Guadalcanal, Harrington directs the unloading of casualties into a waiting ambulance. (NARA.)

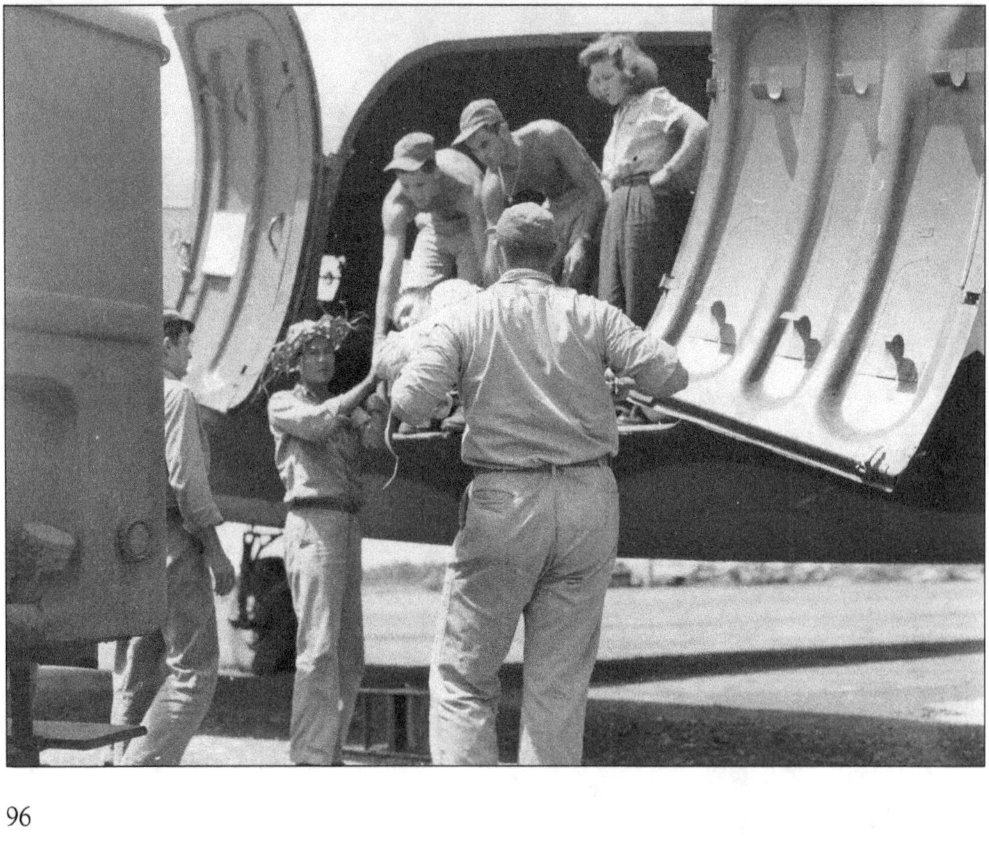

Lieutenant Harrington looks on with concern as a wounded man is passed out of the aircraft. These evacuees were destined for Guadalcanal's 137th Station Hospital, one of three 500-bed station hospitals then operating on the island. By this point, Bougainville had excellent field hospital units deployed within the perimeter, quickly tending to and evacuating critically wounded patients, nearly all of whom left the island by air. (NARA.)

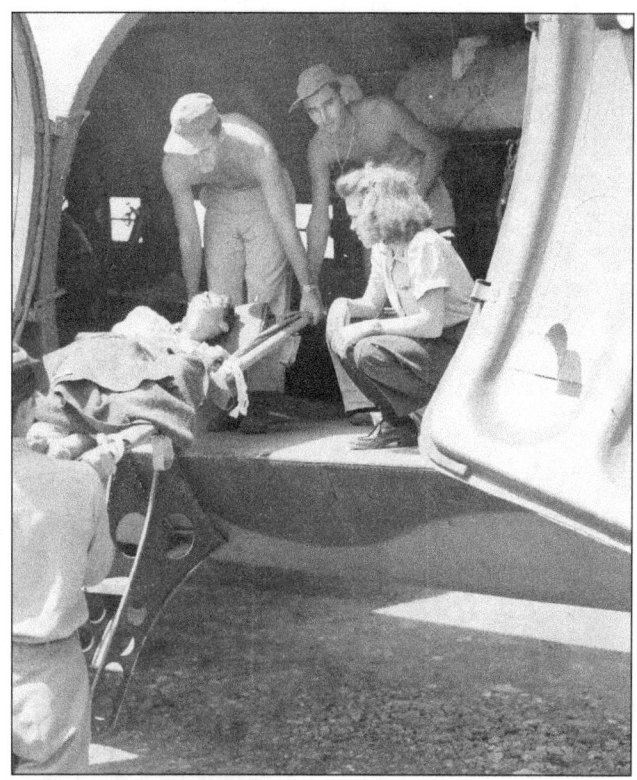

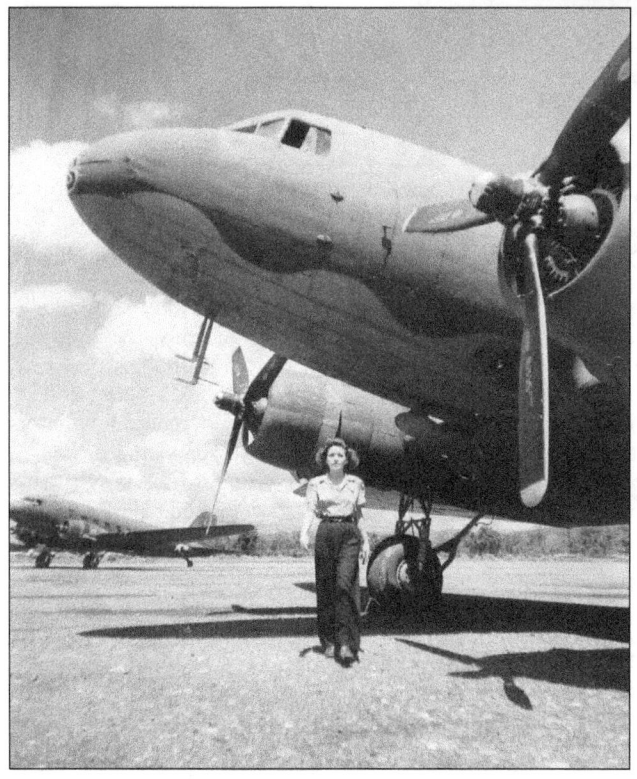

Lieutenant Harrington walks beneath the nose of her R4D after the mission. In the background is R4D "93" (39073), lost in May 1944 (see page 107). The American offensive on Bougainville continued until April 18, 1944. Afterward, the number of evacuees decreased significantly. Despite large numbers, estimated at over 40,000 men, the surviving Japanese forces on the island were cut off from supplies, in poor health, and badly demoralized. (NARA.)

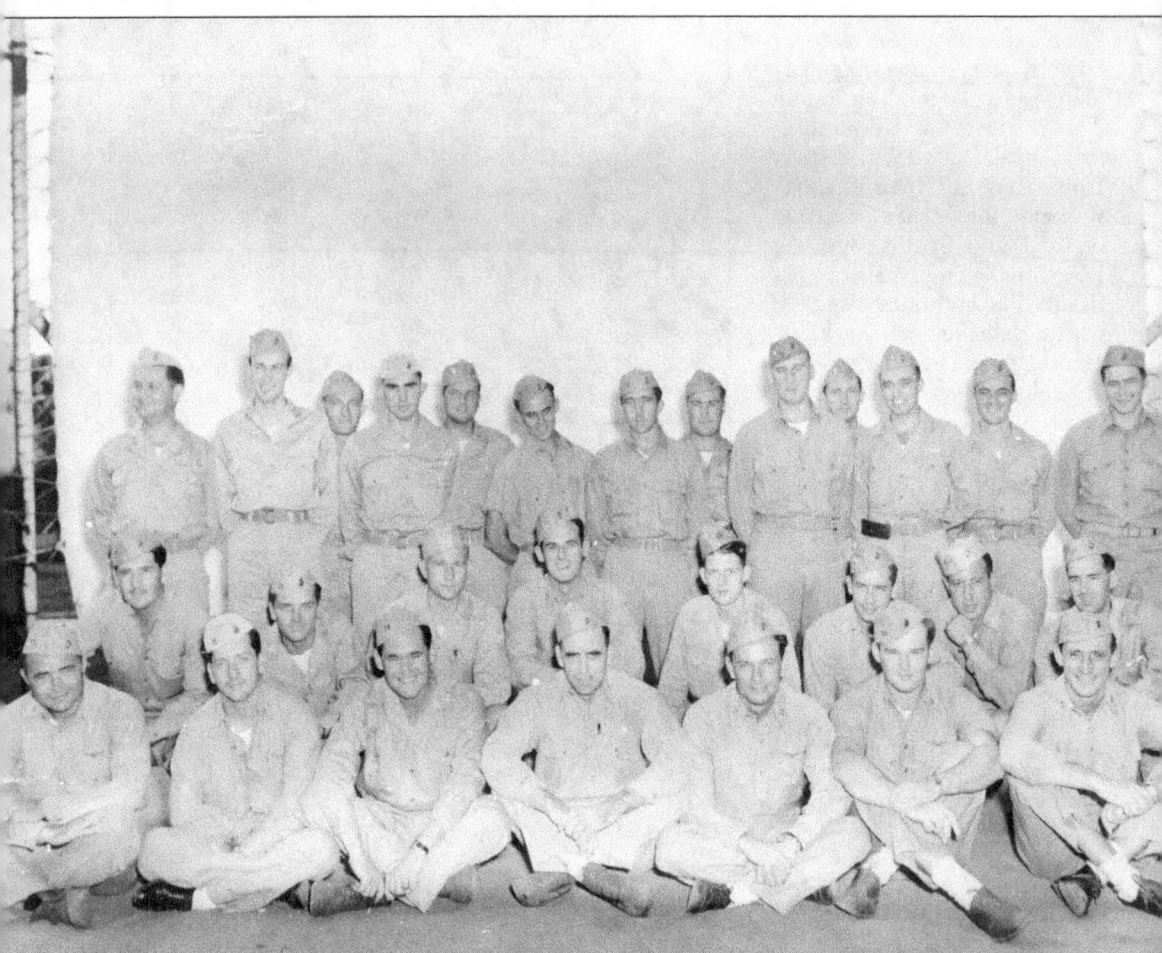

Officers of VMJ-253 pose for a partial squadron photograph at Tontouta in April 1944. Pictured from left to right are (first row) Capt. Fred Bresee, Capt. Donald McGee, Capt. John Ashe, Maj. James Moran, Capt. Robert Schroeder, Capt. John Walker Jr., and Capt. Paul Albright; (second row) 2nd Lt. Mark Freeman, Capt. William Parton, Maj. William A. Miller, Capt. Jerome Gordon, Capt. Edwin Rounds, 1st Lt. William Marks Jr., 2nd Lt. Philip Mattia, and 1st Lt. John L. Reynolds; (third row) Capt. Wilfred Findeisen, 1st Lt. William Heckman, 1st Lt. George Sealy, 1st Lt. Sidney Haidlin, 1st Lt. William Osbourne, 1st Lt. Willard Trimm, 1st Lt. Orson Wilhelmson, 1st Lt. Gordon Shull, 2nd Lt. Myron Boyce, CWO3 Meade Warthen, 1st Lt. Kenneth Mayberry, 2nd Lt. Clovis Davis, and 2nd Lt. Robert Lucas. All were naval aviators except for Boyce and navigators Davis, Freeman, Lucas, and Warthen. Warthen, formerly the squadron sergeant major, was an original member of VMJ-253 and a recipient of the Distinguished Flying Cross. Many in this group were ending their second combat tour. On June 15, VMJ-253 was detached from MAG-25. (MAG-25/SCAT.)

Some crews of the 13th TCS preparing to depart the South Pacific for the United States posed for photographs with their aircraft, as the crew of *Snafu* did on Espiritu Santo on April 8, 1944. From left to right are (first row) crew chief S.Sgt. Vincent Kelley and radio operator S.Sgt. Manuel Mello; (second row) copilot 1st Lt. Howard Leibundguth, pilot 1st Lt. Robert Folatko, and navigator 1st Lt. Abraham Cohen. (AFHRA.)

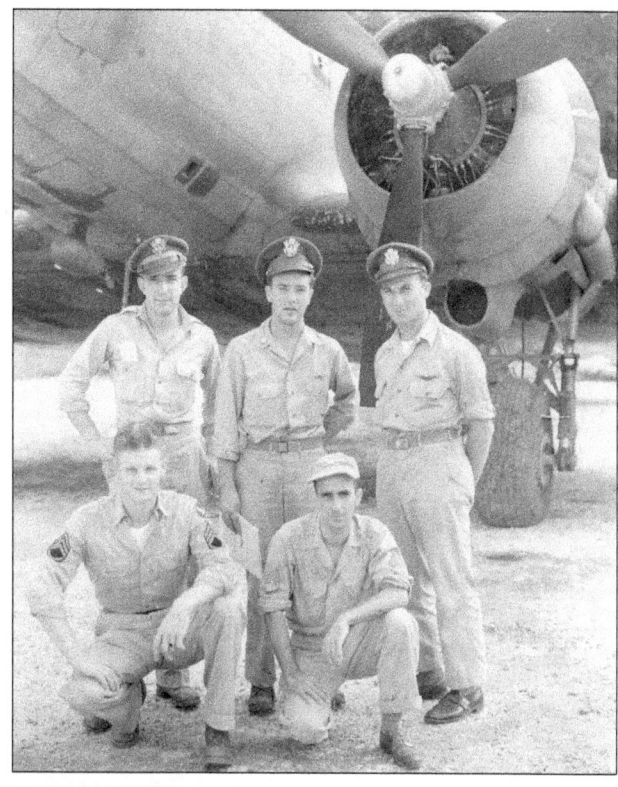

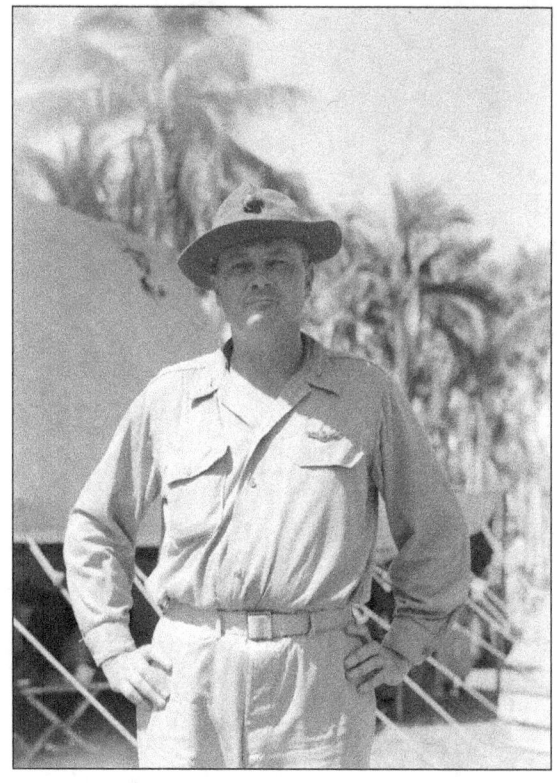

Col. William A. Willis commanded MAG-25 during the first seven months of 1944. A regular officer, Willis joined the Marines in 1929. His prewar assignments included fighting, scouting, and observation squadrons at Quantico and later VMJ-2/252 in San Diego and Hawaii, where he was stationed at the outbreak of war. He is shown in the Philippines after taking command of MAG-12, a fighter-bomber group, in September 1944. (NARA.)

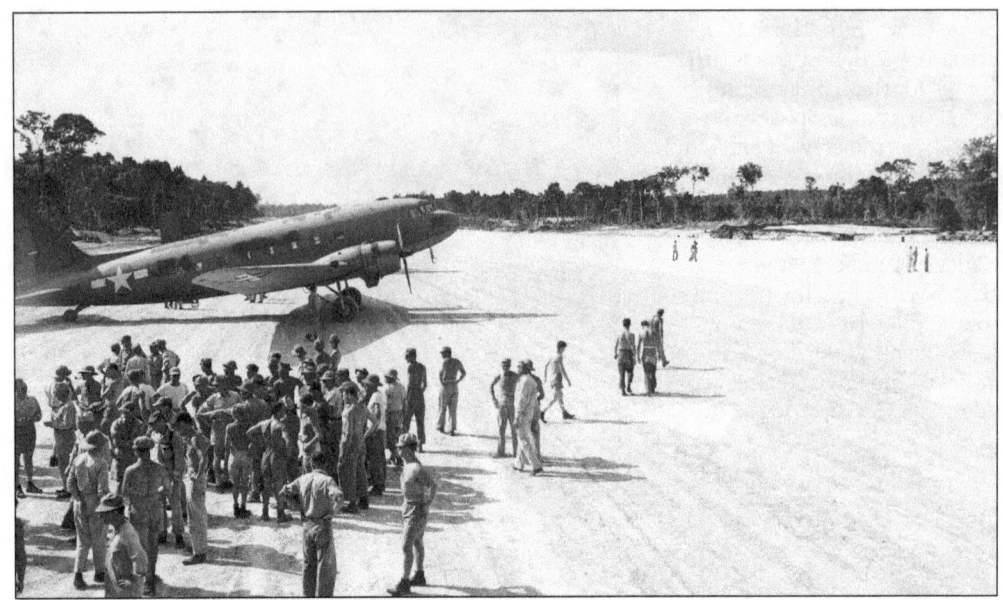

On March 20, 1944, Allied forces continued bypassing Rabaul, occupying the island of Emirau in the northern Bismarck Archipelago without opposition. Seabees completed Emirau's runway within five weeks. R4D "85," with its distinctive patchwork paint concealing earlier markings (likely those of Headquarters Squadron, MAG-15), was among the first SCAT arrivals on April 29, 1944. (NARA.)

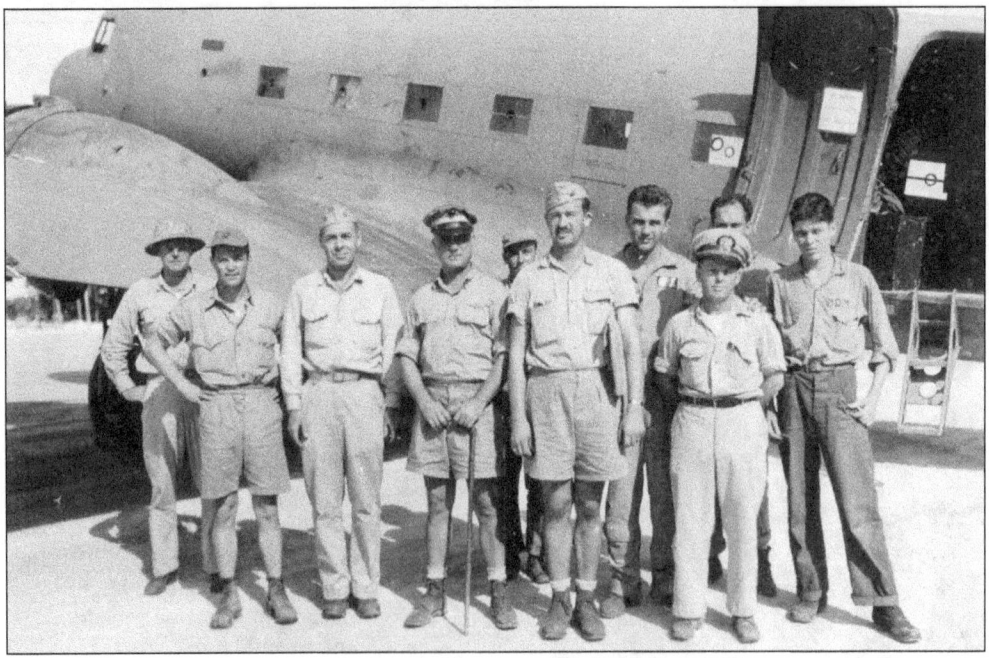

Maj. Gen. James T. Moore (fourth from left) poses with the first SCAT crewmen on Emirau on April 29, 1944. Second from left is pilot Capt. George "Dock" Kimball of VMJ-253. Sixth from left is Maj. Jonathan "Chic" Dyer of Headquarters Squadron 25. Unfortunately, the rest of the men are unidentified. Kimball's crew were 2nd Lt. Robert Sidak, MTSgt. Phillip Kroening Jr., Sgt. Reginald Parrish, and S.Sgt. Charles Nixon. (NARA.)

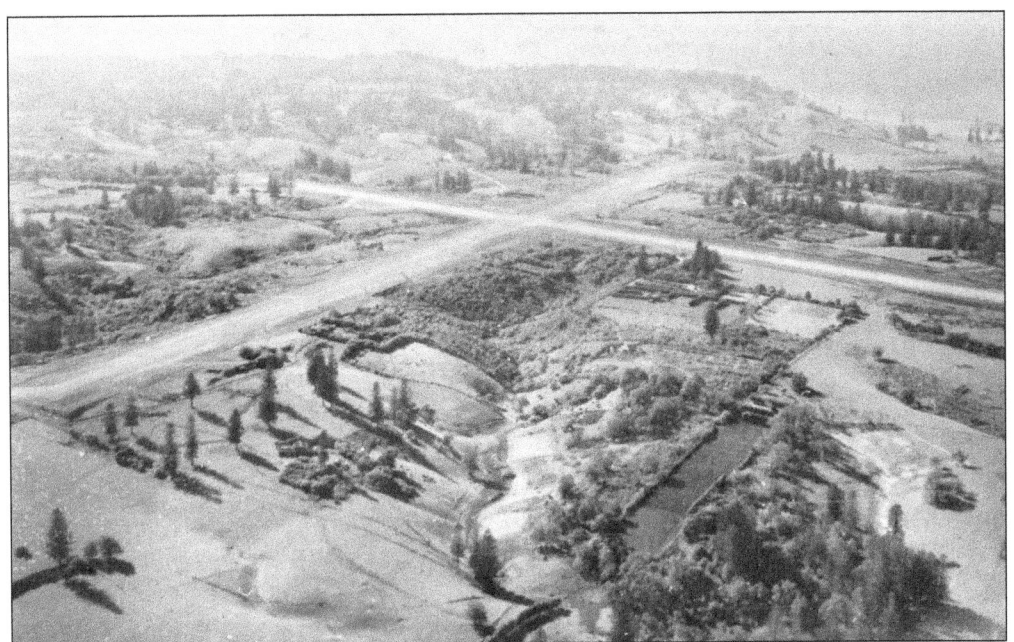

David Douglas Duncan took this photograph of Norfolk Island from a SCAT R4D. The island's wartime history, including the razing of its historic mile-long avenue lined by towering Norfolk pines in order to build this airstrip, formed a colorful backdrop to part of James A. Michener's novel *Tales of the South Pacific*. Norfolk's inhabitants were mostly descendants of the HMS *Bounty* mutineers, relocated from Pitcairn Island in 1856. (NARA.)

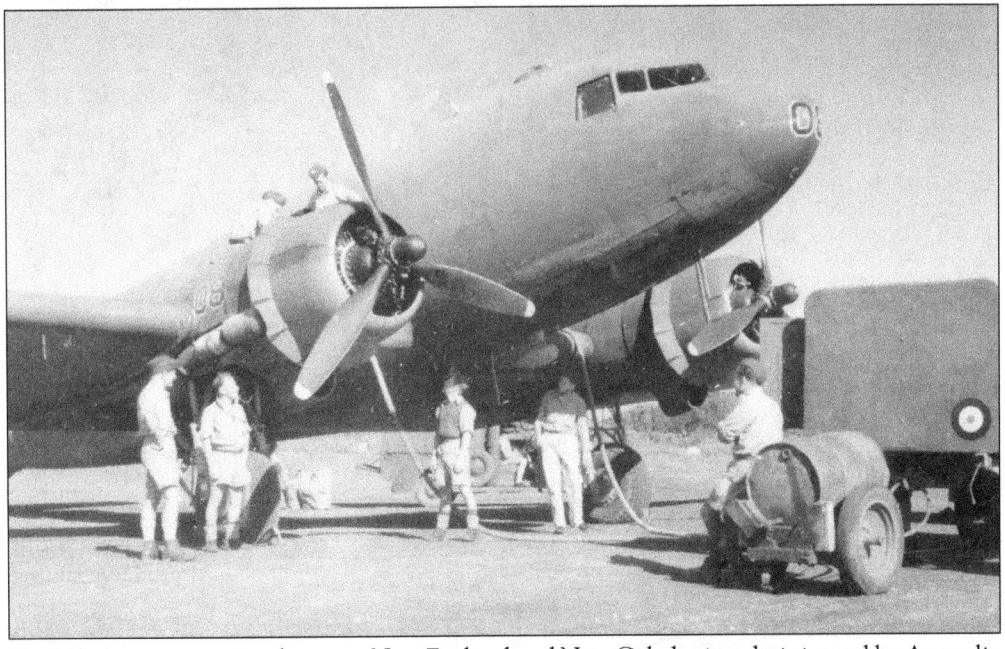

Norfolk was a way station between New Zealand and New Caledonia, administered by Australia but garrisoned by New Zealand. In addition to occasional cargo flights, SCAT sometimes used the airfield to avoid extremely severe weather. Here, a Royal New Zealand Air Force ground crew refuels R4D "08" in April 1944. (NARA.)

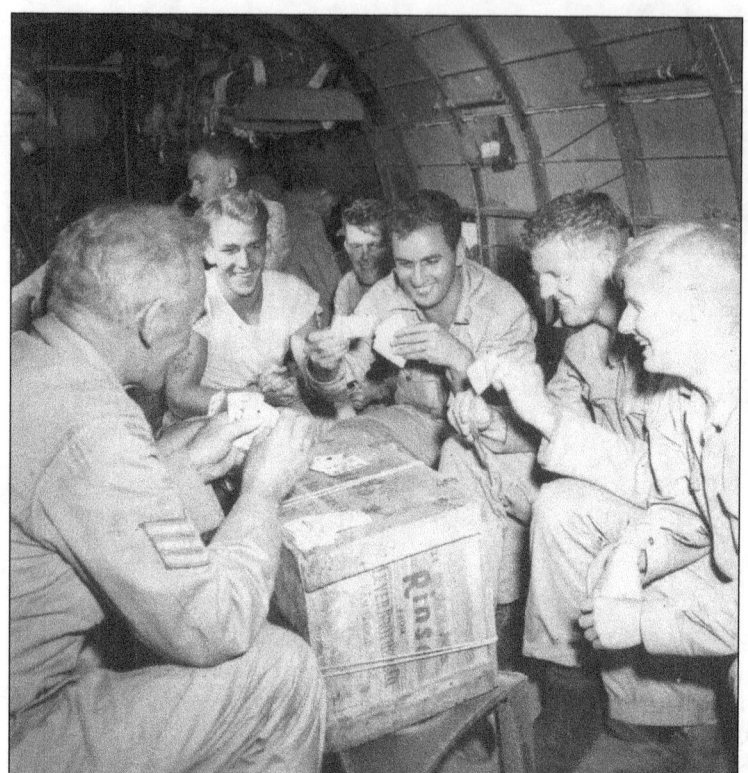

There was no flight like the flight home. These buoyant New Zealanders are headed homeward on a SCAT transport in March 1944 after spending over two years deployed to forward areas. New Zealand, struggling to meet manpower demands, withdrew its 3rd New Zealand Division from the Solomons in mid-1944. Many of its veterans were reassigned to the 2nd New Zealand Division fighting in Italy. (NARA.)

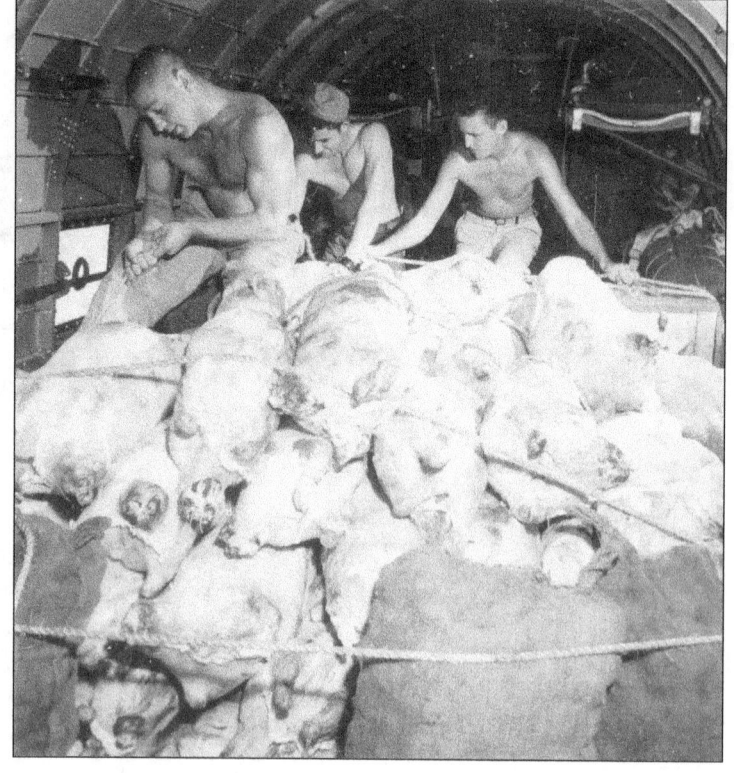

There were many reasons to appreciate SCAT, which received mentions in many units' war diaries, and among them was its role as a food-delivery service. This is a load of frozen Australian mutton. Meat and produce were frequent SCAT cargo, especially to areas housing combat aircrews, who had special dietary requirements. (NARA.)

Although aircrews received the most attention, SCAT also owed its success to the outstanding logisticians who organized each flight. Here, US Navy clerks of Headquarters Squadron 25 man the passenger desk at Henderson Field's operations building on April 24, 1944. Behind them is the SCAT flight assignment board. Due to the stifling heat and humidity, uniforms were frequently shunned in the South Pacific, even by clerical workers. (NARA.)

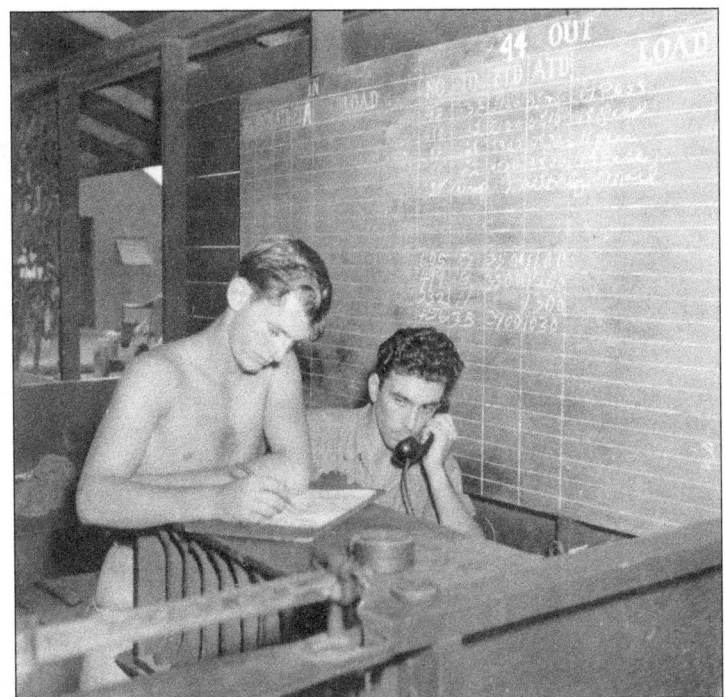

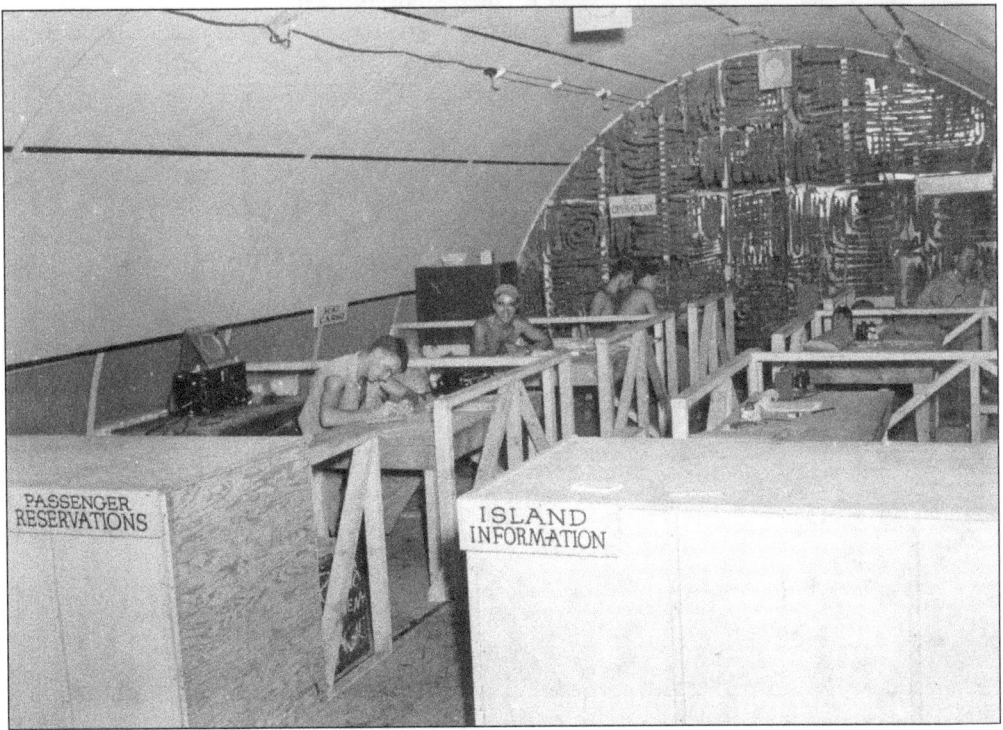

It was no cosmopolitan travel agency, but the SCAT operations office on Green Island was complete with passenger, cargo, and even island information services dutifully provided by members of Headquarters Squadron 25. SCAT's buildings on Green Island were constructed by Seabees of the US Navy's 33rd Naval Construction Battalion. (NARA.)

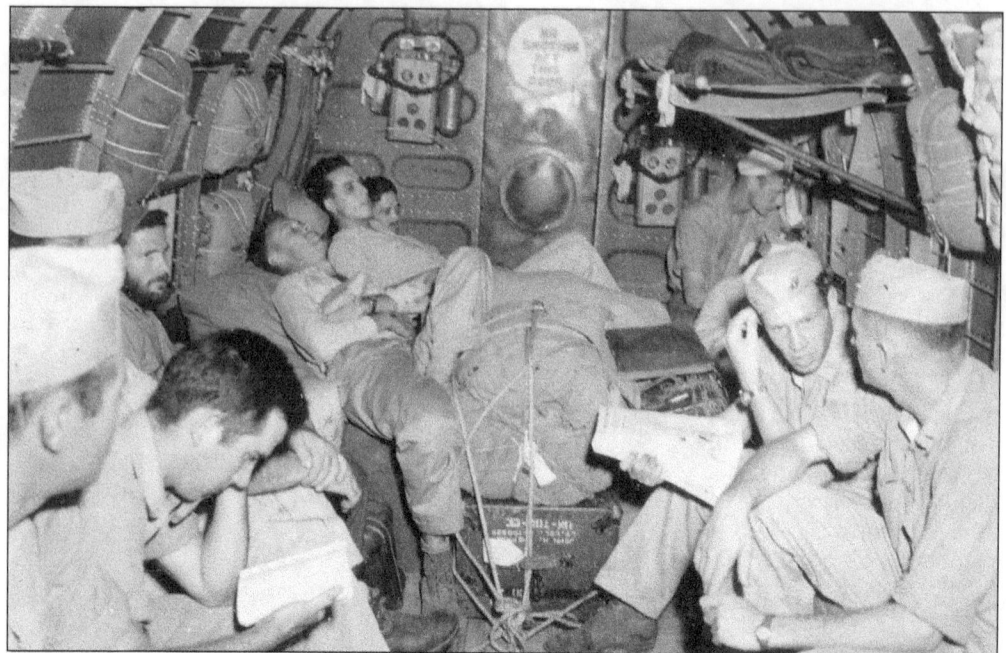

This was a typical scene aboard a scheduled SCAT flight, on this occasion an R4D of VMJ-153 headed from Guadalcanal to Espiritu Santo. The passengers are a mix of soldiers, sailors, and Marines, both officer and enlisted. It was a SCAT mantra that the private who absolutely had to get somewhere would always take precedence over the general who just fancied a trip. (NARA.)

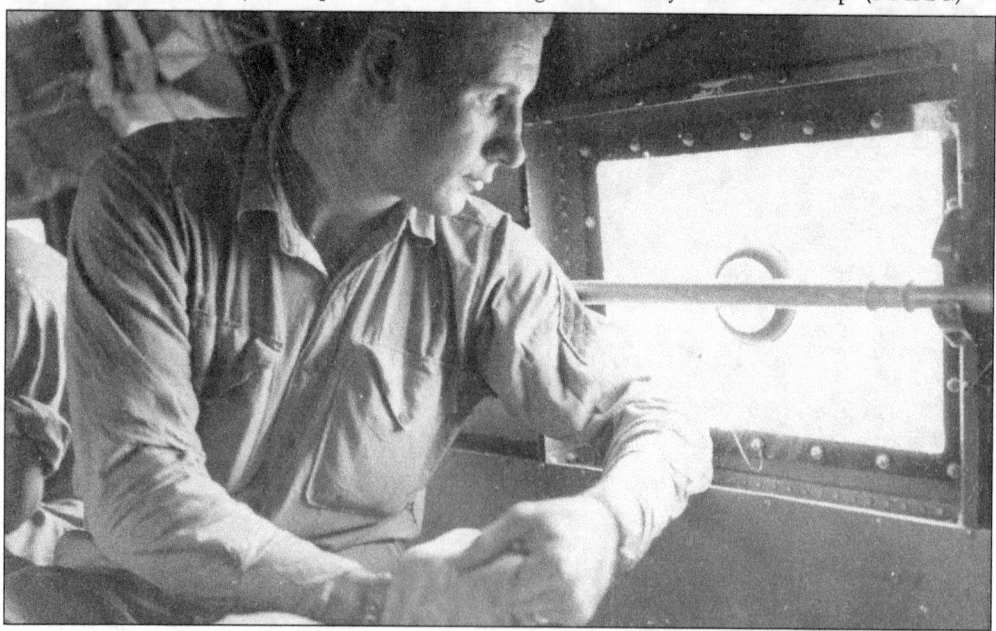

A SCAT passenger takes in what was likely a spectacular view. The circular object in the middle of the window is a gun port, a rubber grommet with a removable clear plastic plug. In theory, these allowed infantry weapons to be used in defense against enemy aircraft, but their practical value was extremely dubious. Flight crews did frequently carry sidearms, and oftentimes a Thompson submachine gun was stowed aboard. (NARA.)

The photographs on this page were taken at the SCAT maintenance area at Tontouta Air Base in April 1944. Here, SCAT maintenance personnel tend to an R4D-5. This former MAG-15 aircraft, with its unusual markings, may have belonged to Headquarters Squadron, 1st Marine Aircraft Wing, which typically operated two R4Ds. (NARA.)

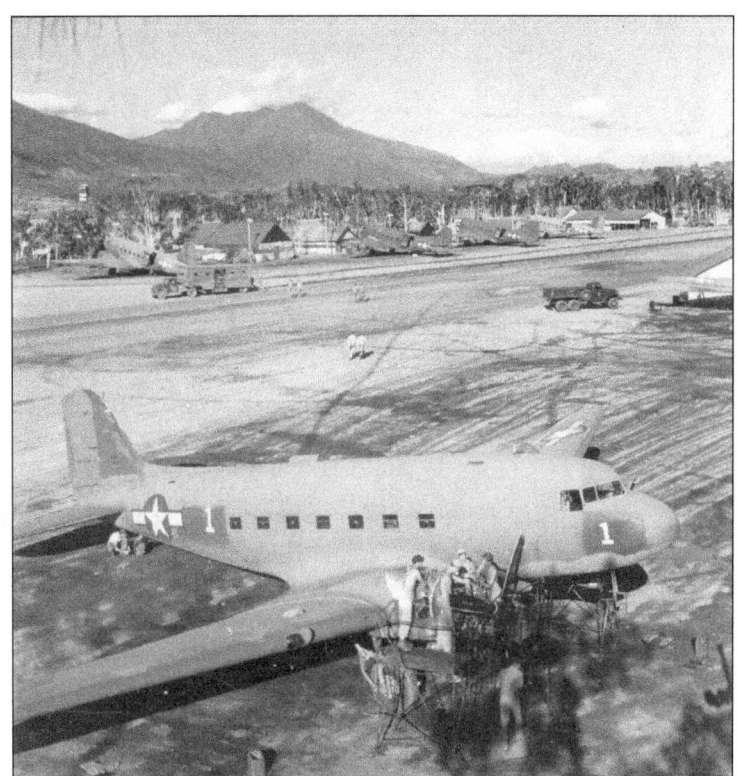

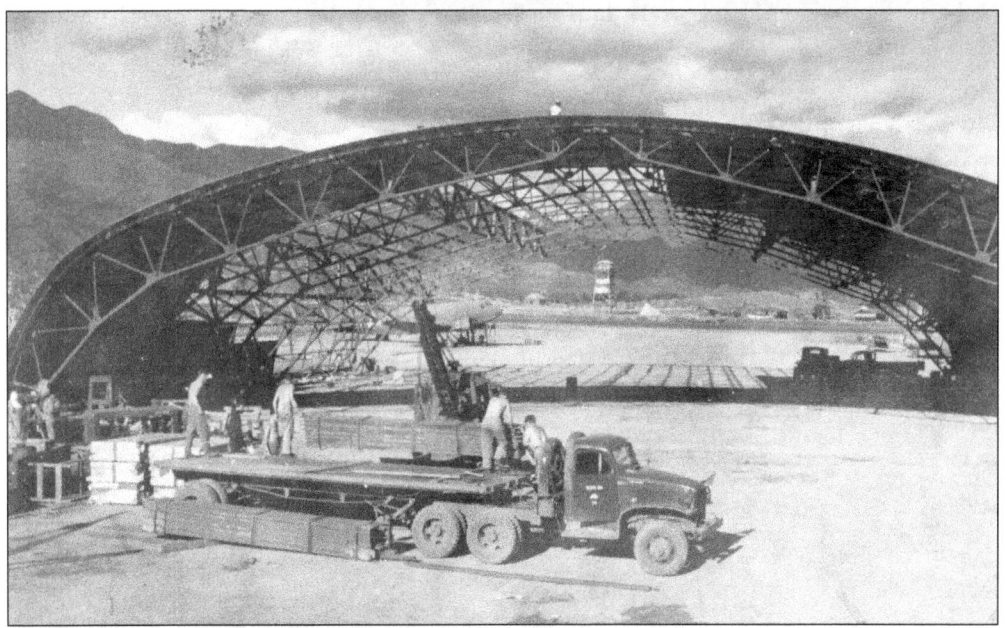

MAG-25 personnel disassemble the group's maintenance hangar in preparation for their move north to support operations beyond the Solomons. Group headquarters moved to Bougainville beginning on June 17, 1944, followed by VMR-153 in July and VMR-152 on August 1. Concurrently, on July 3, South Pacific Combat Air Transport Command was dissolved. SCAT did not disappear, however, living on as Solomons Combat Air Transport Command. (NARA.)

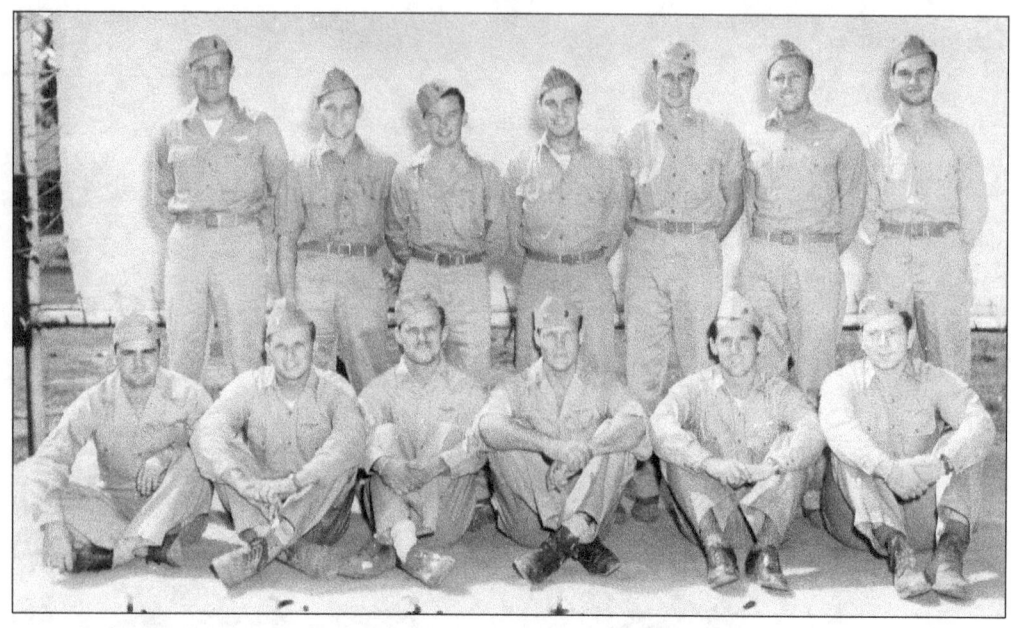

Many MAG-25 crewmen posed for photographs in mid-1944. The partial squadron photograph above shows naval aviators of VMJ-152 at Tontouta in May. From left to right are (first row) 1st Lt. Thomas "Tommy" Walker, 1st Lt. Wayne McLaughlin, 1st Lt. Leo Kabat, Capt. Lawrence "Skin" Davis, 1st Lt. James Kile, and 1st Lt. Harold Klesath; (second row) 1st Lt. Lester Hauge, 1st Lt. Richard "Stub" Haralson, 1st Lt. Paul "Hookie" Wynn, 1st Lt. Jack Glover, 1st Lt. John Sinderholm Jr., 1st Lt. Edgar Lancaster, and Lt. Roger Brown. Pictured below, from left to right, Capt. Max Dix, Capt. George Kimball, Capt. Gerald "Jerry" Shea, and Capt. Ellsworth T. "Terry" Nobles pose at Tontouta. Shea was with VMJ-152, the others with VMJ-253. Dix, Kimball, and Nobles were all recipients of the Distinguished Flying Cross. (Both, Author's collection.)

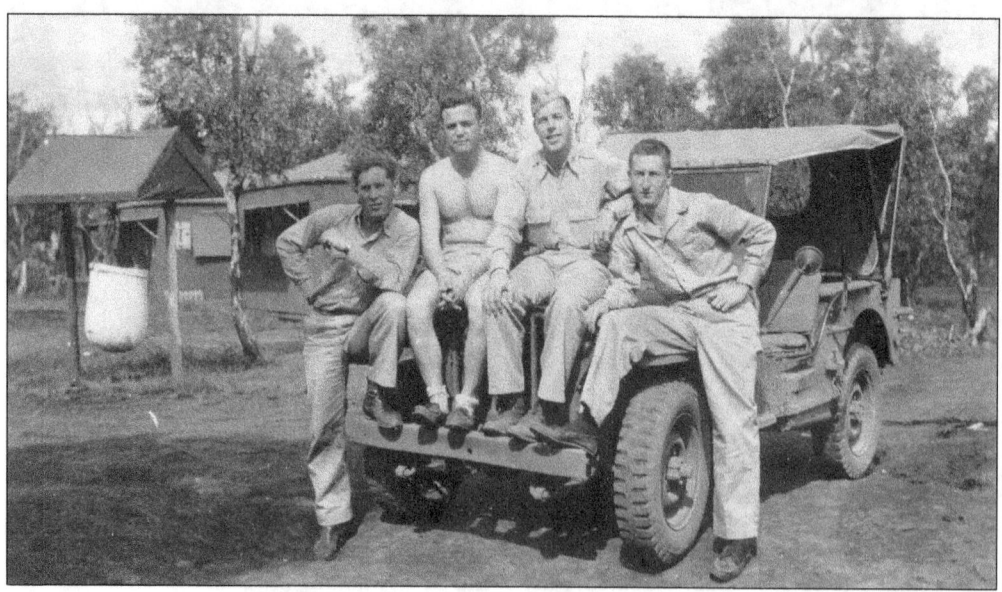

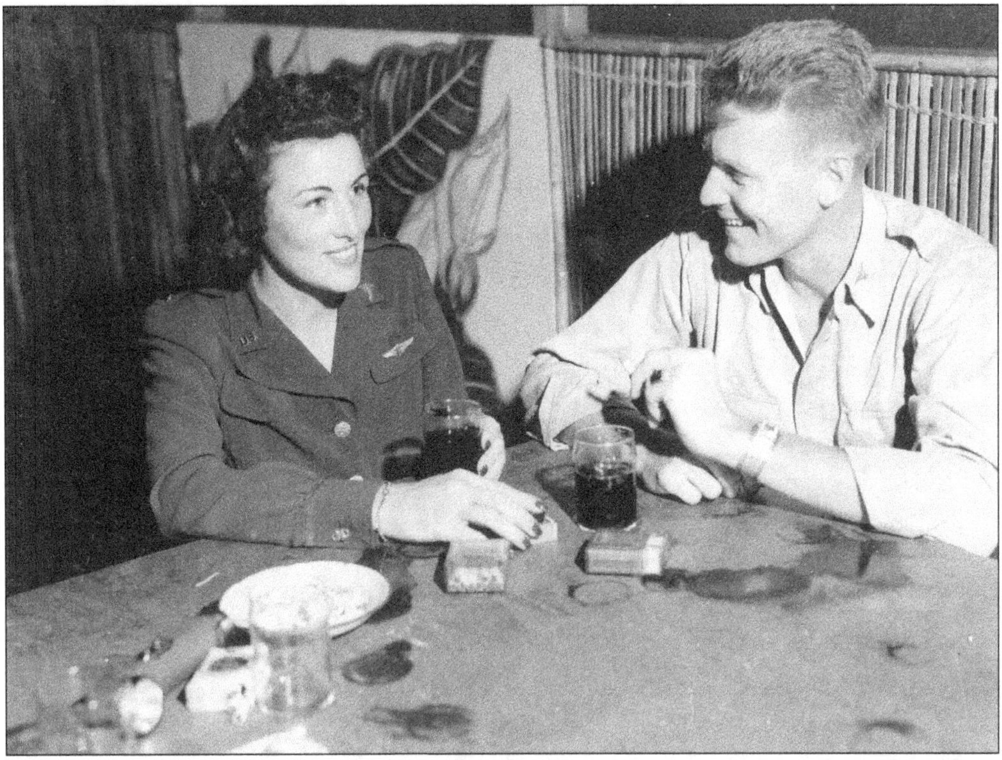

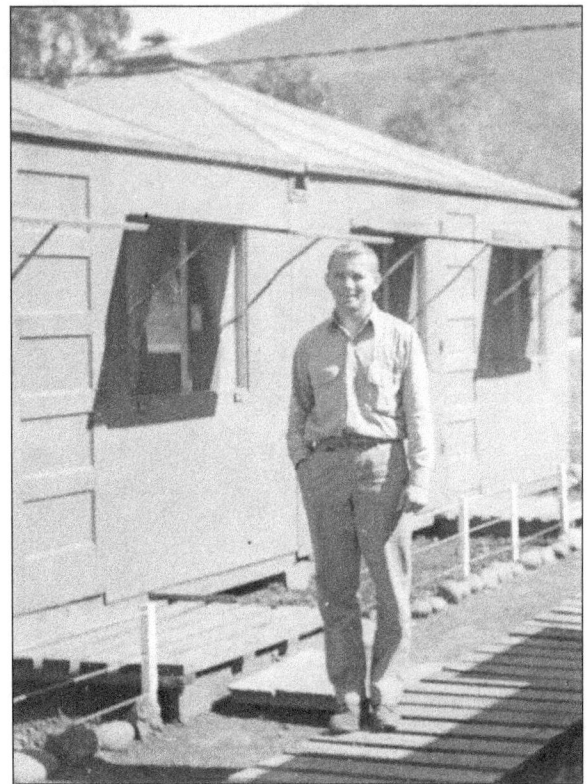

This may be the last photograph ever taken of flight nurse 2nd Lt. Eloise Richardson, shown at the officers' mess on Guadalcanal with 1st Lt. John Buehler of the US Army's 137th Station Hospital. Richardson, of the newly redesignated 801st Medical Air Evacuation Squadron (MAES), was declared missing in action aboard R4D-5 39073 of VMJ-152, lost due to unknown causes on May 18, 1944. (NARA.)

This photograph is among the last taken of 1st Lt. Richard Haralson, first pilot of R4D-5 39073 on its fatal flight. His crew, in addition to Lieutenant Richardson, were radio operator Pfc. Charles Bakewell, navigator Sgt. Daniel Bate Jr., copilot 1st Lt. Jack Glover, trainee navigator MTSgt. William Lane, and crew chief S.Sgt. Norman Myers. Sixteen passengers were also aboard. All are memorialized at Manila American Cemetery. (Author's collection.)

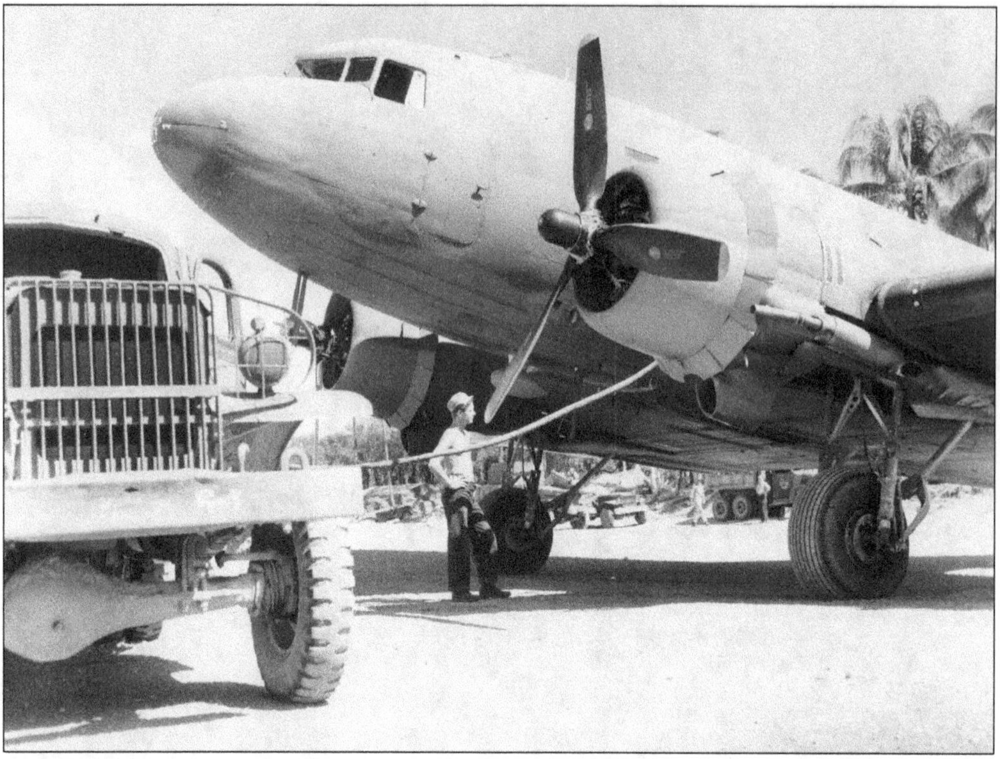

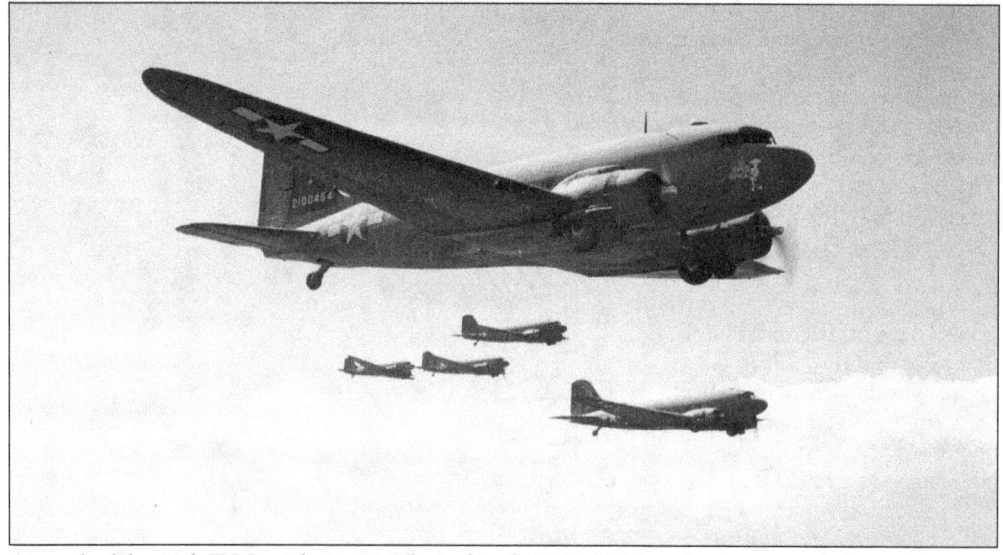

Dedicated Marine and USAAF ground crews leapt to work on newly arrived SCAT aircraft. Here, a ground crewman refuels R4D "11" from a GMC CCKW fuel truck on Bougainville in June 1944. Pilots, crew chiefs, and flight mechanics made sure to inspect their ships for damage and maintenance issues before and after each flight. (NARA.)

Aircraft of the 13th TCS, with C-47A *The Sad Sack* (42-100454) in the foreground, fly over Espiritu Santo in this photograph taken from the lead aircraft's cargo door in July 1944, the month that the squadron and the rest of the 403rd Troop Carrier Group separated from SCAT. The 13th TCS would go on to serve in New Guinea, the Netherlands East Indies, and the Philippines. (AFHRA.)

Five

FROM PELELIU TO TSINGTAO

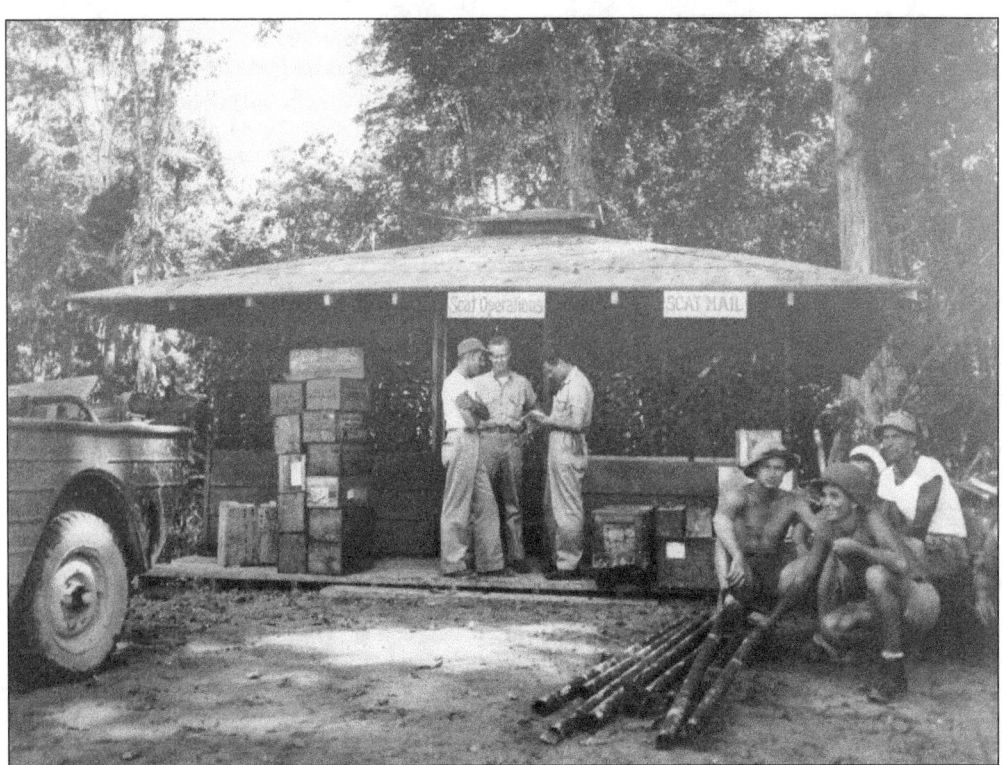

This leisurely scene at the shaded SCAT Operations hut at Segi Point, New Georgia, belies the intensity of SCAT's daily operations. By the time this picture was taken in September 1944, combat operations in the Solomons had waned and MAG-25 had moved its headquarters north to Bougainville to support operations there and in New Guinea and the Philippines. The vehicle at left is a Ford GPA amphibious jeep. (NARA.)

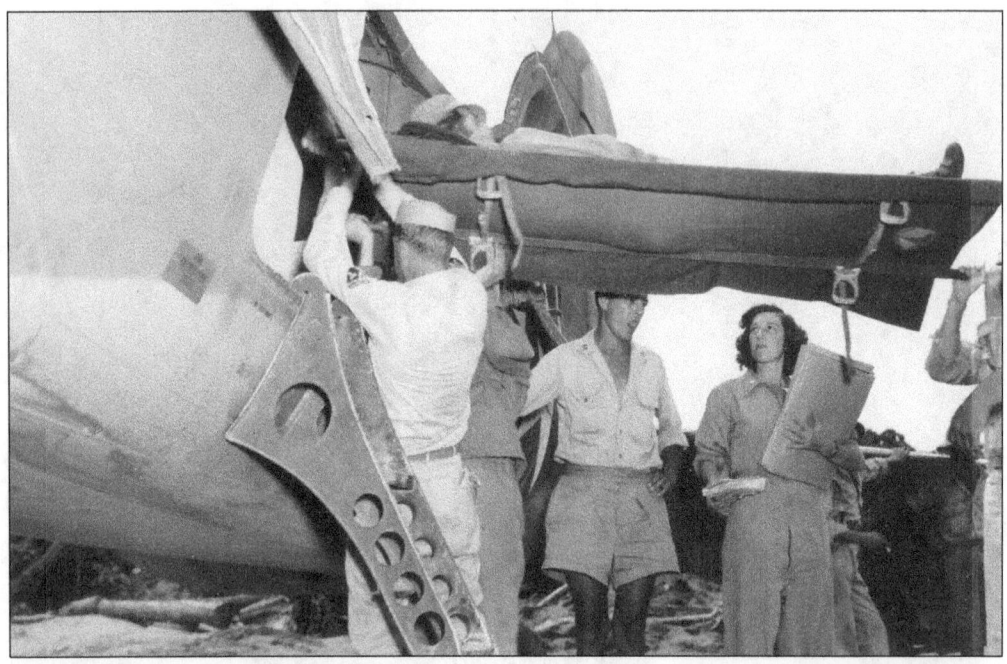

Second Lt. Ada Endres of the 801st MAES, a veteran of SCAT operations in the Northern Solomons and the Bismarck Archipelago, supervises the transfer of patients into a C-47 on Bougainville in late summer 1944. Endres later received an Air Medal. In September 1944, the 801st MAES separated from SCAT, joining the 54th Troop Carrier Wing, 5th Air Force, in New Guinea. (NARA.)

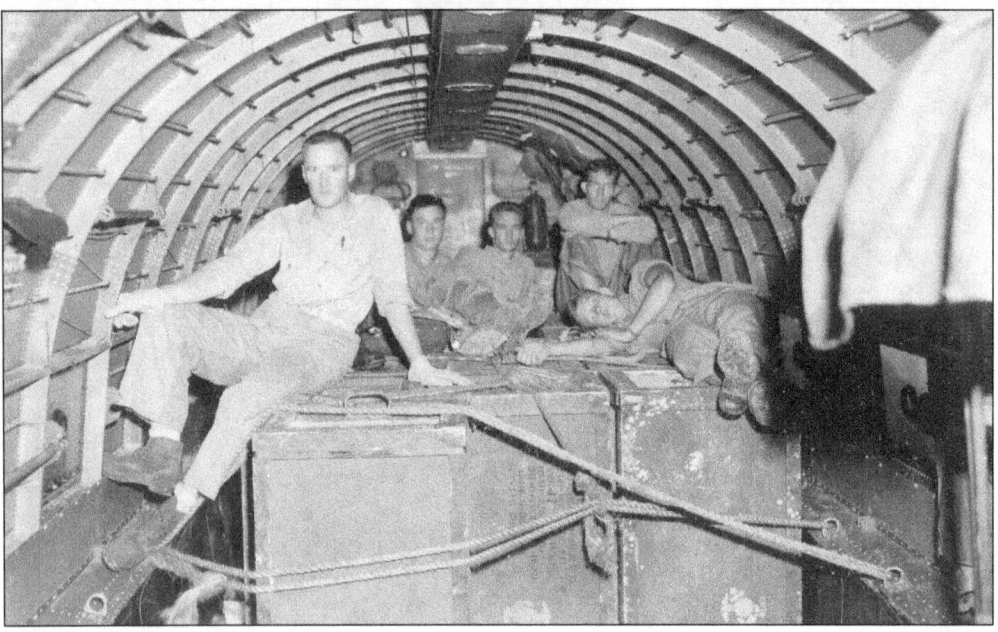

During the brutal fight to dislodge Japanese defenders from the caves and crevices of Peleliu, SCAT received an urgent request to ship additional flamethrowers, requiring a long overwater flight through poor weather. Maj. Theodore Sanford Jr.'s VMR-153 crew was the first to arrive, on October 15, 1944. From left to right are Major Sanford, flight mechanic Sgt. Leland Blackwell, Sgt. Raymond Boyer, S.Sgt. Charles Wilson, and radio operator S.Sgt. Lawrence Gregory. (NARA.)

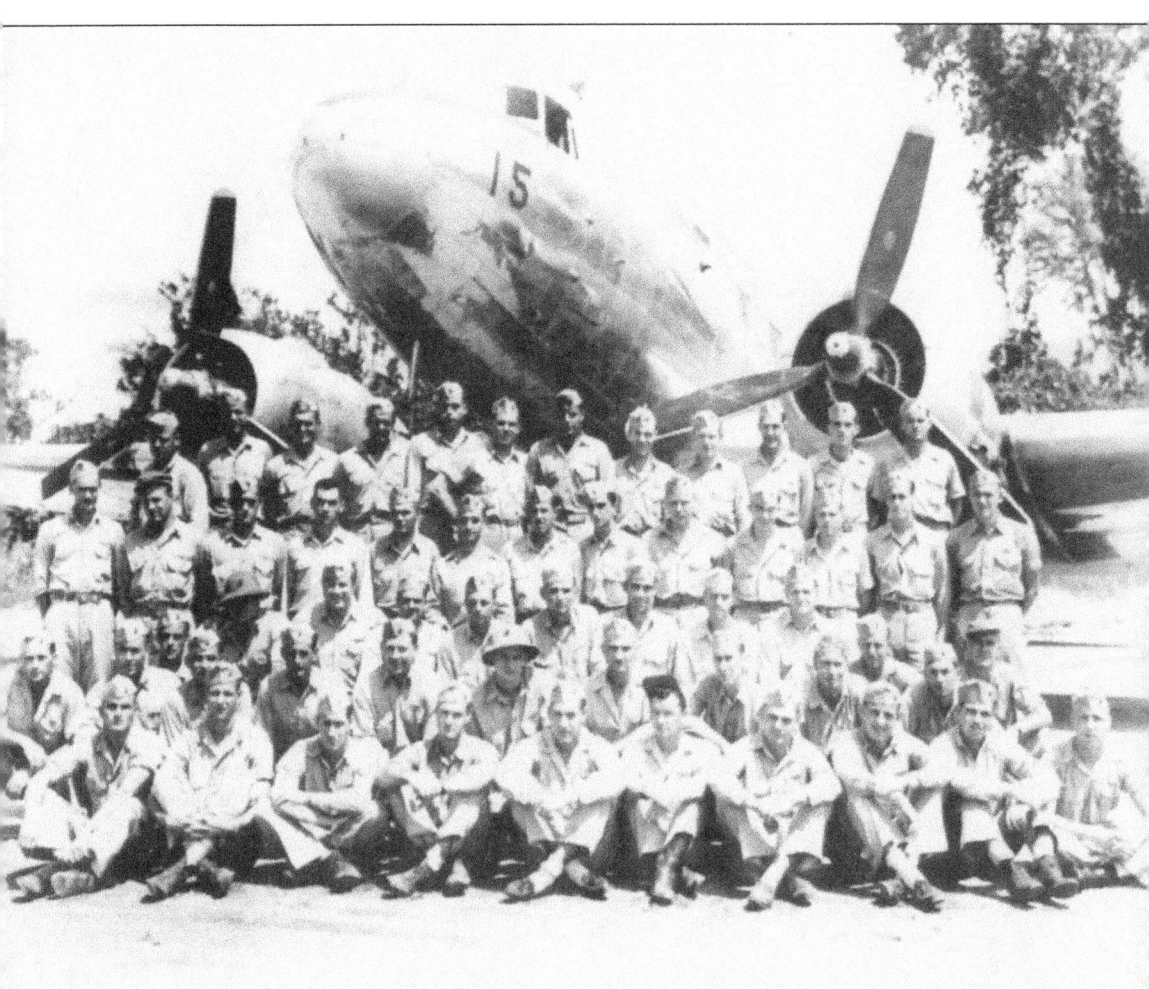

Officers of VMR-152 pose for a photograph with R4D "15" on Bougainville. The aircraft is in the penultimate marking scheme applied to wartime MAG-25 aircraft, stripped to bare metal and polished, with black stenciling and anti-glare panels. With the threat of Japanese air power greatly diminished, SCAT began maximizing its aircraft's performance by removing their lusterless camouflage paint, decreasing weight and drag. A full coat of camouflage paint reportedly weighed 250 pounds, and its removal could increase speed by 10 to 20 knots. Aircraft numbers, which still often bore no relation to BuAer numbers, were now applied to the sides of the nose and in large numerals on the vertical stabilizer. At some point, in a return to pre-war customs, crews began stenciling "U.S. MARINES" and the aircraft's BuAer number prominently on the vertical stabilizer, and adding a Marine Corps "Eagle, Globe, and Anchor" just aft of the cockpit windows. (Author's collection, courtesy of Maj. Paul E. Wynn.)

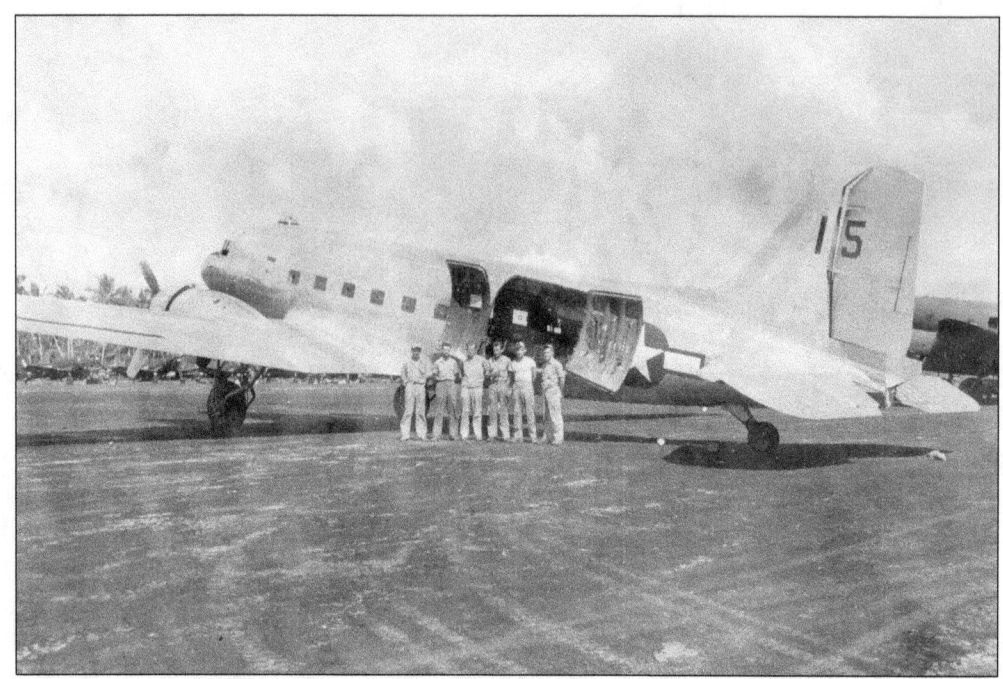

Another view of R4D "15" shows an unidentified crew on Leyte, likely at Tanauan where the four F4U Corsair squadrons of MAG-12 were then stationed, on December 28, 1944. By that time, MAG-25 was dedicated to fulfilling the air transport needs of the 1st Marine Aircraft Wing, which flew fighter, bomber, and close air support missions in support of US Army ground forces in the Philippines. (NARA.)

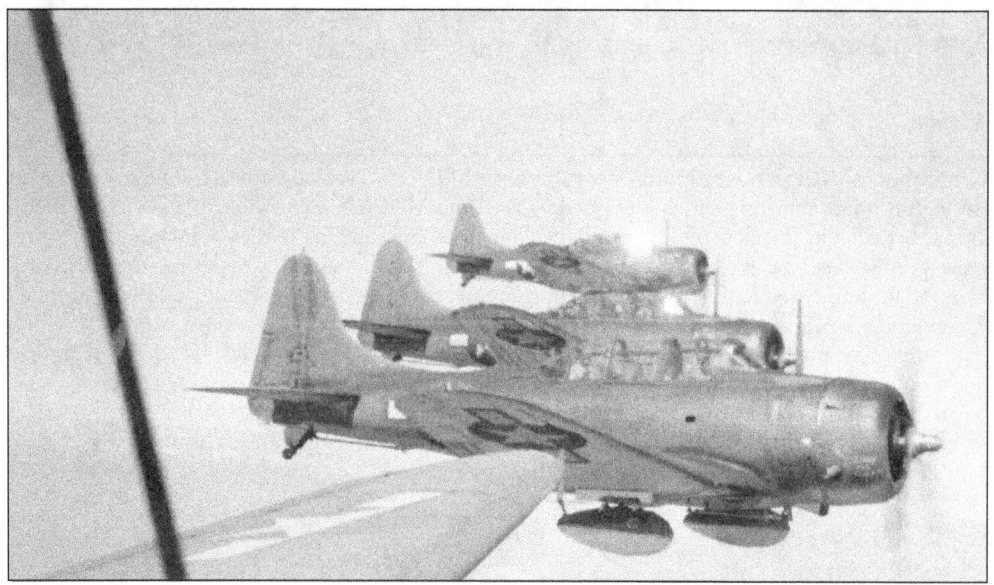

These SBDs are receiving navigational escort from a VMJ/VMR-152 R4D in 1944, keeping in close formation per standard practice. Navigational guidance, already a routine procedure, was one of MAG-25's major contributions during operations north of New Guinea, escorting short-range fighters and bombers to bases throughout the Philippines and as far north as Okinawa and Iwo Jima. The diagonal line is the edge of the pilot's open side window. (Author's collection.)

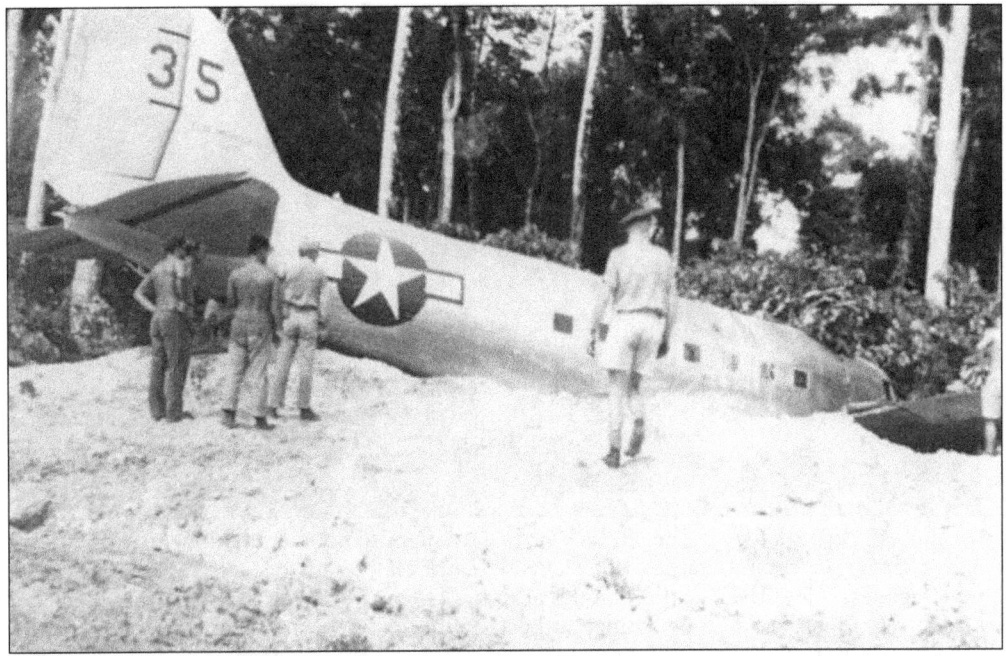

R4D "35" (17208) of VMR-153 crashed on takeoff on Emirau on the morning of May 5, 1945, plowing into an embankment beside the runway and drawing a curious crowd. There were no injuries, but the aircraft was salvaged for parts. This photograph was taken by Leading Aircraftman James Crarer of No. 5 Servicing Unit, Royal New Zealand Air Force. (Courtesy of Tony Crarer.)

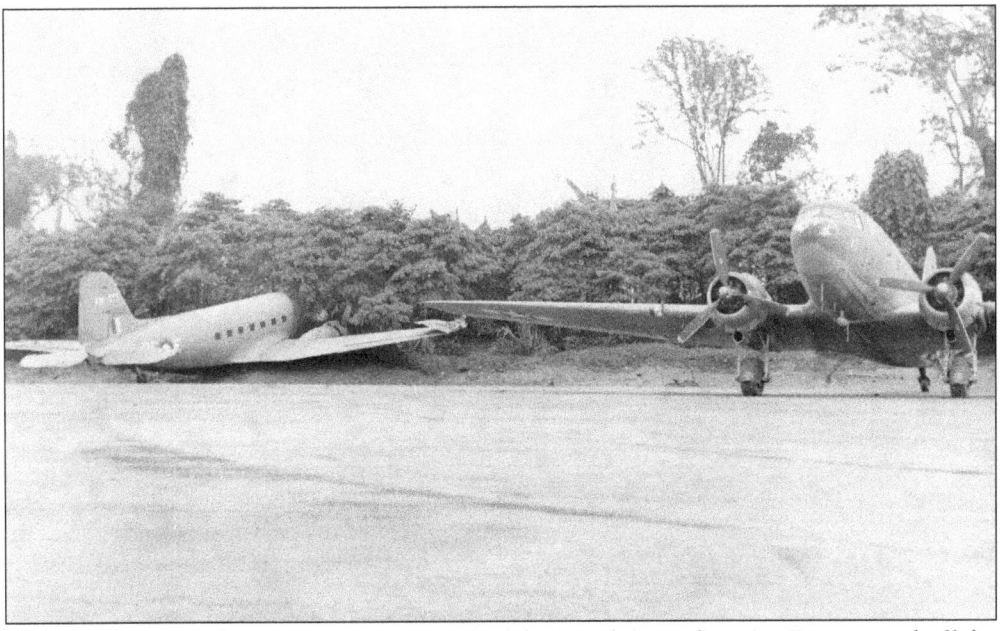

On July 20, 1945, Dakota A65-27 (VH-CTY) of the Royal Australian Air Force veered off the taxiway at Piva Uncle after suffering a hydraulic brake failure, grazing R4D "10" (17095) of VMR-152. The Marine aircraft was formerly "95," the old number peeking through faded paint on the nose, and now wears atypical MAG-25 markings, with small white side numbers and an "Eagle, Globe, and Anchor" aft of the cockpit. (NARA.)

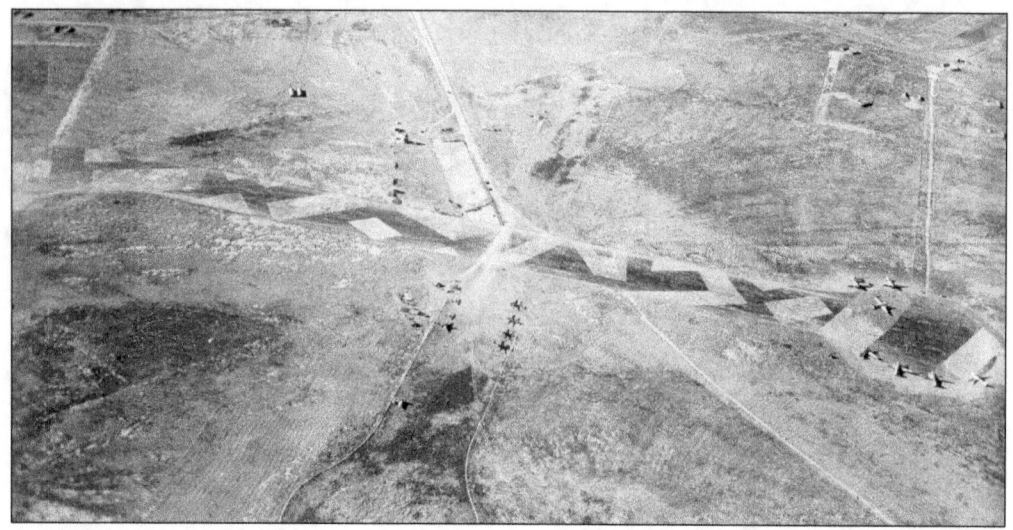

On October 6, 1945, VMR-153 began MAG-25's movement to northern China, arriving here at Chanweichang aerodrome southeast of Tientsin (Tianjin), formerly occupied and camouflaged by the Japanese. Note the squadron's R4Ds at right. The movement was part of the American effort to repatriate Japanese personnel and those who had been imprisoned or pressed into Japanese wartime service. MAG-25 supported both the 1st Marine Aircraft Wing and 3rd Marine Amphibious Corps. (NARA.)

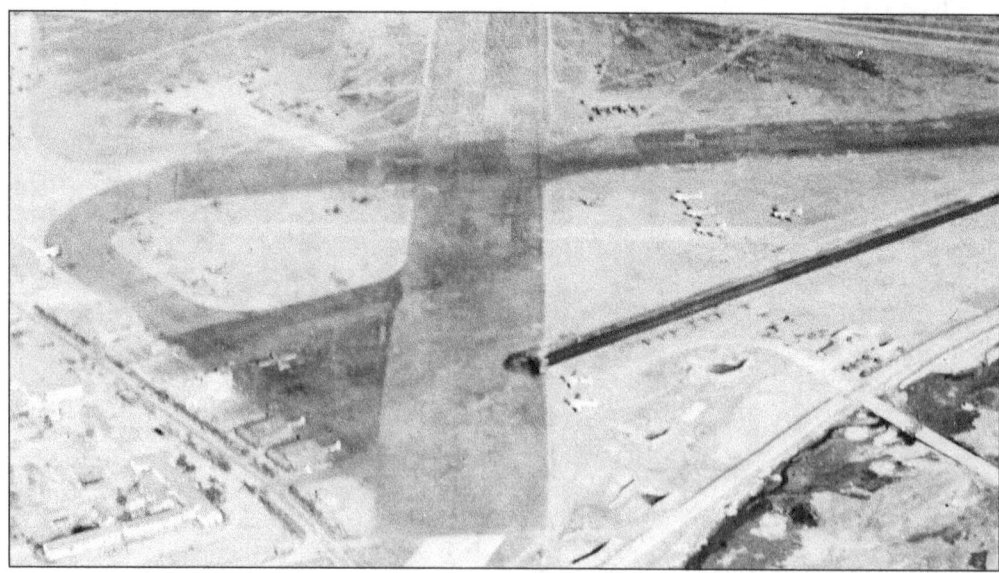

On October 24, MAG-25 headquarters and VMR-153 relocated to the Tsankou aerodrome north of Tsingtao (Qingdao). They were joined by VMR-152 on November 16, shortly after this photograph was taken. Most flights were to Peiping/Peking (Beijing), Tientsin, and Shanghai. Numerous VMR-153 R4Ds can be seen on the field, at left, along with larger R5C Commando transports, smaller OY-1 observation aircraft, and F4U Corsairs. (NARA.)

During the war, Japan held many Allied civilian prisoners in the Weihsien (Weixian) Internment Camp (also spelled Weihsin or Wei H'sin in contemporary American documents). On August 17, 1945, a total of 1,497 surviving prisoners, including 204 Americans, were liberated. Here, a USAAF B-29 Superfortress drops food and medical supplies to cheering survivors just outside the camp on August 27. (NARA.)

On October 12, after the survivors were medically cleared, MAG-25 began the first daily evacuation flights from Weihsien. Here, on October 16, a scarlet fever patient is loaded into R4D "25" (17219) of VMR-153. Among those who had died in the camp's primitive conditions was Scottish missionary and Olympic medalist Eric Liddell, whose earlier life was portrayed in the 1981 film *Chariots of Fire*. (NARA.)

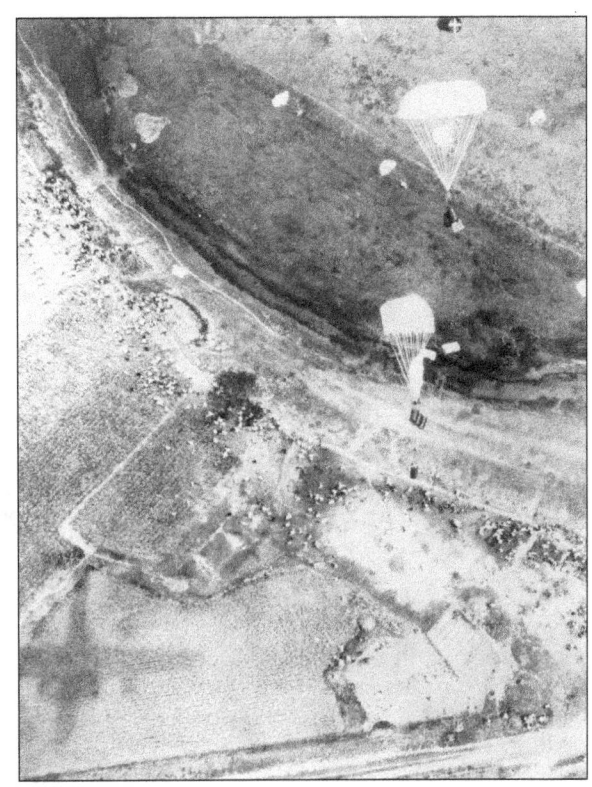

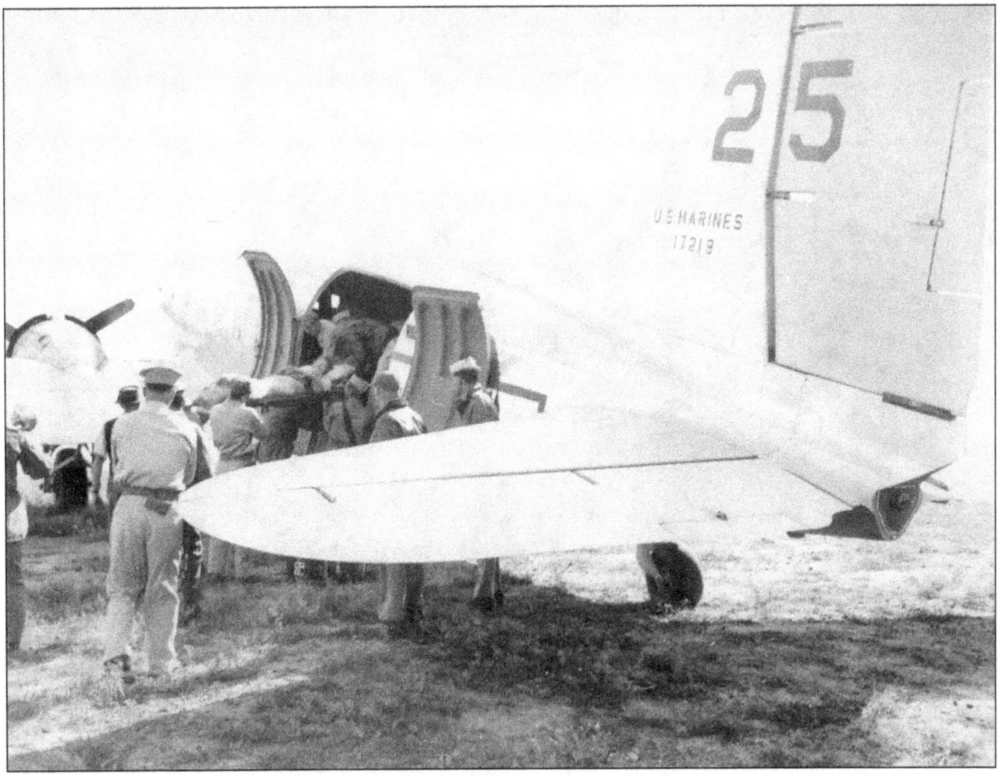

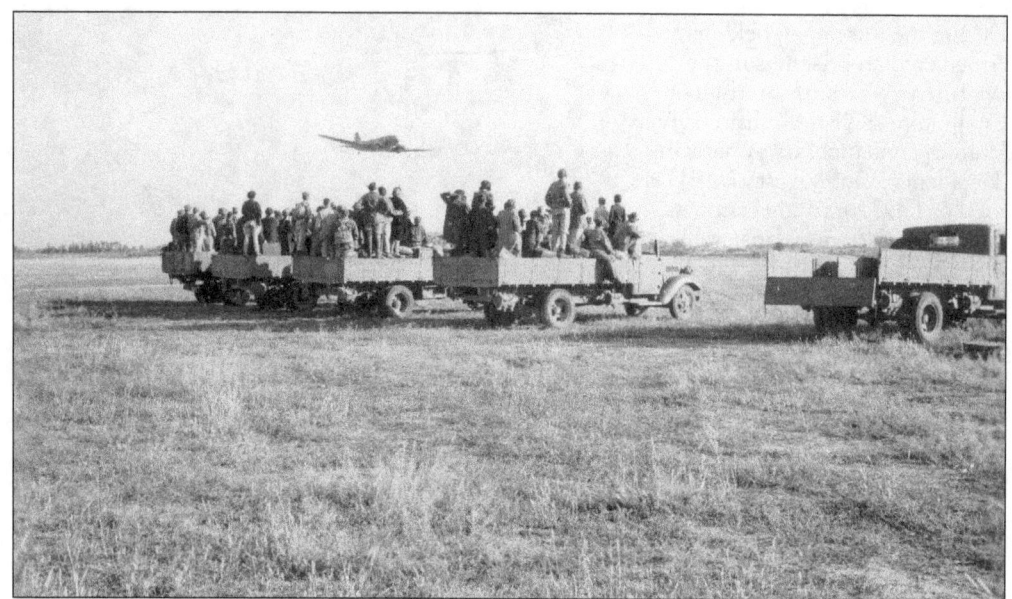

Above, internees loaded into trucks for the trip from the camp area to the airstrip await the transport that will take them to Tientsin. Below, VMR-153 crewmen assist survivors into R4D "38" (17149) on October 17, 1945. Most of the former prisoners were British, American, Canadian, or Australian, many of them missionaries or academics, plus many dependent children. Among them was future US ambassador to China Arthur W. Hummel Jr., who had been a postgraduate student in 1941. The squadron averaged 80 evacuees per day, providing a vital link since communist guerrillas often threatened the rail line between Weihsien and Tientsin. (Both, NARA.)

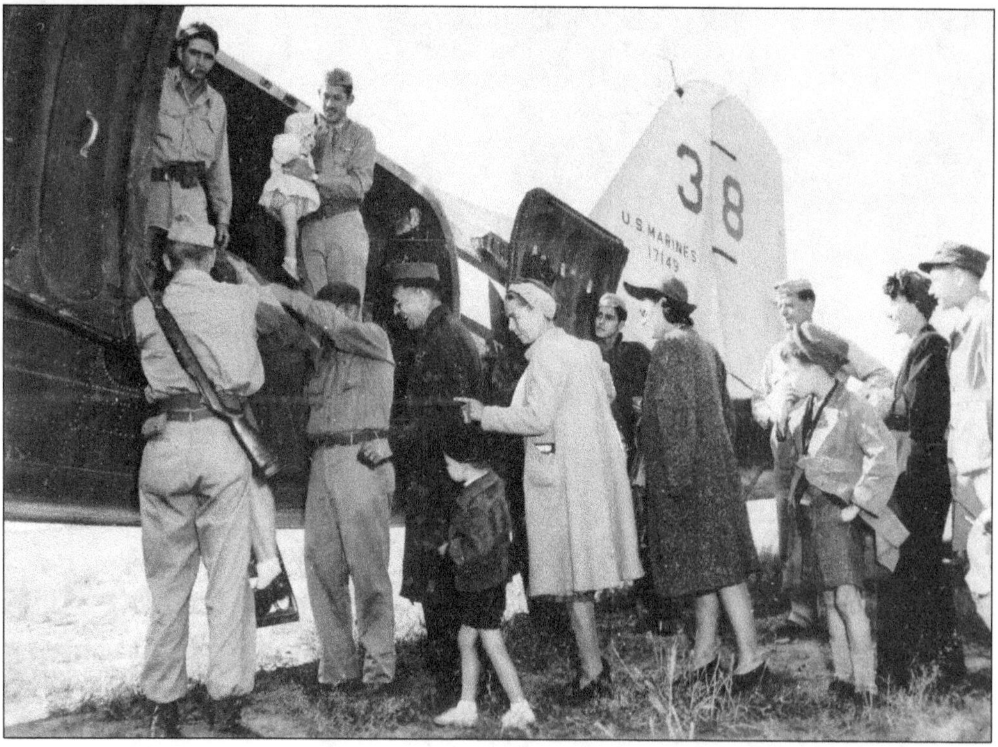

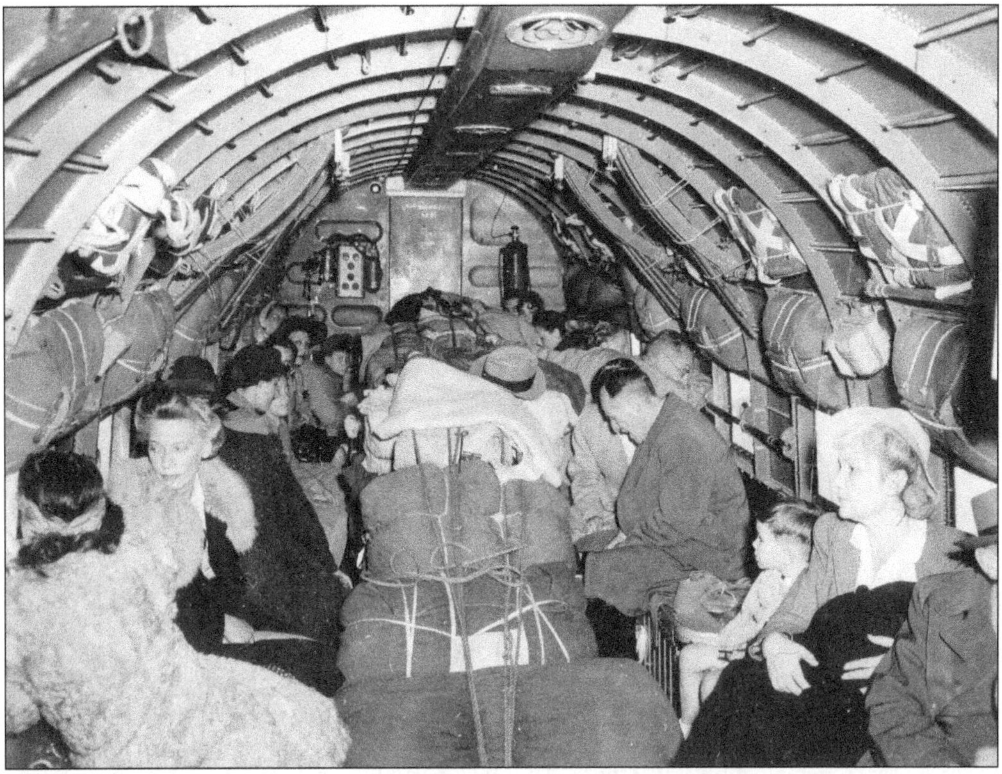

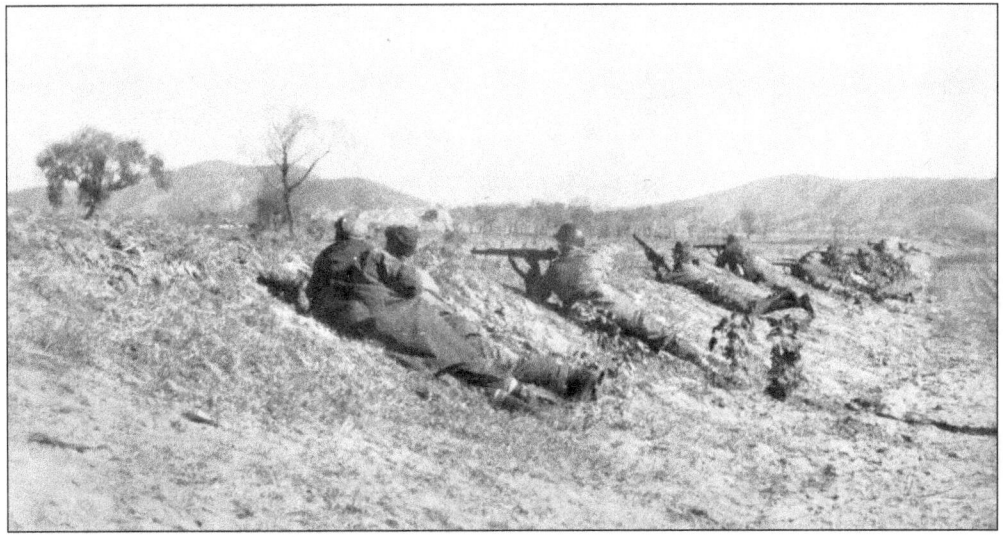

Although the lasting image of the Weihsien evacuation was that of grateful prisoners returning to freedom, such as those crowding the VMR-153 R4D above, it was a deadly prelude to the Cold War that made an airlift necessary. Below, in a scene eerily similar to events in Korea less than five years later, US Marines exchange fire with communist guerrillas along the road between Tientsin and Chinwangtao (Qinhuangdao) on November 14, 1945. The guerrillas had fired toward an American convoy, a common occurrence along major roads as China fell further into civil war. These riflemen eventually called in close air support from Marine F4U Corsairs against a nearby village. (Both, NARA.)

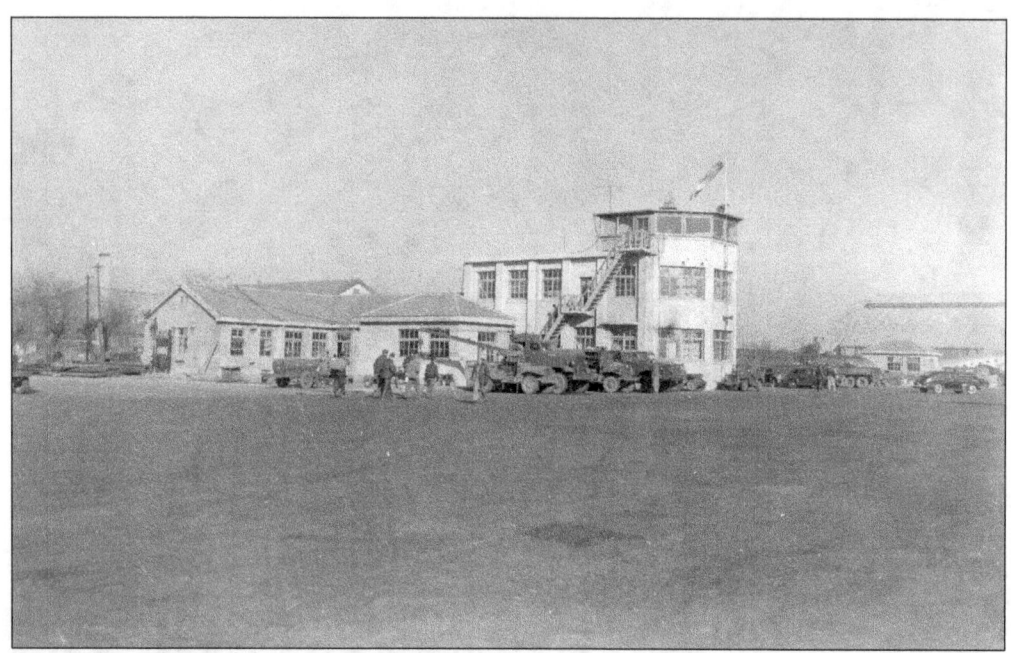

During its China service, MAG-25 transported 1,774,282 pounds of cargo and 22,685 passengers over 10,653 flying hours. MAG-25 remained at Tsingtao's Tsankou aerodrome, a former Imperial Japanese Army Air Force flying school, until June 6, 1946, the same month that these photographs were taken. However, VMR-153 remained at the base until February 1949. Above, the control tower appears to remain a hive of activity. An R4D is partially visible at far right, along with the wingtip of another. Below, an R4D, possibly from Headquarters Squadron, 1st Marine Aircraft Wing, sits in Tsankou's engineering hangar. The wingtip of another R4D is visible at right, while at left a crew works on a weary-looking Grumman J2F Duck amphibian. The airfield was eventually developed into the modern Qingdao International Airport. (Both, NARA.)

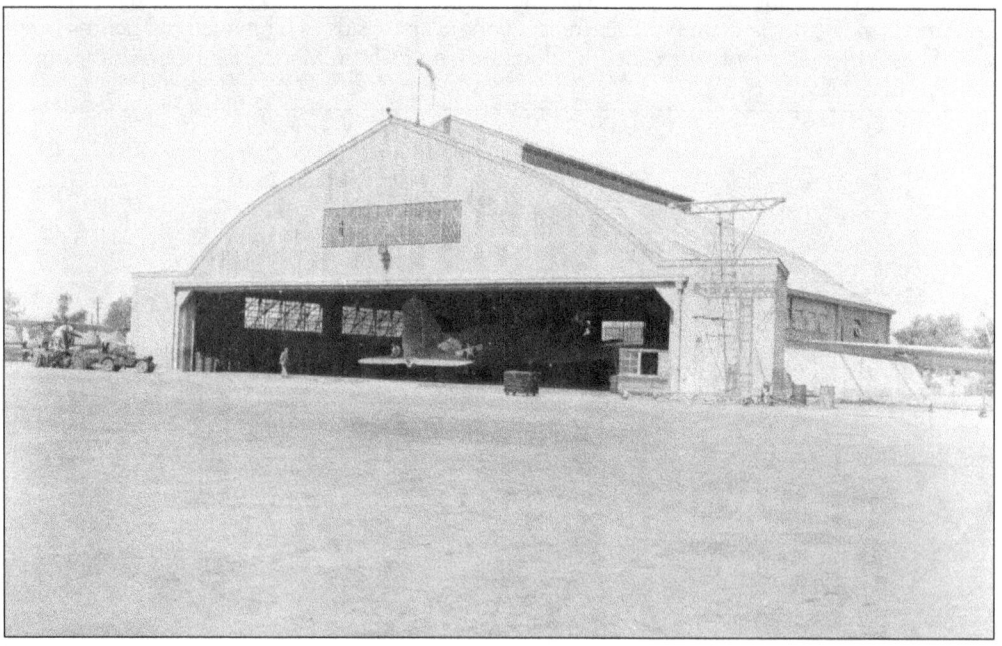

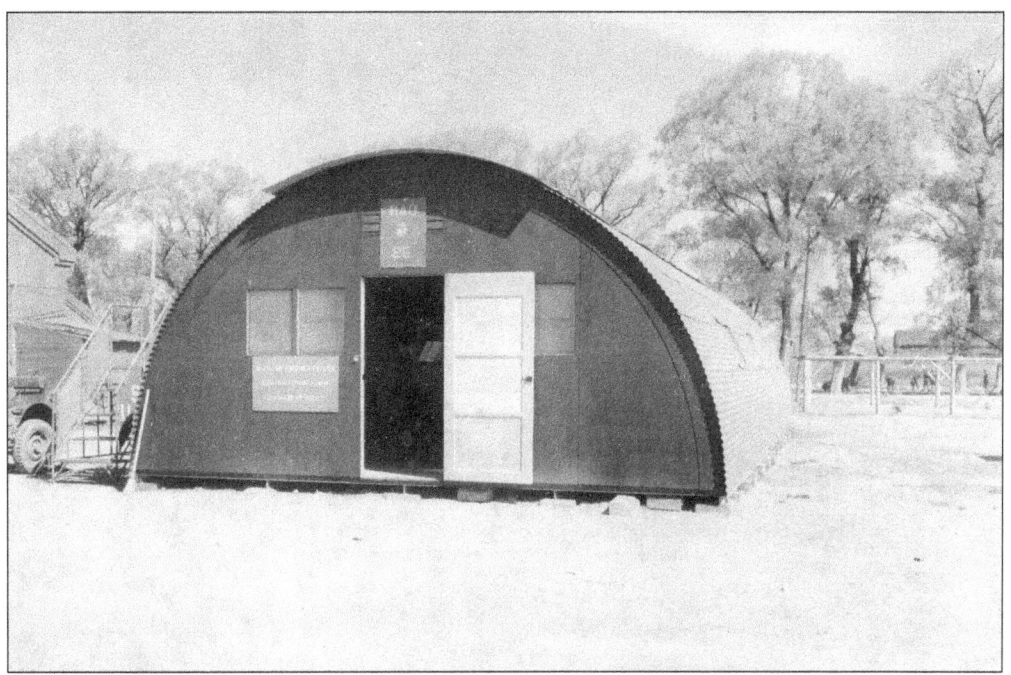

MAG-25's Quonset hut operations building at Peiping looked little different from its predecessors in the South Pacific, with the notable exception of its operating hours: "0730–1600" and closed on Sunday. This photograph was taken in May 1946, shortly before MAG-25 returned to the United States. It would be seven more months before President Truman formally ended America's participation in World War II, on December 31, 1946. (NARA.)

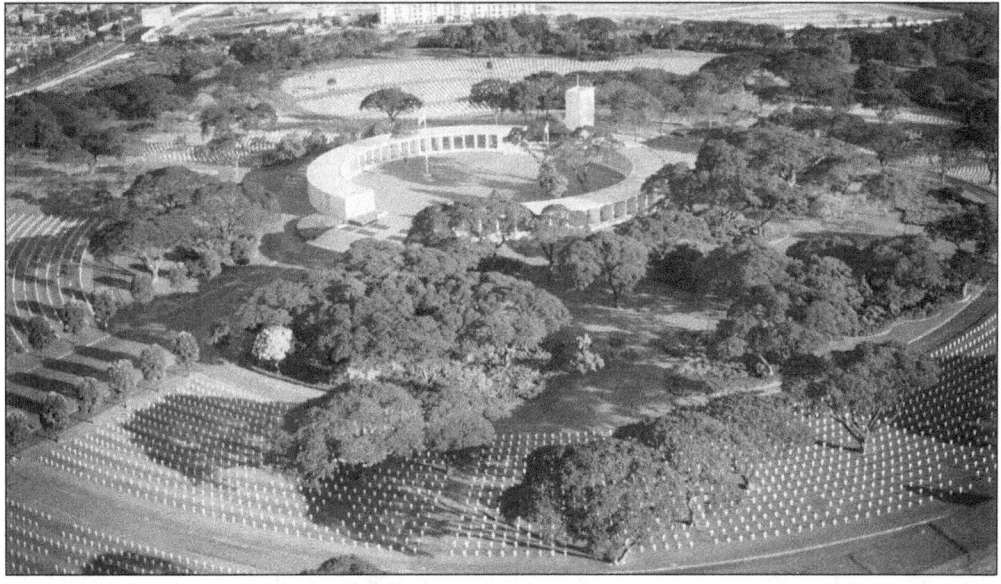

Many MAG-25/SCAT personnel killed or missing in action are interred or memorialized at Manila American Cemetery. They include 1st Lt. Neal Allen, 2nd Lt. Philip Anders, Maj. Max Clinkinbeard, 1st Lt. Burton Hall, 2nd Lt. Howard Kirk Jr., 2nd Lt. Joseph Kolkmeyer, 2nd Lt. Louis Nelson, Cpl. Rudolph Noga, M.Sgt. John Rinaldi, 2nd Lt. Ralph Saltsman, Cpl. James Stratton, and 2nd Lt. William Tangney. (Courtesy of the American Battle Monuments Commission.)

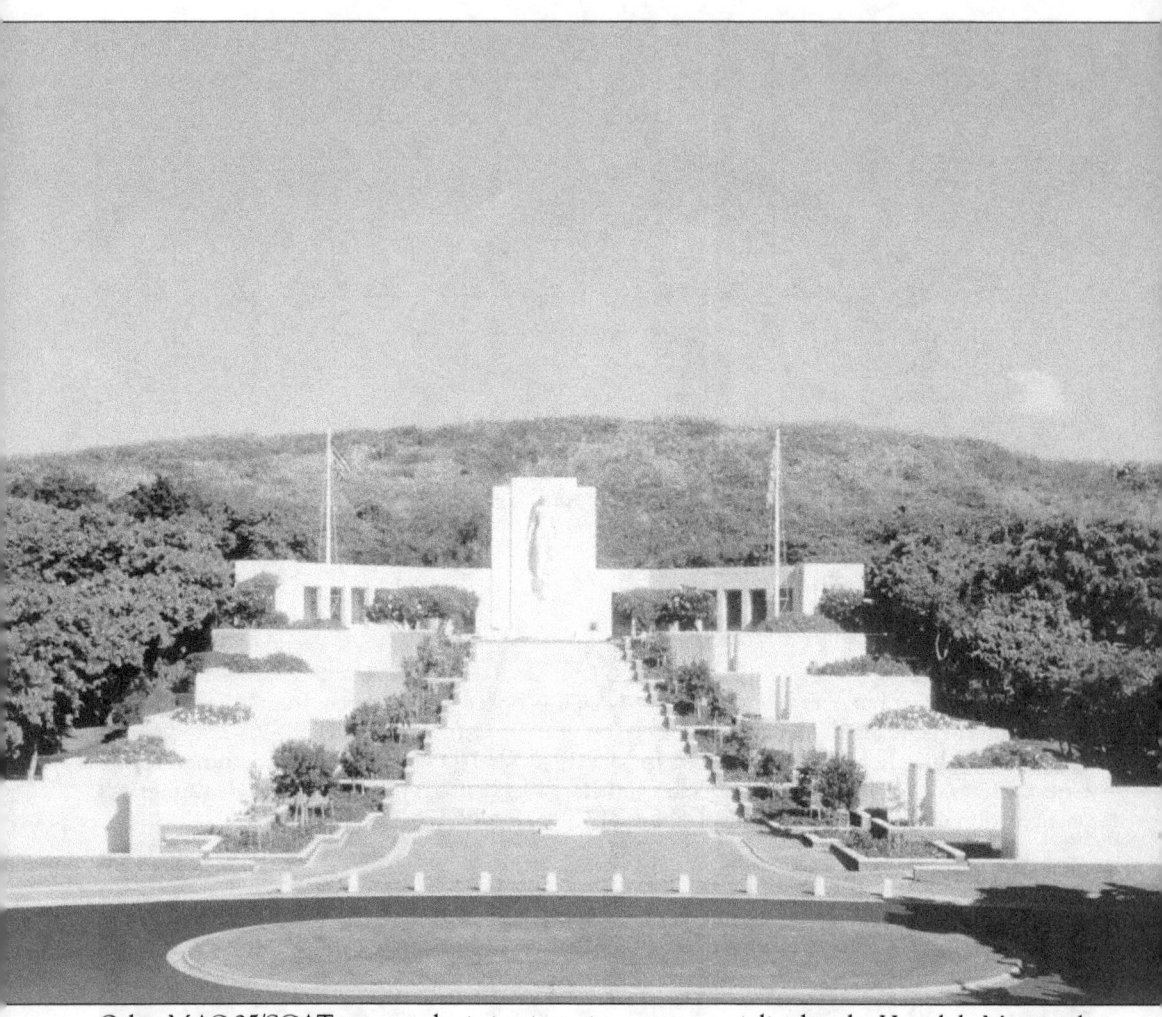

Other MAG-25/SCAT personnel missing in action are memorialized at the Honolulu Memorial. They include Cpl. Lewis Baughman, S.Sgt. Carl Boeckmann, 2nd Lt. Russel Buzard, S.Sgt. Edward Croteau, Sgt. James Duignan, 2nd Lt. John Felts Jr., 1st Lt. Merrill Fink, 2nd Lt. Richard Harpe, MTSgt. Opal Hughes, Capt. Reynolds Knotts, CPhM Clarence Latham, MTSgt. Louis McCay, S.Sgt. Robert Mock, 2nd Lt. Joshua Morris, S.Sgt. Lawrence Pitkus, 2nd Lt. George Richardson, and Pvt. Norman Weinstein. Those interred elsewhere include T3 Eugene Barr, Cpl. John Chapman, Sgt. Philip Greenberg, 1st Lt. Robert Healy, Cpl. Curtis Holt, S.Sgt. James E. Kaufield, Pfc. John Keniery, Capt. Thomas Keppelman, Maj. Edward Megson, Cpl. Joseph Mendelsohn, 2nd Lt. Augustus Miller, Cpl. Oscar Mueller, Cpl. Joseph O'Connell, T.Sgt. William Pappageorge, Sgt. Richard Roos, 2nd Lt. David Schwartz, Capt. Charles Shaeffer, Cpl. Kenneth Singley, 2nd Lt. John Talbot, 1st Lt. James A. Walker, Capt. Joseph Wheeler, 1st Lt. Donald Wilkie, and M.Sgt. Harry Wlodarsky. (Courtesy of the American Battle Monuments Commission.)

Six

KOREA

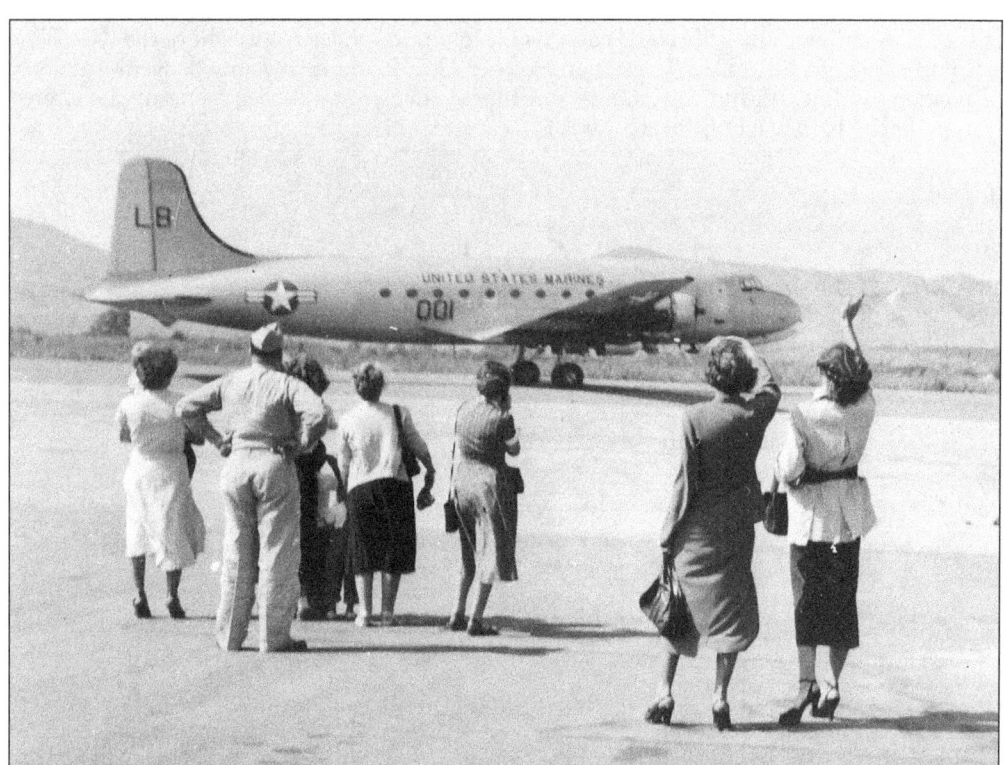

MAG-25 was reactivated just months before the Korean War, in February 1950, with VMR-152 and VMR-352 attached. Here, draftees' relatives wave farewell as a VMR-352 R5D departs Camp Pendleton loaded with Marines of the 1st Replacement Draft on September 29, 1950. The replacements would bolster the 1st Marine Division, which had spearheaded the Inchon amphibious landings and the liberation of Seoul, and was preparing to assault Wonsan, North Korea. (NARA.)

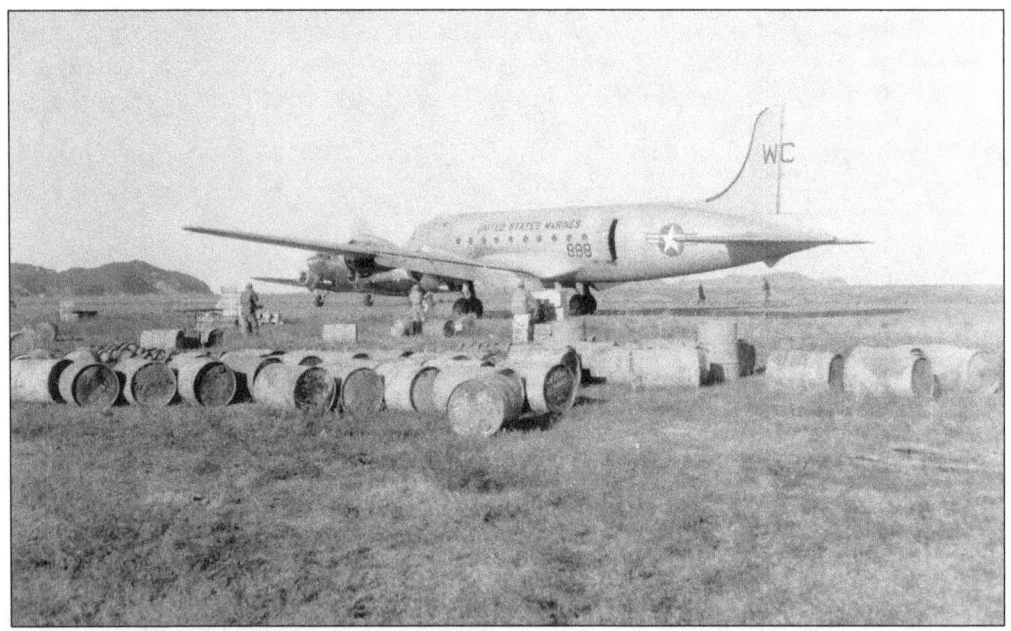

Both VMR-152 and VMR-352 were equipped with the Douglas R5D Skymaster, the naval version of the DC-4 airliner. The R5D could carry nearly four times the cargo weight of the R4D. This is R5D-3 91998 of VMR-152 at Wonsan on October 23, 1950, departing after delivering a supply of aviation gasoline. Within days, a massive Chinese offensive would begin erasing the United Nations forces' hard-fought gains. (NARA.)

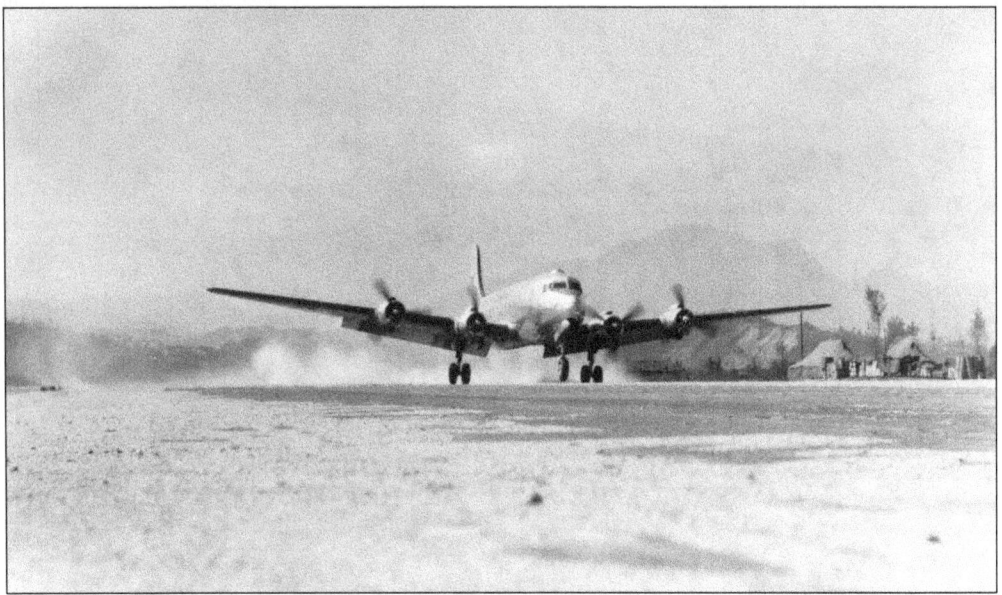

MAG-25, flying from Itami, Japan, continued its mission of transporting personnel and priority cargo. Beginning in November 1950, Chinese intervention had succeeded in driving the United Nations forces deep into South Korea, overrunning many airfields. By summer 1951, counterattacking United Nations forces again pushed north beyond the 38th Parallel. Here a VMR-152 R5D arrives at K-47 airfield near newly-liberated Chunchon (Chuncheon), South Korea, carrying food and medical supplies. (NARA.)

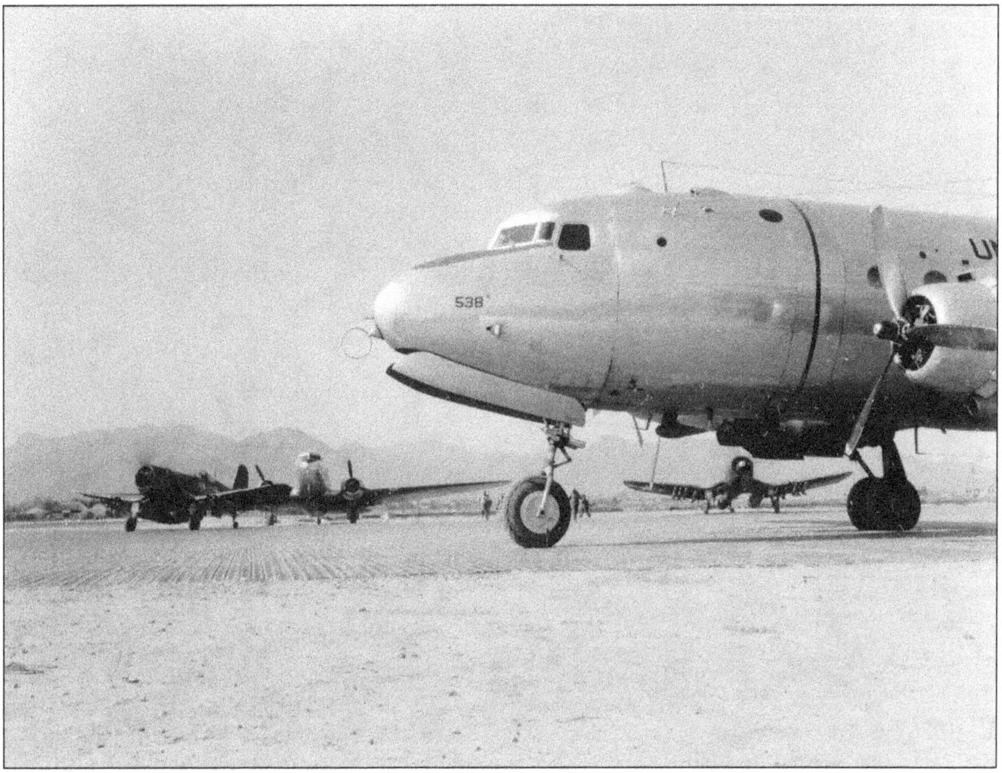

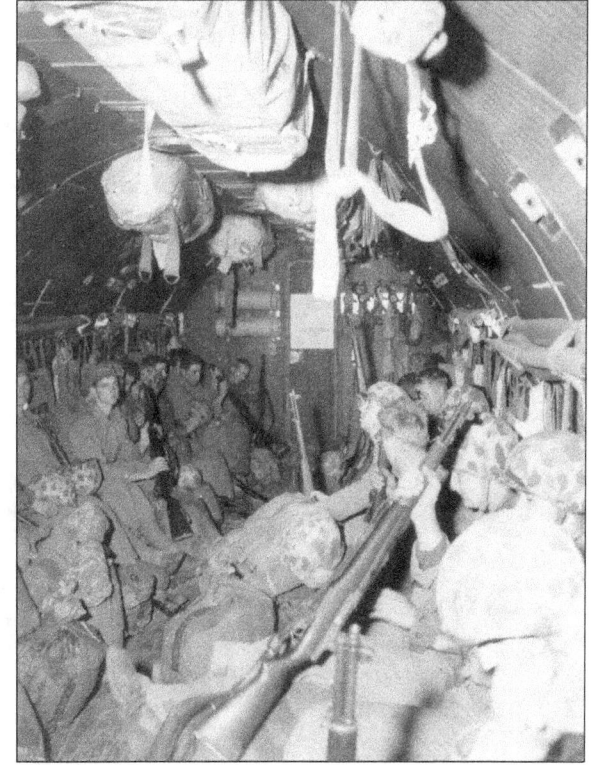

F4U-4 Corsairs taxi out past a VMR-152 R5D and a 1st Marine Aircraft Wing R4D at K-1 (Pusan West) airfield on April 26, 1951. On May 30, VMR-152 would suffer its only aircraft loss in Korea when R5D 56513 struck a mountain south of K-1 in poor weather. Killed were T.Sgt. James Becker, Capt. William DeVinney, M.Sgt. Charles Edwards, T.Sgt. John Higgs Jr., and Capt. Robert Moore Jr. (NARA.)

During the Battle of Chosin Reservoir, the 1st Marine Division conducted a fighting retreat and breakout that inflicted heavy Chinese losses. Afterward, the division assisted in pushing back toward the 38th Parallel. From the summer of 1951 until the armistice of July 27, 1953, the war was relatively static but still exacted a deadly cost. Here, replacement Marines head to Korea aboard a VMR-152 R5D on May 5, 1952. (NARA.)

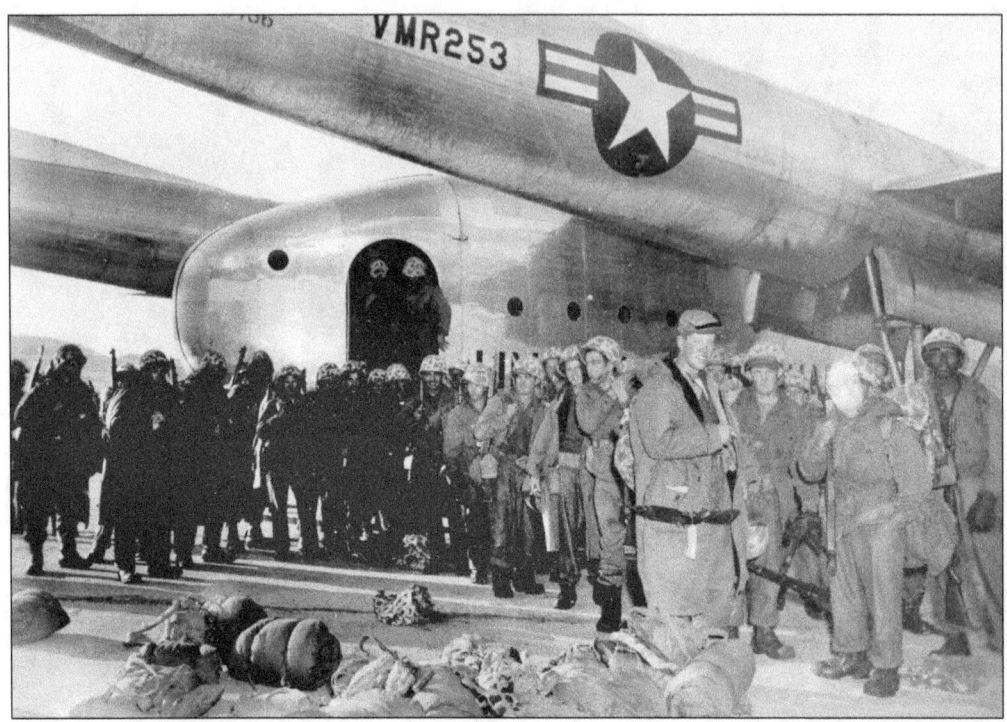

VMR-253 was also reactivated under MAG-25 but did not immediately report to Korea. Equipped with the Curtiss R5C and (shown here) the Fairchild R4Q, the squadron initially operated out of the group's home at Marine Corps Air Station El Toro, California. Above, R4Q-1 128736 delivers replacement Marines in cold weather gear to Camp Pendleton during training on March 18, 1952. There would be 31 wartime "replacement drafts" to maintain the 1st Marine Division. Below, R4Q-1 128735 participates in AIRLEX-1 in August 1952. Loaded at Camp Pendleton, the squadron established an "airhead" at Camp Hawthorne, Nevada, testing Marine Corps techniques for airlift rather than amphibious assault. (Both, NARA.)

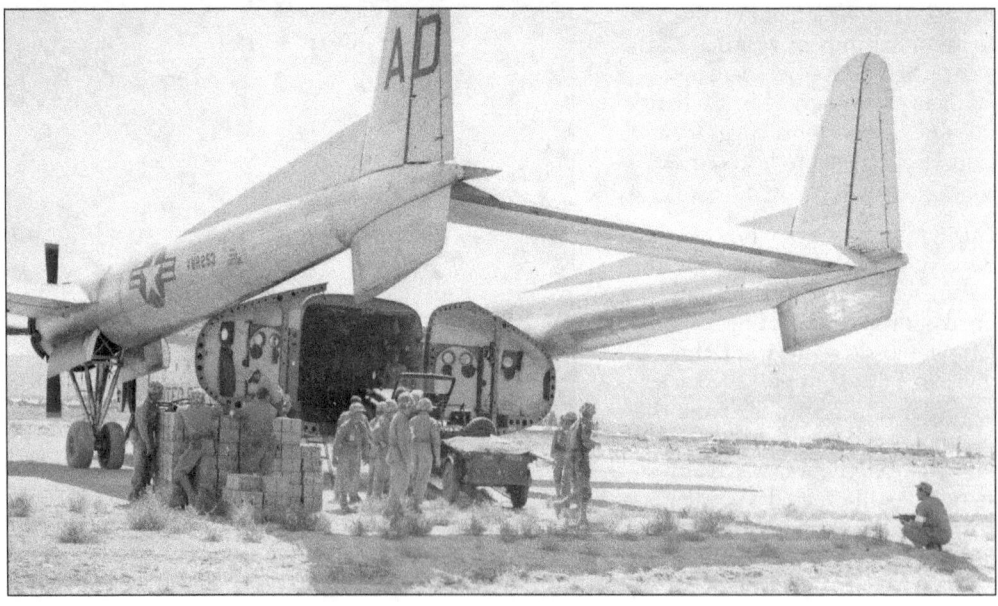

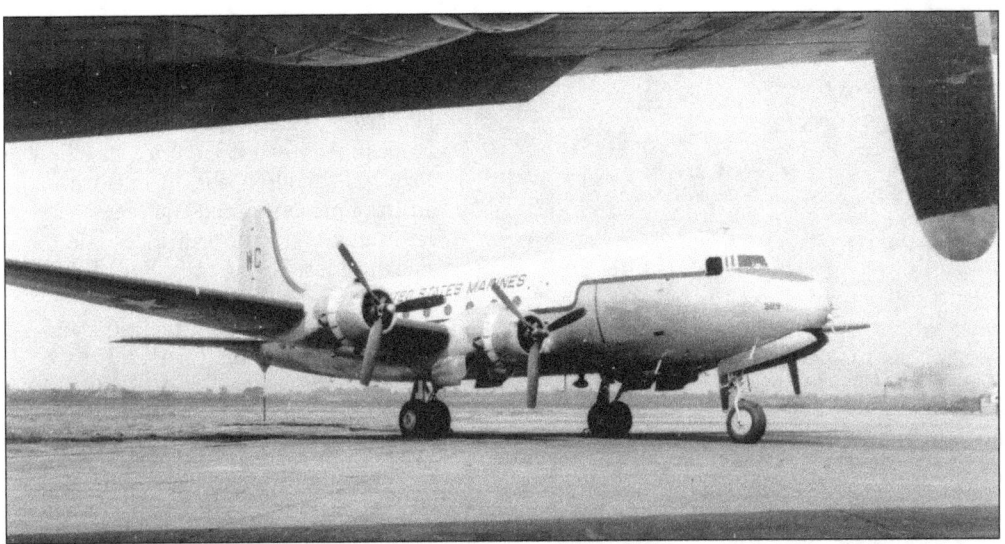

MAG-25 flew throughout the Korean War, its forward echelons attached directly to the 1st Marine Aircraft Wing. Its wartime commanding officers included SCAT veterans Col. Allen Koonce (1952) and Col. P.K. Smith (1952–1953). This VMR-152 R5D-2 (90389), photographed in Korea on May 15, 1953, has the white-painted upper fuselage that was introduced on US military transports to reduce cabin temperatures. Later registered N44906, it is currently derelict in Arizona. (NARA.)

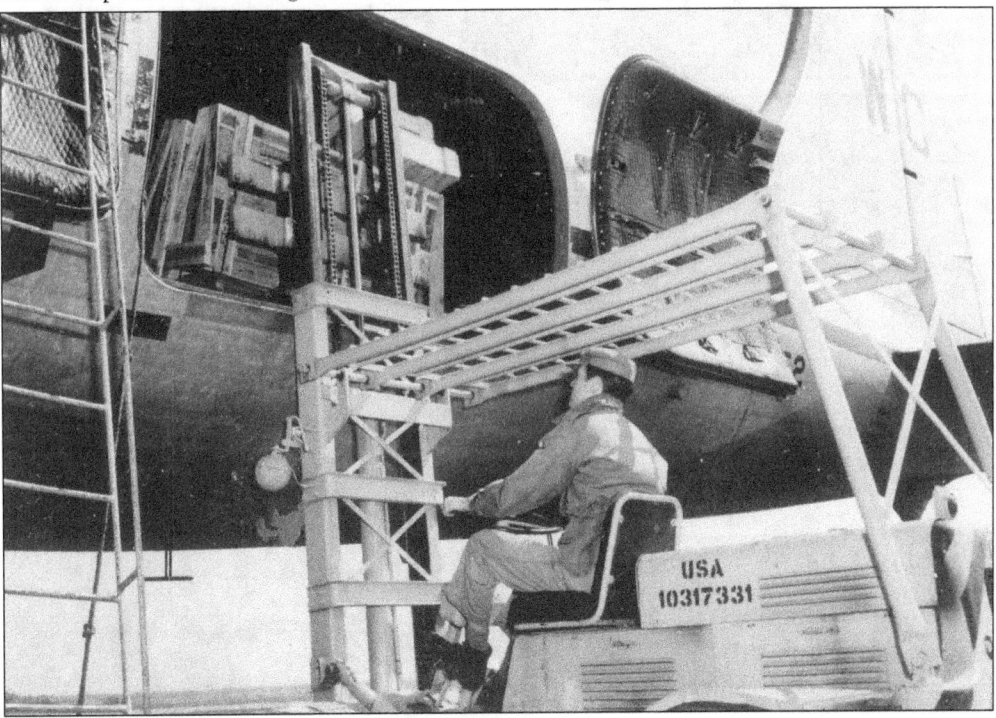

An R5D of VMR-152 delivers bread and other foodstuffs from Japan to K-1 on October 21, 1953. The R5D carried more and had wider cargo doors than the R4D and R4Q, but the cargo compartment's height above the ground was less than ideal. The Lockheed GV (C-130) Hercules, with a rear-loading cargo ramp near ground level, soon proved a superior combat transport and remains in production in 2017. (NARA.)

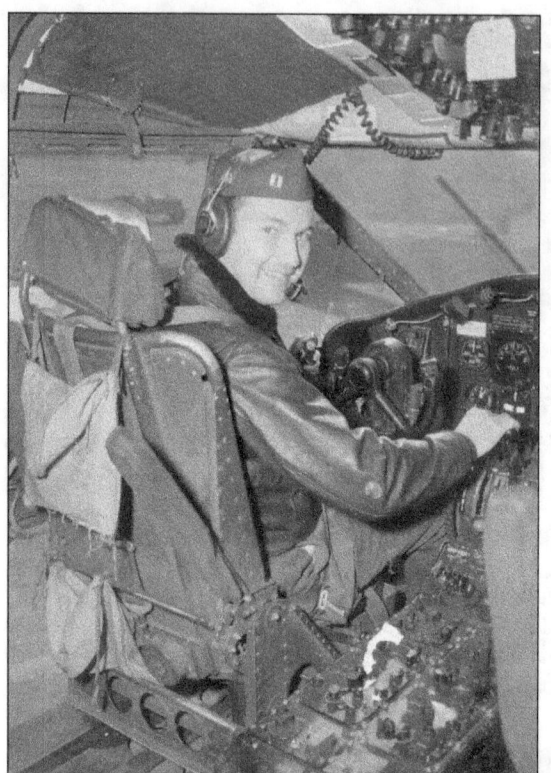

Capt. Robert Rippetoe of VMR-253, a World War II veteran, sits at the controls of his R4Q in Korea on January 19, 1954. VMR-253 arrived at Itami in August 1953, joining its fellow MAG-25 squadrons for the massive airlift of personnel and equipment set in motion by the armistice. The squadron lost one aircraft, R4Q 126579, along with crewmen Maj. Gene Badgley, S.Sgt. William McBride, and Capt. Rupert Nelson. (NARA.)

An R5D of VMR-352 sits on the ramp at Marine Corps Air Station El Toro on August 1, 1957. The squadron tail code had recently changed from LB to QB. The Korean War was MAG-25's last conflict. However, VMR-352 is one of two former MAG-25 squadrons to live on, flying the KC-130J Hercules, as Marine Aerial Refueler Transport Squadron 352 (VMGR-352). VMR-253 has been redesignated, somewhat confusingly, as VMGR-152. (NARA.)

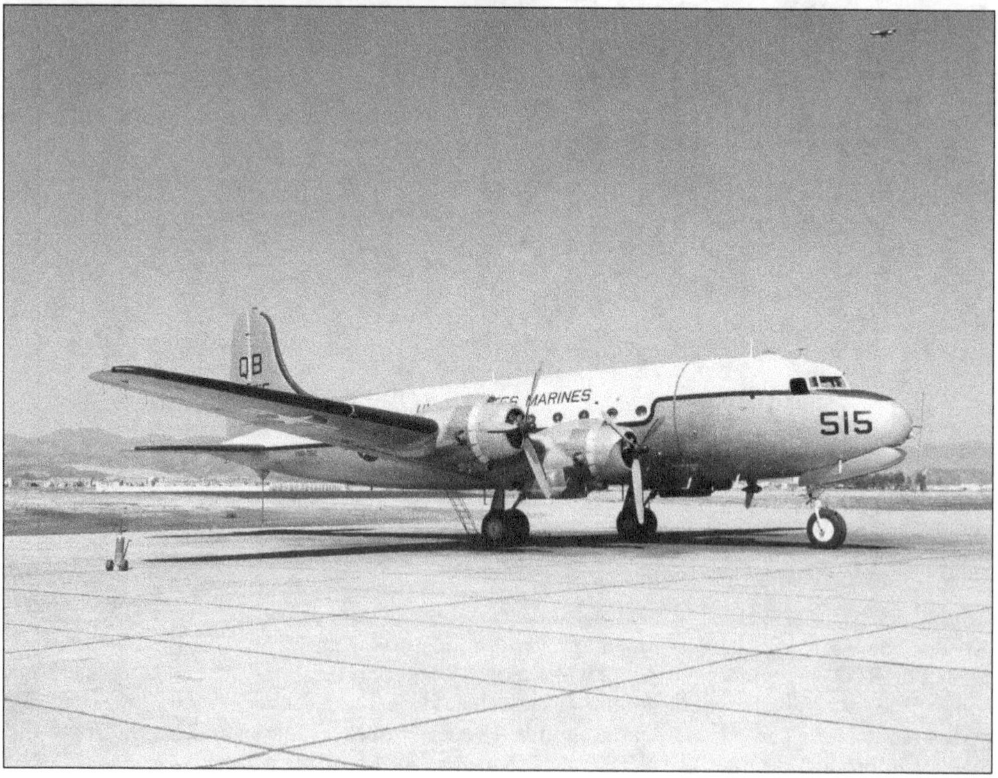

SELECTED BIBLIOGRAPHY

Allen, Robert J., and Otis Carney. "The Story of SCAT. Part I." *Air Transport*, December 1944, 22–27.

———. "The Story of SCAT. Part II." *Air Transport*, January 1945, 28–32.

Anderson, Norman J., and William K. Snyder. "SCAT." *Marine Corps Gazette*, September 1992, 54–60.

Elliott, John M. *Marine Aviation at Quantico 1918–1941*. Denver, CO: Outskirts Press, 2012.

Goodwin, Hal. "SCAT!" *Skyways*, March 1944, 35, 64, 88.

Hubler, Richard G., and John A. Dechant. *Flying Leathernecks: The Complete Record of Marine Corps Aviation in Action 1941–1944*. Garden City, NY: Doubleday, Doran & Co., 1944.

Johnson, Pendleton T. "I Was a Patient from Guadalcanal." *Hygeia*, December 1943, 860–863, 882–883.

Miller, Robert C. "Guadalcanal Fast Freight." *Douglas Airview*, May 1943, 4–7, 40.

Page, Evelyn, ed. *The Story of Air Evacuation, 1942–1989*. Dallas, TX: Taylor Publishing Company, 1989.

"SCAT." *Flying*, October 1944, 118–119, 282, 286.

Sherrod, Robert L. *History of Marine Corps Aviation in World War II*. Washington, DC: Combat Forces Press, 1952.

Washburne, Seth P. *The Thirsty 13th: The U.S. Army Air Forces 13th Troop Carrier Squadron, 1940–1945*. Chelsea, MI: Thirsty 13th LLC, 2011.

In addition to the above volumes, factual material for this book was drawn from unit war diaries, muster and casualty rolls, historical and operations reports, technical manuals, missing air crew reports, and other official records held by the Air Force Historical Research Agency and within the following record groups at the National Archives and Records Administration in College Park, Maryland: Publications of the US Government (RG 287); US Army Air Forces (RG 18); Office of the Chief of Naval Operations (RG 38); US Navy Bureau of Aeronautics (RG 72); Department of the Navy (RG 80); US Army, Office of the Chief Signal Officer (RG 111); US Marine Corps (RG 127); and US Air Force Commands, Activities, and Organizations (RG 342).

DISCOVER THOUSANDS OF LOCAL HISTORY BOOKS
FEATURING MILLIONS OF VINTAGE IMAGES

Arcadia Publishing, the leading local history publisher in the United States, is committed to making history accessible and meaningful through publishing books that celebrate and preserve the heritage of America's people and places.

Find more books like this at
www.arcadiapublishing.com

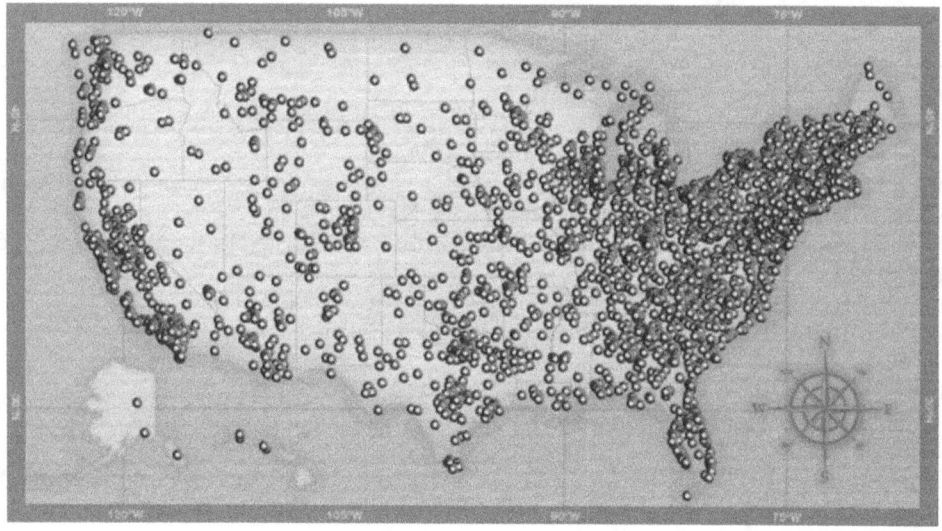

Search for your hometown history, your old stomping grounds, and even your favorite sports team.

Consistent with our mission to preserve history on a local level, this book was printed in South Carolina on American-made paper and manufactured entirely in the United States. Products carrying the accredited Forest Stewardship Council (FSC) label are printed on 100 percent FSC-certified paper.

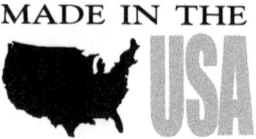

MADE IN THE USA